Overcoming America /
America Overcoming

Praise for *Overcoming America / America Overcoming*

"This book should go far to establish Rowe as the contemporary American social critic who has inherited the mantle of Christopher Lasch. Rowe continues Lasch's trenchant observations of the sickness of our times, sounds the prophetic call to conversion for the sake of the true American promise, and carries the reader forward with strong, clear, well-chosen words and convincing argument. The text reads as if it were spoken onto the page and the reader hears it as much as sees it. Rowe has created a style of writing most fitting for our 'post-traditional' era; it is intimate, engaged, conversational, reflective, personal, anecdotal. Rowe speaks as directly as any text can to the souls of his fellow citizens desperately seeking to make sense of who we are and who we should be in this overwhelming, disorienting globalizing world. Make no mistake about it, however, Rowe is not out to betray the modern liberal project, but to save it, and the America that did so much to create it, by setting it on new and firmer ground. He convincingly claims that relational liberalism is the transformative reality of American culture and history at its best, and that we will overcome the malaise of contemporary America by our faith in the human capacity to rise above circumstance and exercise choice, even of our worldview. This elevated awareness and choice is the only way to overcome the modern condition as it now paralyzes the human spirit. Rowe brings his firsthand experience with inter-cultural dialogue, and in depth knowledge of Chinese culture, as well as his lifelong devotion to liberal education as a way for citizens in a democracy to grow morally and spiritually together, to the contemporary public conversation he so celebrates and augments in this book. This is a summary statement of Rowe's philosophy of life, one his fellow citizens (and academics!) would do well to engage, understand, rebut, if they can, and take to heart."—**J. Ronald Engel**, Senior Scholar at the Center for Humans and Nature (Chicago, New York), and Professor Emeritus at Meadville/Lombard Theological School, is both activist and author in the vital overlap between religious humanism, democratic life, and ecological sustainability, and one of the framers of *The Earth Charter*

"Recommended for the panoramic vision holding this very substantive work together, its faithfulness to the pragmatic vision of democracy, and its responsiveness to dialogue with non-Western traditions."—**Sor-hoon Tan**, Associate Professor of Philosophy at the National University of Singapore, author of *Confucian Democracy: A Deweyan Reconstruction*, and editor of *Democracy as Culture: Deweyan Pragmatism in a Globalizing World*.

"America was once the hope of the world through its rediscovery of the meaning of being human and of working together to protect the rights and obligations that are generated by both the possible greatness and the actual frailty of human nature. Even with all the pragmatically necessary compromises, the fundamental principles of the idea of America were first incarnated in its inspired forms of government and supported by the blessings of its land. These principles remain eternal and unchangeable. The question is how to protect and continually rediscover these unchanging principles in a world of rapidly accelerating change—change that is transforming the forms of human life within and among nations and peoples, involving forms of communication, the immensity of technological progress, and its equally immense dangers in angry or greedy hands—not to mention the fearful loss of the work of listening to each other that is the real root of democracy and civil discourse, and is therefore the root of truly human qualities of thought and ethics. The eternal principles embedded in the idea of America stand in greater danger than ever; and America, and therefore the world, needs high guidance in making the necessary secondary adaptations of its forms of life and government in order to maintain all that is essentially America, and therefore essentially human, in a world that is in great danger of losing its humanity forever. *Overcoming America / America Overcoming* represents a pioneering vision of the lineaments of the new map of eternal America as it struggles to stay America—with all the hope for the world which that entails—while the world changes within and around us."—**Jacob Needleman**, author of *The American Soul* and many other books, and Professor of Philosophy at San Francisco State University

"Professor Rowe's thoughtful and timely effort to engage us in a dialogue between traditions and modernity beyond closed particularism is a source of inspiration for all public intellectuals in America. His proposal for a new American cultural identity is open, pluralistic, and self-reflexive. His critique of instrumental rationality articulates with persuasive power the proper role of reason in a just society essential for human flourishing."—**Tu Weiming**, author of *Confucian Thought: Selfhood as Creative Transformation* and other books, a United Nations designated Eminent Person, Harvard Professor, and Director of the Institute for Advanced Humanistic Studies at Peking University

Overcoming America /
America Overcoming

Can We Survive Modernity?

Stephen C. Rowe

LEXINGTON BOOKS
Lanham • Boulder • New York • Toronto • Plymouth, UK

Published by Lexington Books
A wholly owned subsidiary of The Rowman & Littlefield Publishing Group, Inc.
4501 Forbes Boulevard, Suite 200, Lanham, Maryland 20706
www.lexingtonbooks.com

Estover Road, Plymouth PL6 7PY, United Kingdom

Copyright © 2012 by Lexington Books

All rights reserved. No part of this book may be reproduced in any form or by any
electronic or mechanical means, including information storage and retrieval systems,
without written permission from the publisher, except by a reviewer who may quote
passages in a review.

British Library Cataloguing in Publication Information Available

Library of Congress Cataloging-in-Publication Data

Rowe, Stephen C., 1945–
Overcoming America, America overcoming : can we survive modernity? / Stephen Rowe.
  p. cm.
Includes bibliographical references and index.
ISBN 978-0-7391-7140-0 (cloth : alk. paper) — ISBN 978-0-7391-7141-7 (ebook)
1. United States—Politics and government—Philosophy. 2. Democracy—United States. I. Title.
JK31.R68 2012
973.932—dc23
                                                    2011036217

♾™ The paper used in this publication meets the minimum requirements of American
National Standard for Information Sciences Permanence of Paper for Printed Library
Materials, ANSI/NISO Z39.48-1992.

Printed in the United States of America

"I call upon heaven and earth to witness against you this day, that I have set before you life and death, blessing and curse: therefore choose life, that you and your descendents may live."—Deuteronomy 30:19

"It is not the Way that makes the human great, but the human that makes the Way great."—Confucius, *Analects*, 15:29

Contents

Foreword

Make no mistake: *Overcoming America / America Overcoming* is a work of public philosophy. Works in this genre are as old as Aristotle, but they have come back into prominence in recent decades as serious Americans are trying to project their discontents and proposals on a larger screen than that which campus, congress, and media provide.

For some decades, prominent professional philosophers had exited the public stage and divided into camps, where many did profound work, most of which failed to touch on issues of our common life. Today many thinkers called "public intellectuals" and "public scholars" are back and busy, and it is in their company that we locate Stephen Rowe. Some dismiss their approach as *haute vulgarization* or "pop" ventures. There is no danger that Professor Rowe will be dismissed with such classifications, because he makes strenuous demands on his readers. Yet merely to put a conventional label on him can also be a form of dismissal. For a first example, substantively his accent is not one with which all publics are familiar, because he is so at home with religious motifs, as many in the "public" readership are not. In fact, he is claiming that our problems are religious at root.

For a second example, note his style, to which I was implicitly referring when I mentioned the demands his book makes. A quick page-through might convince readers that he deals in abstractions, and they can be forbidding. If to many of us in the "general public," this book's languages may at first sound foreign because of those abstractions, we must remember that there are abstractions and there are abstractions. There are impoverishing abstractions and enriching abstractions, and you will find Rowe in the "enriching" camp, ready as he is to make practical applications, to cite a whole gallery of thinkers who have intended to deal with concrete situations, and have successfully done so. He takes readers on a literary stroll down a gallery where one expects the busts of William James, Confucius, John Dewey, and their kin and kind, to erupt in speech or to whisper quiet counsel. No one has accused such public thinkers of having retreated into abstractions, enriching or otherwise. And so it is with Rowe.

Still, if not fair warning, here at least is an alert: it takes only a few pages for most readers to recognize that Rowe's subject deals with urgent and immediate matters, but he clearly does not believe that meaningful contributions can be exhausted if dealt with only superficially, as if by raiding parties who run off with terse bright ideas from their repository of options. No, he wants ideas to be explored, probed, mulled over, to the point that they can become integrated into our "worldview"—a favorite Rowe term—since he wants to help see a fresh worldview emerge among public-minded Americans and the larger public. He wants us to *think*.

Further along the lines of "fair warning": Rowe's landscape, the horizon to which he beckons, is vast. Insofar as his thinking and proposals are concerned, his calendar does not call anyone back to a pre-modern time and style or presently to an anti-modern stance. Instead he defines what he means by "modernity" and what José Ortega y Gasset called "the modern theme," and then shows how to transcend its limits and enjoy new philosophical and democratic vistas. But his call is so rich and his promises so daring that one is left—at least *this* one is left, at first, with intellectual vertigo and spiritual breathlessness. An experiential metaphor comes to mind:

Aeons, or at least decades ago, I was for a time in a calling which led me to have to lead young people to places of recreation and amusement, as in Amusement Parks. The "kids," to use their concrete language, liked to cajole or dare their counselor to ride with them on roller coasters, fast-circling centrifugally-forced merry-go-rounds, and other instruments of torture, and then listen for my shrieks and squeals. I was too terrified to squeal, and this thought prevailed over all others: "They should not let them run this device or get anyone to ride it!" "They": the manufacturer, the operator, the ticket-seller? So now as a reader I felt at times, when hanging on for dear life as Rowe begins by hurtling us readers across the landscape of possibilities, dares, invitations, and speculations. But suddenly the whole project began to make sense, since Rowe is at heart a concrete-minded thinker. His opening epigraph invokes a biblical call to "choose" He could have chosen to experiment with some form or other of idealism, but he chose, or was called to, pragmatism and to invoke thinkers who relish the concepts related to it—and whose ventures he integrates into a coherent and satisfying whole. Gone are the vertigo and the breathlessness, and readers are left with firm terrain on various scenes such as "America" or "Liberal Education"—and even the experiential ground of "Democracy."

The scene of liberal education, the college and the university, is Rowe's natural turf, the place where the abstract gets concretized in the practical issues of curriculum, academic mission, career and vocation, and ethics. He has been a leader on that scene for decades, and on an occasion or two where he reminisces about it to make a point, he will be recognized by many other products or agents of liberal education. Liberal education: about which more than a word or two, since when Rowe talks about "Overcoming America / America Overcoming," his instrument, symbolized by that slant bar ("/") is liberal education and its near-identity with democracy. Whoever may have underestimated the daring of public philosophers, or at least of Rowe in their company and who has kept up to date on recent cultural trends, political arguments, and practical trends, has to be aware of how treacherous life on its scene has become.

You know the charges: parents complain about paying for an education that does not assure a guaranteed income and security. "For-profit" universities—though not all of them—advertise that they can guide students past arts and letters and other frivolous educational diversions, direct to the troughs where they can feast on fattening foods which will prepare them for "the market." Some political camps charge that liberal education has become too "liberal" in another sense, and that people in charge of its mission(s) are "liberal" in their ideological wrongness. Legislators ask why the public should pay for liberal education, which they dismiss as "elite," and therefore bad. Maybe worst of all, some liberal educators have lost sight of the goals and intents of classical, modern, and, one hopes, post-modern liberal education, have turned against themselves and their kind, and become nihilists. (By the way, Rowe's paragraphs on "nihilism" and its cognates are brilliant, their diagnoses not to be missed.)

What a scene of danger and tumult is Rowe's "chosen" milieu or battle ground! I thought of what he is trying to do here, and in which he succeeds, I am persuaded, is to show an awareness of that scene, chose not to be "overcome," as the book's title suggests, and to go about his business so serenely and almost nonchalantly that he can enrich his argument through illuminating forays into Chinese thought and literature. To keep my own bearings, I reached for metaphor, and came up with cooking omelets. In this case it implied risk, the risk "The Great Blondin" took at Niagara Falls so long ago, as described by Thomas Kaplan in *The New York Times*, August 5, 2011);

> . . . The great Blondin, [who] crossed the gorge [at the Falls] on a wire in 1859 and repeated his feat as a regular attraction at the falls. On occasion, Blondin would wear a sack over his head, or push a wheelbarrow, or even carry his business manager. In one variant of his act, he donned a chef's hat and stopped above the gorge to cook an omelet for passengers on the Maid of the Mist sightseeing boat, bobbing in the waters beneath him.

To continue using the metaphor at precarious length, let me note that "anybody" or almost anybody—I am not sure of myself—can cook an omelet, but not in anything like Blondin's circumstances. And here we bobbers in the figurative waters beneath him, see Professor Rowe doing his own version of such cooking.

Make the case for "liberal education" (or for "democracy" as a way of living), now, and in these circumstances? I think of an old epitaph which paid tribute to someone who had done "the best things in the worst times." Rowe, readers will discover, has set out to do things like the best things in times which rank high (or is it "low"?)—among the "worst times." One of the reasons he bids fare to be successful is because of his trust in readers. Instead of proclaiming, he appeals for and sets the terms for conversation. In the nature of things, a book appears to be a monologue, but Rowe's mode, manner, and substance is invitational. He has convictions and sets them forth, but his commitment is to process and democratic conversation, in order to demonstrate readiness for change—which he shows is not the same thing as rendering him and his argument "relativistic." His word for all this is "dialogue," a term which he lifts far above the language of cliché. We "the public" have to believe we know, and we do know, some things which will contribute to the "Overcoming" task for Americans today and tomorrow. He's listening—while at the same time representing the nearly silent democratic sub-tradition of American life he calls "relational liberalism."

A crucial element in all of the above is a theology which frames and inspires this act of conversing. I mentioned before that his voice is distinctive because it is explicitly religious. I gave it only a half-line, but it deserves notice because religion from and with a wide horizon is diffused through the book. He did not bring it in covertly, but he does define its content and intentions in fresh ways, and in ways which have the paradoxical quality of both unifying and affirming diversity. Rowe invites us, "the public," to engage in "the public philosophy" with him, with no need for hierarchy, and with faith that the overcoming we need will emerge from this engagement. Let us accept his invitation.

Martin E. Marty
University of Chicago

Acknowledgments

I am fortunate to work in an ambitious and energetic public university that is deeply committed to liberal education, and to liberal education understood as cultivation of the fully developed human being and the possibility of a democratic life. So, unlike many other representatives of the broad yet endangered subtradition of relational liberalism, I have been spared the fate of becoming isolated, frustrated, and pessimistic under the weight of the late twentieth and early twenty-first centuries—at least on my home ground. So my first acknowledgment must be to the splendidly (mostly) diverse group of people who each give their contribution plus a little more to that commonly shared life known as Grand Valley State University—that America and the world could be like this!

And I am blessed with some friends and colleagues who keep me alive within a worldwide network of conversation and care. I mention a few here who have been particularly helpful, in one way or another, with this project: Joan and Ronald Engel, Vandana Pednekar-Magal, Fred Dallmayr, Kevin A. Rowe, Peimin Ni, Cheryl Jones, Jacob Needleman, Rosemary Yokoi, Sydney Burrows, Geling Shang, Barbara Roos, and Tong Shijun.

Then there is family, with whom I am at home: Lihua, my wife and *sine qua non*, my children, Kristin, Matthew, Kevin, and Yiqing, and grandchildren, Connor, Anna, Sylvie, and Peter Behn.

And, after all these decades, there is Martin Marty, with whom I share not so much agreement as a profound and profoundly significant sentiment.

Part I

America and the Problem of Modernity

Chapter One

Worldview, Choice, and Dialogue

One night on a 747, stuck in a typhoon in the middle of the Pacific: radical instability, heavy blows, total unpredictability in the midst of vast, unknowable forces and great distance from land. Did they not see this on the radar? Shouldn't they have flown around it? Did someone miscalculate the altitude? I remember observing that my fellow travelers looked pretty good, despite the deep distraction of fear—or were some of these people just not that concerned for one reason or another? The atmosphere was one of striking human silence, except for a few exclamations with the most severe thumps, as backdrop to airplane noise—the squeaking of stressing plastic, and some truly disturbing sounds from down in the structure. After the storm finally passed, wariness remained.

It occurred to me that this situation could be seen as America in miniature: curious human silence, distressing technology, an environment of radical uncertainty and unpredictable thumps.

America is the very front edge of modernity, that now-global way of life and worldview which revolves around the rationalization and quantification of everything, endlessly expanding commodification, insistence on instant gratification, and competitive individualism spreading to all relationships. The heavy turbulence of this time is indicative of this life-way breaking up, becoming, as we have come to say, "unsustainable." America's vexing and never-ending problems are expressive of a deep historical shift, tremblings on the threshold of transition to a profoundly new era. And of course there is real possibility—as with the 747—that we might be on the verge of catastrophic breakup rather than transition in any positive sense.

But America should not be underestimated.

The genius of America is overcoming.

At its best, America overcomes incredible adversity, both externally and internally, progressively extending and more deeply embodying the ideal of "liberty and justice for all." America is the land of new beginning, the land to which people migrate for a better life, the nation which has embraced revolution.

Yet now it is America itself which needs to be overcome. For the best of America has been eclipsed by the worst features of modernity, a fate which is shared to some degree by virtually all societies on the planet. Modernity threatens to shade out and suffocate all values associated with higher or deeper meanings, including those most intimate to the living of a human life. And the worst of the modern is its pretense to sufficiency, the way it enfolds and intoxicates, anesthetizing in a pleasant degradation.

Surviving the modern requires a developed awareness of its limiting and ultimately lethal character, reappropriation of traditional sources for the cultivation of human vitality, and activation of these sources through dialogue with those of other traditions who are also addressing the limitations of the modern. This is profoundly different from fundamentalist reaction which asserts "good" tradition against "bad" modernity. The overcoming I am recommending is a much more nuanced approach which entails conscious affirmation not only of some elements of "tradition," but also of what is valuable in the modern, as against its all too obvious limitations.

In this book I address these dimensions of overcoming—awareness, reappropriation (again, of both some traditional values and the best of the modern), and activation. And I suggest that America, having been so influential in spreading the modern condition across the globe, is now in a position to lead a movement beyond the modern, into a new era in which globalization can mean something quite different from homogenized modernization. For at its best America embodies a dialogue between the traditional and the modern which leaves the worst features of both behind, and fuses their best features as the radiant center of its vitality.

WORLDVIEW AS ISSUE AND CHOICE

America is struggling to cross the treacherous ocean over which we find ourselves after humans have been alienated from traditional cultures. Beginning in the late 19th century and intensifying through the 20th, traditions, those age-old containers of human life, have been discovered to be other—amidst wildly mixed feelings of sorrow/loss and critique/anger. Either way, traditional cultures no longer provide a home. We live in the midst of fragments of tradition, as well as desperate attempts to *get back*, to absolutize the order and authority of tradition against the insufficiency of the modern. But fundamentalism never proves to be viable, since it inevitably results in some form of *jihad* against life in the present. However, this does not change the fact that sooner or later the post-traditional, modern confusion does indeed become intolerable. It is the "wasteland" of which T.S. Eliot spoke, a barren ground of unrelenting competition and relativistic indifference to all value except those of number/money, and the consumer preferences of overly entitled but otherwise undistinguished individuals. It is an insult to the human spirit, if not to Dao/Allah/Heaven/God.

In this situation, the deep dilemma of our era becomes one of either absolutism reasserted or relativism unconstrained: either "clash of civilizations," each asserting its own superiority against the modern confusion, or the "end of history" reduction of all to consumerism and the war of all against all; either one right way or else no way that is any better than any other; either oppressive unity or chaotic diversity, homogenization or incommensurability, sameness or difference. . . . Two options, each unacceptable, forced choice—"catch 22" as the underlying reality of our time.

Yet there are also in our midst pockets of beauty and potential, goodness and hope. Some actually do live beyond fanaticism, decadence, and despair; some find a way to cross over to a new ground beyond the limitations of the modern, a way which includes awareness of the largely obscured dignity of America and what is worth saving in the modern Enlightenment project.

Another option becomes available. Most of us have glimpses of it from time to time. There is still something great here, something worth standing up for, something beyond just privileges. The problem is that access to it requires a certain faith, and the courage to enter into a developmental process in which vulnerability and openness to growth are necessary. It also requires maintenance of wakefulness in the midst of never-ending modern temptations to narcosis, through "lifestyles" of multiple tasking and entertainment, and/or ideologies which insulate against the need to think. Wakefulness, in turn, requires support, confirmation, companionship, nurturance. And it also takes *interpretation*, as the necessary connective tissue between ethereal vision and the embodied presence of ordinary life.

In this book I want to engage the art of interpretation in ways which are as practical as possible, in relation to the developmental challenge we face today. I want to interpret the emergence of a new worldview as the underlying drama and hope of our era, and as intimately connected with the quality of our everyday lives.

In our time, worldview has become conscious, and hence a matter of choice and responsibility. We experience this consciousness, for example, in liberationist movements, environmental awareness, criticisms of capitalist greed and the politics of self-interest, and calls for inclusion and affirmation of diversity—all of which point to the problematic nature of our inherited worldview, and the necessity of change at this level.

But to identify worldview as problem is extremely difficult. In fact, it indicates the sort of difficulty societies of the past did not survive. For the vast majority of our ancestors, worldview—that comprehensive lens through which we apprehend and assign value in all of life, the perspective which informs the way we set priorities—including those having to do with who gives and who receives, how we identify issues and evaluate consequences— lay beneath conscious awareness, as something given in such a way that it was not seen. The movement beyond the traditional period of human history, as well as movement beyond the crises of our time with which it ends, require that we make conscious that which has been unconscious, choose values that are more life-affirming than those we inherited, *and* act from the perspective of that conscious choice. [1]

Our challenge is nothing less than the conscious reinvention and choosing the best of *culture itself* under post-traditional circumstances. The imperative is one of growth, and it is inherently religious in nature: it has everything to do with how we orient ourselves in relation to the broadest horizons of meaning and value, and how we are able to transcend ego and draw on energies which lie beyond what we can ordinarily comprehend or control. We need religion as William James defined it, as "the belief that there is an unseen order, and that our supreme good lies in harmoniously adjusting ourselves thereto." [2] We need the kind of belief which comes as close as possible to being identical with "adjusting;" the kind of religion that is closer to what some today call "spirituality," as distinct from "religion" insofar as the latter is associated with dogma, institution, hierarchy, and command.

The survival of America—perhaps the world—turns on whether we can become aware of the limitations of the worldview we have inherited, and choose a better one, one which is more conducive to well-being, more conducive to *life*. America, as the leading edge of the modern departure from tradition, is at a crucial point of transition: either it will be lost, assuming— with greater or lesser degrees of violence in the transition—the subservient position of an empire whose time has past, *or* it will become one of several societies—along with Australia, New Zealand, Bhutan, Brazil, Costa Rica, Germany, and Netherlands—which lead the way in being not only post-traditional but also post-modern, as societies which are democratic and sustainable, societies in which material well-being is embraced and disciplined within a deeper and more broadly life-affirming sense of value. This is to say that it may not be too late, that people like Morris Berman who have concluded about America that "there is no warding off the Dark Age" may be speaking prematurely. [3] The positive alternative, which certainly exists in many of our hearts, and in some relationships/communities in our nation and in quite a few other places across the Earth, could be stronger than it appears.

This choice can be thought of on the analogy of the moment in the history of our species when prehistoric ancestors came to stand erect; when, unlike other animals, forelimbs ascended from the ground, allowing face and attention to rise upward, to live in a world of greatly expanded horizons. For the first time, humans were able to "lift mine eyes up unto the hills," withdrawing attention from the urgent immediacy of life on Earth, to contemplate the mountaintops and the heavens, matters of value and meaning, within the kind of expanded consciousness which perhaps gave rise to the Axial Age foundation of the historic traditions (which I will discuss very shortly). Whether this is so or not, the point is that our survival into the future depends on an analogous opening of horizons—most simply stated as an opening from short term, individual interest to longer term, communal interests, and from regard for life on the planet as a trial to the capacity of a conscious mortal being to embrace life as a gift.

However, this dramatic image could be misleading, since emergence of a new worldview is *already going on in our midst,* though a certain refocusing may be necessary to be able to see it. For Americans, focus must be adjusted to include the whole world, and to eliminate a certain distortion related to democracy. Amartya Sen, champion of democracy as a commonly shared global heritage, describes this distortion:

> The apparent Western modesty that takes the form of a humble reluctance to promote 'Western ideas of democracy' in the non-Western world includes an imperious appropriation of a global heritage as exclusively the West's own. The self-doubt with regard to 'pushing' Western ideas on non-Western societies is combined with the absence of doubt in viewing democracy as a quintessentially Western idea, an immaculate Western conception. . . . This misconception results from gross neglect of the intellectual history of non-Western societies.[4]

Because of this distortion, America could fail to see the new worldview emerging in other parts of the world, for example, in the countries just mentioned, or in its early stirrings in the Middle Eastern Arab Spring of 2011. America could, quite ironically, forget its own roots in the commonly shared heritage of democracy as government by discussion and public reasoning, confusing democracy with corporate capitalism on one hand, and with what Sor-hoon Tan calls "anti-democratic culturalism"[5] on the other—the relativistic policy of non-intervention or, in the vernacular, "whatever."

In my work I have been fortunate to avoid over-specialization, and to participate in several circles of conversation through which the emergence of a new worldview is occurring quite visibly: the intercultural and inter-religious dialogue movements, process philosophy, feminism, Third Epoch Confucianism, the environmental movement, higher education, postmodern philosophy, and American pragmatism. There is remarkable consistency among these conversations and the broader movement which together they carry. They all insist that our times require us to become conscious of the limitations of the worldview we inherit, responsible for the conscious task of choosing a more adequate worldview, and they all point toward the emergence of a new worldview which is life-affirming, pluralistic, relational, ecologically responsible, and oriented to human transformation in the direction of thriving. Some of these conversations point as well to the ways in which this "new" worldview also involves the re-valuing and re-appropriation of values which can be found in most of the world's traditions, including the American democratic tradition. My aim is to make this new worldview, and the developmental adventure which is integral to it, available in a way which is *practical*—oriented to the transformation we so urgently need.[6]

Consideration of "worldview" need not take us away from the world of politics and policy, as in so much of the "consciousness rising" activity of the past several decades. It is essential to the new worldview that it makes it possible for us to live in the world with greater zest and joy, less ego inhibition, more responsiveness and appreciation, and greater compassion. It is a worldview of full presence, a worldview of ordinary human experience—of "return." This quality was brought home to me recently through talking with my son. He is a student of politics, both academically and in his various associational and institutional engagements, and one who is well acquainted with the ominous quality of our times and the vastness of the issues before us. Despite and through this awareness, he gives his best to the world, living in the perception of another possibility, something like what his father calls a new worldview. In our conversation we sailed out into the deep waters of the real issues of our day, the moral issues of health care, income distribution, military and environmental policies, and education. These issues then led to questions as to whether American politics will remain jammed up in ideological conflict and self interest, how we will deal with the fact that our present way of living is a way of unjustified privilege in relation to the rest of the world, and how we will overcome the fact that the directive forces of corporate capitalism and technological advancement are deaf to both the citizenly voice and the common good. These questions then opened onto the region of that most general problem of worldview, of that underlying and unifying set of assumptions and values by which America navigates in the world. Acknowledging the problem, and after a short but poignant moment of silence, my son then "returned" by remarking that what we really need is exercise of civic virtue. I am pretty sure—from previous conversations—that what he meant was acting not only to affirm and support the other in their full personhood, as in much of traditional ethics, but also acting in such a way as to create a world in which this kind of relationship is as available as possible to others also. He also spoke of the need to educate people so they become capable of understanding and engaging this virtue, as one in which there is an amazing coincidence between what is good for the other and what is good for self—one that involves a certain kind of love, *Amor Mundi*, love of the world.

Awareness at the level of worldview can support us in the understanding that practice of civic virtue is quite different from a burden of self-sacrifice, or a duty which compromises individuality. It can help us transition to a new worldview in which practice of civic virtue is discovered to be among the very best things we can do for *ourselves* as well for as others, through participation in the life-giving paradox of vital relationship. Healthy worldview can help us live more fully alive, at the same time it liberates us to care for/in the world. This applies to you and me in our local situations, and it also applies to the role of America and other nations in the larger world.

So the "new worldview" is not something abstracted from how we are living right now. It is practical in the sense that it is connected not only to that which we perceive to be ultimate in life, but also to how we move within the webs of relationship and community which constitute the immediacy of our life-situation. We can work on worldview and practice civic virtue at the same time. In fact, the one requires the other, as we come to discover the joy of an entirely synergistic relation between the two. To put the matter somewhat crudely, (re)discovery of the value of civic virtue can be seen as analogous to discovery of the need for regular physical exercise. It is an essential element of a good and healthy life.

NEW WORLDVIEW

The conversation with my son described above is but one very local instance of new worldview emerging in both interpretation and action, this sense of "another possibility" which can bring us out of despair and into the kind of action which exhibits a distinctively post-traditional and post-modern *Amor Mundi*, a love of the world that motivates creative engagement. It is emerging through many localities, through many very particular conversations in America and on the planet.

But at some point the question arises: What can we say in more general terms about the nature of new worldview? How can we support the many local emergences without insisting that they be either totally the same or completely different? This is not an easy question, especially if it is assumed that "answer" must come in the form of a doctrine or a superior set of ideas, some grand and final abstraction to which all local instances must correspond, as was assumed historically within the dominant Western worldview. However, through the many descriptions of the new worldview which are contained in the pages that follow (and which one hears in local conversations such as that with my son), there are four points which are widely shared. First, they understand that ideas are relative to living, not the other way around; our lives cannot be either reduced to or derived from the ideas through/about which we speak. Rather, the quality of the life we live is either supported and enhanced by the ideas we adopt—or not. This implies that we have some perspective on the worldview we represent, as at least in part a limited human response to that which we and/or our ancestors perceive to be ultimate in life. In philosophical terms, this is to say we have achieved some degree of hermeneutical sophistication, understanding that human beings inevitably have an interpretation, though no one has *the* interpretation—that all of us are in a lifelong process of refining our interpretations. Second, they agree that the new worldview is, above all, *relational,* that the purity of its presence is dependent on the quality of our relationships with others, the quality of our responsiveness, communication, and compassion. Further, the new worldview is *pluralistic,* reflective of *alterity* or otherness as a second root imperative and challenge of our era: encounter with the other who is different, maintaining relationship which neither reduces the other to the same, nor pushes them to the incommensurable, living in the paradox of sameness and difference where human well-being occurs. This implies that we are able to affirm ongoing growth and refinement in relation to both the articulation and the practice of our worldview, along with others who are doing the same. The third point is affirmation of life, including the vast interdependence of the natural world within which life is given, in Hannah Arendt's words, as "a free gift from nowhere (secularly speaking)."[7] The new worldview entails movement beyond the earth and life-denying tendencies of both traditional and modern cultures, into a life way which values faithfulness to Earth as what William James calls "our common mother."[8] The fourth point is *development.* The new worldview which is emerging in our time both generates and depends on a maturity which has been known at the foundation of the great traditions, but which has been largely eclipsed by both the oppressions of tradition and the distractions of the modern.

All of this is to imply that developmental work on worldview involves the willingness *to think,* which is arguably a rare quality in America today, a quality whose absence accounts for many of our difficulties. I don't mean the technical or financial thinking with which so many are obsessed, but the thinking of humans *as* humans—about meaning, value, and purpose. This kind of thinking requires reflexivity or the developed capacity to become conscious of not only what we think but also *how* we think, and thereby become responsible for our choices as to ways of evaluating and prioritizing experience. We need to learn to think about what our values are and why we value them, about our guiding perspective, life-interpretation—our worldview. We need to "choose life."

Movement to this crucial choice involves three developmental steps, or stages. First we must understand that the Western myth of the detached, transparent, objective observer has past, as has the absolutistic period in human history in which (especially Western) people and cultures claimed that their view of reality had "universal validity" and hence superiority over all others. We need to become conscious of worldview as an essential human and cultural function, maturing beyond it as an unconscious given, and in the process move on from the age-old need for an absolutized One Correct Way of thinking/valuing, to appreciate there being more than one right answer to life's most important questions.

Second, we must develop beyond the temptation—in a world which has been de-absolutized more by modern/consumer values than by conscious resolve—to adopt the shallow and relativistic surrogate worldview of materialism/capitalism/scientism which comes to the fore after traditional worldviews have ceased to function. Still in the second stage, we must avoid pitfalls of corrosive cynicism and moral degradation which are implicit in the surrogate worldview, as well as the seductions of fundamentalist and even fascist *re*absolutizings, once the insufficiency of the surrogate has been discovered.

The third step is into the stage in which we are able to move beyond the pessimistic reduction of life to power relations which is inherent to the modern. This occurs as we dare the initially terrible encounter with the Nothingness which lurks within modern life, an encounter which first occurs in the form of the nihilistic conclusion: that the emptiness of modern life means that life is about nothing more than the clashing of interest and power. This phase fades and passes as the encounter with Nothingness deepens and we discover—if we do not become arrested in nihilism, or a victim of some fundamentalist recoil and/or terrorist reaction—Nothingness as *source* and *life-affirmation.* This more mature understanding of Nothingness, reflective of awareness of the radical ineffability of that which is ultimate in life, or of the gift quality of life itself, makes it possible for us to participate in the liberating awareness that a worldview is humanly inevitable and a reflection of how we live, as well as of the uniqueness of our local situation—culturally, socially, and personally, and hence a matter of choice and responsibility. Worldview is at least in part a choice, a human creation, a *response* to the gift quality of life and its deepest source (whether we call it the Dao, God, Allah, Gaia, or the Force). We become able to affirm worldview as a human response to the commonly shared source of life, as expression of our own life-affirmation, and hence also as a part of our lives which grows and develops, becoming ever more global over time in ongoing reciprocity with the way we live, think, and the web of relationships in which we live. Here we become capable to growing beyond the Catch 22 of absolutism versus relativism, into a genuine pluralism which lies beyond mere toleration, and hence into the willingness to learn and grow through relationship with those who are different. All that is needed is for us to acknowledge the inevitably of our having a worldview, our capacity to choose/create at this level, and our ongoing need for growth in both thought and action.

Experience with the enormity of these dynamics and the massive transition they imply has led some to say we are living in a second "axial age," in the midst of a huge historical transition analogous to the Axial Age of the last millennium BCE with the emergence of the world's great traditions, a profound change in human consciousness which occurred simultaneously in parts of the world which were not connected physically.[9] From this perspective, the instability and never-ending crises of our time can be seen as analogous to the trembling of an airplane as it begins to push against the sound barrier. Of course it is not ours to know whether this is actually the case or not—whether, for example, what we are experiencing is something more akin to the decline and fall of a civilization. But the axial hypothesis does serve to underline the depth and urgency of the developmental challenge we face. And I also think it is helpful in that it can provide us with a sense of vocation, a positive vision of a great drama to which we might contribute our effort.

It is important to be aware, though, that visions of a great drama can take us away from ordinary life and actual practice of civic virtue, into realms of abstraction, and universalizing, and thereby into new forms of hegemony based on ideas which turn out to be not universal at all, but unwittingly peculiar to and favoring of our tribe. Indeed, there is a basic paradox to the emergence of the new worldview which has been well-stated in Tu Weiming's phrase, "the globalization of local knowledge."[10] All knowledge universalizes, but at the same time all knowledge can be accounted for by the particularities of its local origin. In our post-traditional time we have learned that visions of the global which are disconnected from humble awareness of their local roots tend toward hegemony, while forms of the local which do not attend to the global dimension become equally problematic. The latter become insular and exceptionalist, without any positive principles for relationships with others who are different, without any appreciation of our common humanity. Either way, vision of great drama which is severed from the global-local paradox becomes dangerous. Ironically, it turns out that both sides of the severing come to the same result, to requiring the presence of others who are identified as less—if not as outright enemy.

In the work which follows, the global aspects of a new worldview are articulated through local efforts in America to reappropriate and revitalize the democratic spirit. Conversely, local articulation arises through dialogue not only with the American past and present, but also with persons from other parts of the globe, especially from China, who struggle with the same basic problem: the need to overcome the limits of the modern, one dimension of which is development of a new worldview which entails fresh reappropriation of traditional resourses. On this crucial point I join others in the global community who see the addictive appeal and tragic limitations of the modern as generating a shared crisis of humankind, what Arendt refers to as the "negative solidarity"[11] of the present, and what Huston Smith describes as "a single common crisis whose cause is the spiritual condition of the modern world. That condition is characterized by loss."[12] America, for all that is great (and all that was new) in its past, gives testimony to this loss and the senses of desperation, frustration, and emptiness which issue from the modern condition. However, I also want to stand by the point I have made previously: that America as aspiration and imperfect embodiment contains great developmental riches as well, including the positive elements of modernity.

DIALOGUE, TRADITION, AND PRACTICE

Dialogue is key in terms of how we can reappropriate traditional sources and the best of modernity, in order to find a remedy for the modern condition, at the same time that it indicates the essential relational dimension of a new worldview. For dialogue represents a new paradigm in which access to the spiritual power of the great traditions becomes surprisingly possible—the *power,* the sustaining energy, not just the ideas and colorful rituals.[13] At the same time, it is also a way in which unity and diversity can be mutually supportive, breaking through the modern opposition between oppressive sameness on one side, and chaotic difference on the other. For within and through dialogue, as the vibrant interplay between the similar and the different, and between the past and the present, we find a new home, a place of not only sustainability but also thriving, including the capacity to work with others on commonly shared problems. Dialogue, then, in one sense *is* the new worldview. Yet some serious developmental work is required in order to get to this place.

Diana Eck indicates how dialogue is fundamentally relational in nature, and how it might be seen as identical with new worldview:

> Dialogue is the process of connection. There is no dialogue among religions as such. Dialogue is always among people. . . . Dialogue is premised not on unanimity, but on difference. Dialogue does not aim at consensus, but understanding. Dialogue does not create agreements, but it creates relationships.[14]

I could only add that the relationship of dialogue is not static, and that developmental movement and transformation occur through ever deeper participation in this relationship—through the practice of it. Through dialogue we find ourselves emerging in our genuineness, as calm and true self, beyond frantic ego, with its endless craving, driven by fear, ignorance, and the urge to control.

This, quite clearly, is to make large claims about dialogue. Understood in the terms I have just used, it can be seen as a contemporary manifestation of the transformative practice which is found in the world's traditions, especially those which focus on transformation through relationship. But at the same time dialogue is also—and rather obviously to those who would look—expressive of vitality in the present, even of the deepest and best potential of modernity itself. So it can be seen as the meeting of traditional wisdom and contemporary vitality, as an intersection at which both come to healthy embodiment.

What I have just said rests on an understanding about human life which needs to be made explicit: There is an unavoidable two-ness or duality about human life which can be described in various ways, but which centers on the transformation of an initial ego self (to continue with the language used above) through the emergence of a deeper true self. Much will need to be said as our conversation continues by way of exploring and testing this bold statement (bold, that is, from the modern perspective, though certainly not from the perspective of the world's historic traditions). For now I just want to say that one of the greatest challenges of the developmental process through which true self emerges is that in its initial stages ego envelopes and normalizes to the point where often it will suffocate true self rather than open to those "higher" or deeper energies which alone can allow redemption of ego and liberation of true self. For ego cannot see beyond its own enclosure, except "through a glass dimly" in extraordinary (and usually very brief) moments of lucidity, self-transcendence, or "religious experience" (just enough to generate poetry, scripture, and hope). The first "moment" in the transformation process, then is our conscious acknowledgment of the tension itself and our need of transformation, our being able to step out of ego just enough to recognize our limitations and affirm the existence of a higher reality which is somehow attuned to the depth of self or "soul"—an awareness which is both "higher" or "deeper," and qualitatively different from that of the ordinary self, an awareness of which others who are different may have some useful perspective.[15]

It is also important to recognize the linkage between this process and the wisdom of the historic traditions. Jacob Needleman says it well: "The idea of a real self behind the appearances forms the central doctrine of every great teaching and tradition throughout the ages."[16] He is speaking of "doctrine" as something much greater than a set of ideas, as something like the "wisdom" which Huston Smith and others recommend as the compelling reason for our reappropriating traditions as very practical resources for our depleted lives in the post-traditional present. The traditions contain wisdom and even energy (or wisdom *as* energy, spirit, in-spiration—something quite different from only ideas) in support of the essential human development from ego-driven to soul-affirming consciousness.

Going back to dialogue and transformation through relationship, one example from a historical tradition is that of Socrates—though I could (and will) also cite the traditions of Confucius, Jesus, and others. We find the center of Socrates' transformative practice in his famous statement about "the examined life:"

> I tell you that to let no day pass without discussing goodness and all the other subjects about which you hear me talking and examining both myself and others is really the very best thing a man [*sic*] can do, and that a life without this sort of examination is not worth living.[17]

"Examining both myself and others" as a daily practice is "the very best thing" a person can do because it moves us from the false knowing of ego to a higher or deeper awareness which Socrates describes as "knowing nothing," which at the same time is the opening through which we develop ever greater access to reality itself and our own "inner" or "prophetic voice."[18] We can find similar examples in the other great traditions.

Returning to "new worldview," I am suggesting that it is indeed new, and that it entails a transformative dimension, a profound response to the imperative of growth. But the transformative dimension itself is not new. It is at least as old as the Axial Age, a dimension which flickers in and out of history as a real possibility for human beings, and one which now intersects in a most fortunate way with that vitality of the present which we know as "dialogue." So perhaps when we speak of a new worldview we are really talking about an idea whose time has finally come.

But, again, the "idea" is really a practice. Hence conscious acknowledgment of the existence of deeper self and our need of transformation presupposes a third basic imperative of our era, and that is the imperative of our adopting—again, consciously—a transformative practice which can carry us across the zone of transition which constitutes the time in which we find ourselves living. And with this post-traditional consciousness of practice we experience the possibility that the wisdom of the traditions might be even more powerfully available to us than it was in the time of our ancestors.[19]

AMERICAN AMBIGUITY

Because of the history of the Western assumption of superiority, which legitimated domination and exploitation of the rest of the world in the modern period, many Western intellectuals—and people generally—are very reticent about speaking of such things as worldview, shy specifically because of the dangers of more or less inadvertent "false universalizing." Those in the Postmodernist conversation often are so occupied with critique and deconstruction of previous instances of Western false or hegemonic universalizing that they become paralyzed in "incommensurability," the understanding that the Other is *so* other that we cannot possibly speak of what is shared or common without becoming imperialists all over again. What I am getting to is that there are serious and subtle inhibitions against speaking of what is great in the Western and American traditions. Yet I also want to say it is worth the risk, worth venturing beyond the shyness which characterizes Western culture in the post-traditional present (an unsteady sort of shyness which can sometimes wear the mask of defensive/aggressive arrogance). For America still has much to offer the world, much beyond that which is attractive, even addictive about modernity.

This raises the question: On what basis do I in particular dare speak of such large things as a new worldview for the global era? Well, first I speak in a radically pluralistic context, offering my interpretation as one among many within the several circles of conversation mentioned above. I write neither from the "ivory tower," nor any other structure of superiority, nor as a display of my individual subjectivity, but from within the larger conversation about the human and planetary future. I do so in appreciation of the fact that my limitations will be identified, and that I will be able to grow with others as conversation continues. Another way to say this might be to say that what is presented in this book is empirically based, a report from the ground of the intertwined conversations I have mentioned and the movements which are both created and reflected by them, as a more or less faithful synthesis and summary which can be challenged where need be. Also, my focus is on the practical value of the view I share, as one which might be conducive to our mutual development and thriving. I write, then, under the criterion that what I say should contribute to the actual embodiment of a new worldview and the reviving of civic virtue in America and the world.

Also by way of being clear about my own location, I want to say that I represent a certain sub-tradition in Western and American history and culture, a tradition of democratic community which, like other traditions, has been eclipsed by modern society and which we urgently need to reclaim. I speak from a kind of "liberalism" which is quite different from the natural rights individualism and corporate capitalism with which that term is usually associated today; I speak from an overshadowed subtradition which emphasizes neither isolation nor collectivism, but relationality.

In addition, I represent a sector of American society which is intimately tied to our democratic aspirations, and that is higher education—which Fareed Zakaria has referred to as "America's best industry."[20] He points to higher education in this way not because of its "career training," but because of its cultivation of the person. More specifically, I represent the tradition of liberal education in America, as a broadly shared tradition of transformation, representation, and deliberation within our shared life as persons who could be capable of democratic relationality—or citizenship, or civic virtue. I will want to say more later on about this great but undervalued American asset.

Finally, I write from a certain understanding of America. America, unlike other nations, has been from the beginning an ideal and a conscious "experiment," a vastly imperfect attempt to create a "republic of man[*sic*]kind," and a social order whose unity arises from its plurality: out of many, one—*E pluribus unum.* It has been a laboratory in which people from all over the world have attempted to live in harmony, within a worldview which is both commonly shared and affirming of difference, and in which care for the common good is given religious significance through a non-ecclesiastical civil religion as well as through practices of participation and service in ordinary life. For the distinctively American worldview and its vision of democratic community life is by no means a product of the natural rights tradition alone, the tradition of hyper individualism which is associated with the problematic form of "liberalism."[21] The other, more harmonious tradition to which I point has been substantially influenced and shaped by the Greek tradition of civic republicanism, the democracies of 17th-century left wing Protestantism, actual experiences of self-government, and social activism on behalf of justice for native, African American, and other disadvantaged and/or marginalized groups. Each of these influences has understood there to be a religious quality to the public as a space in which the truth might be uncovered (in Greek, *Alethea,* truth as unveiling), or God's will made manifest, or the best course of policy discovered through the deliberation and reasoning together of citizens who are equal within a commonly shared life which enjoys difference more than sameness.

It is very hard to say what it is that has sustained this most ambitious and fragile understanding and its very limited embodiments in the actualities of American history. Martin E. Marty, our generation's most consistently wise commentator on the American religious condition, adopts Justice Felix Frankfurter's phrase, "the binding tie of cohesive sentiment," to speak of the most illusive and fundamental factor.[22] The content of this sentiment has favored pluralism: the willingness of those who would participate in the public space to acknowledge the limited nature of their views, and the possibility of growth through persuasive contact with those who are different. Marty points out that the principle of cohesion is not that we all assent to the same doctrine or creed. Rather, it is a "sentiment" which arises from the rich and complex interplay of our story telling, our partially overlapping associations, and the conversations we pass through in the course of a day. In other words, the cohesion is a *relational* quality involving much more than only the intellect, a quality Marty refers to as "the spirit of constitutionalism and the soul of the Declaration."[23] Invoking cohesive sentiment, supporting it, and letting it be more inclusive is our most serious and underlying problem today—in America and in the world. My claim is that the most effective way to invoke is through response to the three imperatives that have been identified in this chapter: the imperatives of growth, encounter with the other who is different, and engagement of transformative practice.

Actually, we might simplify these and roll them into one: growth through encounter with otherness as a transformative practice.

NOTES

1. I have found, after many decades of research and teaching, that one of the most profound works on this crucial and very difficult theme is Robert N. Bellah's "Religious Evolution," in *Beyond Belief: Essays on Religion in a Post-Traditional World* (New York: Harper & Row, 1970), pp. 20–45—also in my anthology, *Living Beyond Crisis: Essays on Discovery and Being in the World* (New York: Pilgrim Press, 1980), pp. 91–117. Bellah links consciousness of worldview to our "beginning to understand the laws of the self's own existence" (42), in such a way that "culture and personality themselves have come to be viewed as endlessly revisable" (44).

2. William James, *The Varieties of Religious Experience* (London: Longman, Green, and Co., 1902), p. 53.

3. Morris Berman, *Dark Ages America: The Final Phase of Empire* (NY: Norton, 2006), p. 329. For another current work which speaks of the coming era as one of massive change, and which makes the case that this era can be positive if it is guided by conscious awareness and engagement, see Paul Gilding, *The Great Disruption: Why the Climate Crisis Will Bring on the End of Shopping and the Birth of a New World* (New York: Bloomsbury Press, 2011).

4. Amartya Sen, "Democracy and Its Global Roots," in *The New Republic*, Oct. 6, 2003, p. 35.

5. Sor-hoon Tan, "Reconstructing 'Culture:' A Deweyan Response to Antidemocratic Culturalism," in Sor-hoon Tan and John Whalen-Bridge, eds., *Democracy as Culture: Deweyan Pragmatism in a Globalizing World* (Albany, NY: SUNY, 2008).

6. The dynamics of transformative practice, including reading, writing, and conversation (which I take to be the essential sub-disciplines of liberal education/philosophy as a Western form of transformative practice) have been at the center of my work for a long time. See *Rediscovering the West: An Inquiry into Nothingness and Relatedness* (Albany, NY: SUNY Press, 1994), *Claiming a Liberal Education* (Needham Heights, MA: 1994), *Living Philosophy: Remaining Awake and Moving Toward Maturity in Complicated Times* (St. Paul, MN: Paragon House, 2002), and Shaoxing presentation, "Comparative Philosophy and Practice," later published, in Chinese, in Harvard-Yenching Series, *Globalization and Dialogue Between Civilizations* (Jiangsu: Jiangsu Jiaoyu Press, 2005).

7. Hannah Arendt, in her magnificent Prologue to *The Human Condition* (Chicago: University of Chicago Press, 1958), p. 3.

8. William James, *A Pluralistic Universe*, in *Essays in Radical Empiricism and a Pluralistic Universe*, ed. Richard J. Bernstein (New York: Dutton, 1971), p. 128.

9. In a most general way we could say that the change involved discovery of the One, the single, ultimate principle of reality, *and* that the One can be manifest through human beings as they engage or accept their transformation. See Karl Jaspers, *The Origin and Goal of History* (New Haven: Yale University Press, 1953). A recent articulation of the meaning of the Axial Period and its significance for today, one which especially emphasizes the commonly shared identification of wisdom with compassion at the root of the traditions, before the historic interpretations and orthodoxies were established, is Karen Armstrong's *The Great Transformation: The Beginnings of Our Religious Traditions* (New York: Alfred A. Knopf, 2006).

10. Tu Weiming, "Implications of the Rise of 'Confucian' East Asia," in *Daedalus: Journal of the American Academy of Arts and Sciences,* Vol. 129, no. 1 (winter 2000), pp. 195–218.

11. Hannah Arendt, "Karl Jaspers: Citizen of the World?," in *Men in Dark Times* (New York: Harcourt, Brace and World, 1968), p. 83. In Rowe, ed., *Living Beyond Crisis,* P. 253.

12. Huston Smith, *Why Religion Matters: The Fate of the Human Spirit in an Age of Disbelief* (San Francisco: HarperSanFrancisco, 2001), p. 1.

13. As a post-traditional person who draws on more than one great tradition, I have been aware of this distinction for a long time, and want to mention two mentors who have been especially helpful in understanding the difference between intellectual construction and transformative power: Jacob Needleman, especially in his *The Heart of Philosophy* (New York: Alfred A. Knopf, 1982), and Huston Smith, especially in his *Forgotten Truth* (New York: Harper Collins, 1976).

14. Diana Eck, "Dialogue and the Echo Boom of Terror: Religious Women's Voices after 9/11," in Akbar Ahmed and Brian Forst, eds., *After Terror: Promoting Dialogue Among Civilizations* (Cambridge, UK: Polity Press 2005), p. 28.

15. I am aware that I paint with a broad brush here, and that more fine work will be required later in the conversation. The point is acknowledgment of the limited, anxious, incomplete, and/or problematic self, and the possibility of remedy, redemption, or growth such that a transformed or mature person can emerge. Hence "soul" can be taken to stand alongside Buddhist non-self, Confucian relational self, and the constructions of other traditions which affirm the need of transformation according to their understandings of the human problem and the prescription of practices through which it is addressed.

16. Jacob Needleman, *The Heart of Philosophy,* p. 166.

17. Plato, *Apology* 38a, in *The Collected Dialogues of Plato,* ed. Edith Hamilton and Huntington Cairns, Bollingen Series, no. 71 (New York: Pantheon Books, 1985), p. 23.

18. *Apology* 31d, 40a, *Ibid.,* pp. 17, 24.

19. But, again, let us be clear that the philosophical anthropology or view of human life which I have just presented is by no means shared by all. "Soul" is not in fact acknowledged by all, or maybe even most people in America today, except in vague and tepid ways. The opposite view, one which is deeply entrenched in modern society, would be that of behaviorism and its

claim that stimulus-response conditioning is the bottom line. Perhaps the most direct and authoritative presentation of this view would be B. F. Skinner's *Beyond Freedom and Dignity* (Indianapolis: Hackett, 1971).

20. Fareed Zakaria, *The Post-American World* (New York: W. W. Norton, 2008), p. 190.

21. On the deeper and more substantive meaning of democracy, its roots in many cultures as they can be reappropriated through dialogue in our time, and the radical difference between democracy and the "neo-liberal" meanings with which it has been misunderstood since the Cold War, see Amartya Sen, *The Argumentative Indian: Writings on Indian History, Culture and Identity* (London: Penguin Books, 2005), and Fred Dallmayr, *The Promise of Democracy: Political Agency and Transformation* (Albany, NY: SUNY Press, 2010).

22. Martin E. Marty, *The One and the Many: America's Struggle for the Common Good* (Cambridge: Harvard University Press, 1997), p. 22. See Abraham Lincoln also—1861 "Address in Independence Hall."

23. *Ibid.*, p. 210.

Chapter Two

Ideologues, Nihilists, and the Depressed—and Relationalists

The pathos of our situation in the post-traditional era is that no human description of it is possible, leaving us at the mercy of technologies and systems of commerce which require no description except those of number. This underlying fact is hard for humans to see in the midst of material well-being and/or the promise thereof. Any human description is immediately reduced to the location, interests, and prejudices of the describer, and thereafter dismissed, or it arises from aggregates of interest and power: as markets and voting blocks, mobs of "like" and "dislike," poling, lobbying, and buying as registrations of personal preference. Or any description can be relativized away with ever-available partial and conflicting factuality.

What we don't often notice, and what is so sad and dangerous about our situation from the relational/democratic perspective which was presented in the first chapter, is the impossibility of appeal to "the common good," or "public goods"—such as is envisioned by those components of education which are designed to cultivate the human being and the virtues associated with the living of a democratic life, a life of civil discourse, critical thought, and at least some willingness to sacrifice individual interests to the greater good. These components are seen to be unnecessary, having to do with matters best left to management, or they are met with suspicion as to the hidden interests they might import, or they incite ideological standoff about things which are peripheral to the virtues themselves (all the while demonstrating the consequence of their absence). So we get a life of superficial wrangling and wondering how we can get "an adult in the conversation," all the while the invisible hands of technology and commerce structure and move our world ever more in the direction of a single mechanism which is beyond the reach of any human hand, let alone that of the citizen.

This is not a new or particularly radical description. As early as the 1920s John Dewey spoke of the inability of the public "to identify and distinguish itself":

> . . . the machine age has so enormously expanded, multiplied,intensified and complicated the scope of indirect consequences, have formed such immense and consolidated unions in action, on an impersonal rather than a community basis, that the resultant public cannot identify and distinguish itself.[1]

Alfred North Whitehead, in another classic reading of the modern loss of the public, speaks of the emergence of a new "celibacy of the intellect," professionalism, and "minds in a groove," contributing to a condition in which "the specialized functions of the community are performed better and more progressively, but the generalized direction lacks vision."[2]

Despite persistence and intensification of this problem, some refuse to give up, continue to have faith in the possibility and strength of human goodness to penetrate and transform the world. Some decide and consciously choose to maintain this faith, despite overwhelming evidence against it. Some have "kept the faith," and, who knows, maybe that is the reason why we are still here. Maintaining modesty about what it is possible for humans to know, what if there is something else going on here which we understand only dimly? What if it somehow really matters what we decide and choose— *really* matters, not only that (as some have yet to discover) living as though it did is the best and most healthy way to live?

In order to support that root faith which is no different from life-affirmation or the will to civic virtue, in order to be able to live it into the world as effectively as we can, in order to achieve some measure of grace in the midst of what often seems an impossible situation, we need to be able to speak it to ourselves and each other. This is the purpose of this book.

By way of beginning, I think we need clear-eyed description of the world we share. When this ethereal faith that our action matters and the relational/ democratic vision with which it is associated opens its eyes onto the world, what does it see? This is what I attempt in the next two chapters, this one more macrocosmically, expanding the view which has already been opened up in this first section, and the next more microcosmically, in terms of personhood and the textures of relationship.

CORPORATE CAPITALISM AND THE ABANDONMENT OF AMERICA

The American ideal of democratic community life has been eclipsed by a distinct set of values and sensibilities which grew out of Western Europe in the 17th century, and which later found expression in America and many other parts of the world. It arose with "natural rights individualism" in the social and political sphere, and was supported by the scientific worldview which emerged in parallel and reciprocal reinforcement during the 17th century. America—like many other societies—has been overshadowed by values associated with individualism and the scientific paradigm, putting into the shade earlier values associated with a democratic community life of both liberty and justice in America and elsewhere. With dominance of the natural rights view, society came to be seen as a derivative and artificial entity, a "social contract," with separate individuals being the basic reality. It was thought that society would come to a state of "automatic harmony" as a result of autonomous, rational persons freely pursuing their interests, where this pursuit was understood to be a natural right (and equal possibility), and where "interests" were defined chiefly in terms of the acquisition of property. The tension between this individualism and the other tradition of democratic community life is evident throughout American history, but individualism came to the fore very decisively with transition from the 19th to the 20th century when America underwent its "modernization"—with industrialization, urbanization, immigration, the enthusiasm for science and the beginnings of social science, the development of mass media, and emergence of the corporation.[3] The corporation was defined by direct analogy to the natural rights individual and treated accordingly; it was defined as a super person, as individualism writ large and normatively on the social order.[4] Increasingly democratic values were displaced by corporate values, as "democracy" came to be understood in procedural rather than substantive terms, as a structure of government rather than community, and as the distinctly minimalist form of government most friendly to free market capitalism. And the democratic tradition of citizen action through voluntary associations, community organizations, and the independent sector was largely disqualified from effective participation in public life due to scale, specialization, and a kind of forgetting which came to regard the earlier democratic ideal as "unrealistic."

Corporations gained further power through developing effectiveness in lobbying and in government, and, especially under the leadership of Reagan and Bush, many began to conflate the distinction between democracy and capitalism, to see corporate power as virtually the same as American power, and to reorganize structures of policy-making and taxation accordingly.[5]

Finally, as this view came to dominate American culture and politics, "liberal democracy" came to be all but identified with corporate capitalism and its orienting values of competition and profit. Meanwhile, few noticed expansion of the corporation beyond the nation state, and the irony that the now-global corporations care nothing for America, or any nation state in particular. Despite patriotic rhetoric from corporate leaders, some philanthropy, and public relations programs, the only allegiance of corporations is to their own "bottom line" as determined by cost-benefit analysis and the financial gain of stockholders. America became nothing more than a market, and one more resource to be exploited—and, for many corporate people, a fortress protecting enclaves of privilege.[6]

The problem is structural. Despite the fact that corporations contain many good people, they are structured in a way that requires them to maximize profit above all else. The corporation as an entity has no way—except through programs of philanthropy, which are small in comparison with overall impact, and often driven by PR purposes—to care for the common good, except in the very limited and flawed laissez faire sense that in some circumstances each of us looking out for our own interests will result in a quiet harmony.[7] But in the present world of limited resources, tight interdependence, and awareness of inequalities arising from cultural values, the energizing vision of the corporation and capitalism become radically problematic. Add to these factors the mix of fear and loss of confidence in the future which saturate the current environment, and the possibilities of the corporation being a "good citizen" by contributing to the long-term health of the community becomes an aspiration on the part of good-hearted corporate people with little grounding in reality.

There is a profound irony here, one which may even be among the great ironies in the rise and fall of civilizations. For ours is an era of enormous redistribution and restructuring. Power and resources and cultural energy are flowing out of America and Europe, and into Eastern and Southern societies. Clearly one factor in this is liberationist movements, their unmasking of the dynamics of culture and oppression, and the resulting unwillingness of people to accept the subservient position. That mysterious sense of legitimacy which allowed Western Europe and America to colonize and exploit the rest of the world, assuming, as others more or less did also, its own superiority and privileged status, is gone. And surely another factor in restructuring and redistribution is Western guilt, or at least the Western paralysis and self-criticism which arise once it discovers what has been done. Another factor is the sudden undercutting of the assumption of continuous growth, which legitimates overspending and making pension promises which are unkeepable. Yet another is inability to protect intellectual property and copyrights as protections supporting the ideal of people inventing, producing, and selling something new from their garage.

However, the major factor in the global redistribution of resources arises out of the most intimate center of American aspiration, and that is the convergence of individualism and science in the corporation and its associated investment institutions. Here the sciences of cost-benefit analysis and management are applied ever more deeply and more broadly in the service of individual stockholders,[8] a good number of whom may not even be aware that they are invested in any particular corporation. The corporation seeks competitive advantage wherever it can, under the constant supervision of legions of money managers, and facilitated by an ever more sophisticated managerial revolution with fine-grained measures of planning, effectiveness, systems integration, and productivity—measures which often identify the "human resources" component as more costly and less necessary than it had been before.[9] And in the process, especially in the presence of relatively low costs for labor, natural resources, and transportation outside of America, few notice that this is the major force driving the abandonment of America and the restructuring of the world—again, despite the fluttering of patriotic flags.

HATING REASONABLE DISCOURSE

Why don't Western people *see* this?![10] What blindness—perhaps analogous to that which caused the dinosaurs to wander into swamps, bog down, and die—is at work here?[11] I suggest that this curious condition is due to the fact that Western culture is especially susceptible to what we might call the ideological life orientation, locking into a set of assumptions and subsequent refusal to entertain any new evidence which might call these into question. The particular susceptibility of Westerners to what is surely a basic *human* tendency is associated with the intellectualism of Western history, the need to find meaning and value in a dimension which is *out there,* displaced and static in relation to the complexities and ambiguities of real life. In the post-traditional era we see that intellectualism can be extremely effective in terms of getting things done, but that it is dangerous also, insofar as it can lead to the ideological blindness, especially in times of stress.[12]

This may have been what Socrates had in mind when he said that "there is no worse fate that a person can suffer than to hate reasonable discourse."[13] There is no worse because the alternative to reasonable discourse is ideological dispute. Ideology involves rigid and closed formulation of commitments, purposes, and interpretations, followed by attempt to implement them no matter what the actual circumstance.[14] A close corollary to the ideological is manipulation: the effort, borne of righteous (though usually insecure) certitude, to get people to comply with one's ideology through any means available. Manipulation includes repeated and aggressive assertion of the ideology; "spin," or the packaging of the ideology in positive images, associations, and interests, as well as outright lying—as the attempt to socially construct the situation to conform to the ideology. Within the ideological, the ends justify the means to the extent that the means are hardly noticed. "Reasonable discourse," as the open and dialogical pursuit of the truth and best policy course, is no part of this approach. In fact, reasonable discourse is hated as threatening to ideology.

Hating reasonable discourse is the worst fate for two reasons. First, the ideological hatred of reasonable discourse leads to inflexibility and vulnerability to that which had not been taken into account in the formulation of the ideology, to that which was ignored or denied in the rush from uncomfortable realities into the enclosure of ideology. The defensive arrogance of ideology—its claim to know it all—is especially a temptation in complex and threatening situations. This leads to great danger when the world refuses to comply, or when that which was not noticed suddenly turns out to be decisive. The fate of this kind of position is often failure, not only due to the inadequacy of ideology in general as a response to the complexity of life circumstances, but also because it can so easily be taken by others as provocation and invitation to attack—since the combination of arrogance and ignorance which typifies the ideological orientation is, at best, annoying to those with whom it is not shared.

The second reason hating discourse is the worst fate a person can suffer is that it results in isolation. The ideologue closes her off from fresh insight, emergent discovery, and the inspiration which can occur when we take a position of some openness. In isolation abscesses occur, intellectual, psychological, and spiritual infections which—in the absence of a healthy flow of reflection, criticism, and correction—can lead to various forms of sickness.

Maybe other societies, with long histories of authoritarian rule and corresponding subtraditions of compensation, can handle this orientation better than America can. But America was quite literally founded on reasonable discourse. Nothing has been more fundamental to the American republic than the idea that reasonable people of good will with differing positions on issues within a shared life can deliberate and discover a course of action which is often better than mere compromise. While we may be able to imagine and fear even worse fates for America, a period of sustained despising and defiling of reasonable discourse has undercut its integrity profoundly.

IDEOLOGUES, NIHILISTS, AND THE DEPRESSED

In fact, it seems that in America now there are only three types: ideologues, nihilists, and the depressed. The most obvious kind is the ideologue, the one who takes a fixed and immovable position to such a degree that they have no real interest in what is actually going on. It is understandable: in the midst of the stress and enormous complexity of a suddenly global era, its frustrations and threats, people draw back into the places in which they feel secure. This place, especially for many Westerners, is *knowing*. The ideologue is the one who resides in a structure of knowing they do not entirely trust, and therefore must assert and defend.

Some ideologues are actually nihilists. This distinction is easy to miss—and critical to our situation. The nihilist may champion an ideology, or a series of them, some even in contradiction with others, but they actually believe in none of them. They simply cannot find any other way of relating—or manipulating. The nihilist is the one who has lost all faith in (and/or memory of) the common good and the possibility of civic virtue. They have come to the conclusion that life in the world cannot be about anything more than the pursuit of self-interest and the power-relations associated with ongoing, competitive struggle. There is an essential cynicism to this position, which distinguishes it from the "true believer" attitude of the ideologue, as well as from the earlier natural rights faith that "automatic harmony" and the "common good" would result from people acting on their own interest. The often unwitting arrival at the sad conclusion of the nihilist, and the unconscious awareness that it constitutes a fundamental denial and violation of their humanity—not to mention that of others—lends a fanatical zeal to their presence. It is as though they have committed to the Faustian deal of agreeing that the devil may have their soul at death in exchange for a manic energy in the life that remains. Part of the bargain is an evangelical insistence that all others be brought down to their conclusion. Hence they exhibit envy (of those who still believe in something), manipulation, blaming, lying, and endlessly competitive behavior—ultimately for nothing other than absurd self-aggrandizement.

The nihilist is a former ideologue; he/she has given up on any of the ideologies which fill the air, and become a secret opportunist among them, now insisting on one ideology, now another. But this is not opportunism in the traditional sense, because the nihilist arrives at their opportunistic behavior by way of the conclusion as to the ultimacy of power against a field of utter meaninglessness. Hence they are not selfish like the opportunist, and neither are they selfless in the way that is recommended by the great traditions. Rather, they are empty. They persist and become ever more shrill in their claims to absolute knowing, hardly noticing (or really caring) that

that which they "absolutely know" shifts from one moment to the next, as though to both serve purposes of control and at the same time keep them from encountering their own underlying emptiness. Traditional opportunists look simple-minded by comparison, childish in their self-centeredness, as distinct from the nihilist who has no center.

We are talking about a kind of moral disease which develops at the outer limits of Western individualism, one which requires more full description in the very next chapter, in relation to the late-modern condition of American society. For present purposes perhaps it is sufficient to repeat that it is the emptiness, the absence of integrity—or "soul" in African American terms[15] —that distinguishes the nihilist, the void within themselves which they can neither tolerate nor escape—and the instability that follows from this condition.

The third group is the depressed. They still have faith, but they suffer. They are certainly not very effective in the world, and they are easily marginalized or seduced into the kind of schizophrenia which allows them to accept the dismal state of the world as it is, while projecting their faith into private lives, distant futures, or other cultures. At their best, the depressed know it will take something more than a package of legislation or an adjusted social policy to save us from the disaster which lies ahead on our current course. Since the momentous year 1968 in America, we (now including myself in this third group) have been aware that there must be a fundamental reorientation of consciousness itself, a new worldview, a radical change in the way we think and live.[16] But we have been ineffective in the transmission of this awareness, leaving those in power ever more in power as we retreated further into "consciousness raising" and depression—leaving absolutized ideology and nihilistic assertion to rule in an increasingly hostile public life. Hence since the sixties in America there has been ever-increasing polarization between consciousness types who are politically irresponsible and political types who are unconscious.

Meanwhile, so many of the depressed are caught up in post-modern cultural critique, deconstruction of the traditional worldview, culture wars, guilt, identity politics. They/we have become acutely aware of the sins of the colonizing and hegemonic West in the historical period, and the urgent need for a new worldview which is inclusive and affirming of diversity. But we/ they so easily fall into infighting, suspicion, and paralysis—and often into the nihilistic conclusion as well. In any event, the consequence of all of the above is that they/we have been mostly absent from the actual world of politics and practice of civic virtue.

IDEOLOGICAL AND RELATIONAL WORLDVIEWS

But wait! There is another type, which I will awkwardly describe as the relationalist, as those who participate to some degree in an emerging relational worldview

That great philosopher of the 20th century, Martin Heidegger, famously remarked about a moment like ours that "only a god could save us now." My suggestion is that if some such intervention were to occur, the first thing such a god would do is to help us articulate a new worldview. By "articulate" I do not mean simply the stating of a "philosophy" as a better set of ideas or some abstract dream, but the description and even inspiration of an actual way of living and thriving, right down to the level of child-rearing, education, and personal cultivation in both private and public life—as the essential disciplines of a good life. By "worldview," then, I mean something similar to what the Hebrews were talking about when they said, speaking from a time like our own, "Where there is no vision, the people perish" (Proverbs 29:18).[17]

However, my claim is that such a worldview *already exists*, and does not need to be invented. It is already present, in America today, in world community, and in American history. It only needs to be lifted up and made available. And, of course, people need to be ready to respond.

In fact, the intensity and the dangers of our ideological and nihilistic era reveal that the new worldview—let us call it the Relational Worldview—is really one of two ways of having a worldview, both of which have been present throughout American history. The second, and clearly the more dominant—to the extreme in our time—we can refer to as the Ideological Worldview.

Let me describe the Ideological Worldview first, because we have already been talking about it. It is a worldview which conceives of displaced, static, abstract, *and absolute* sets of rules or laws being *applied* to the complexity and ambiguity of the actual lives we live—as though being in possession of the right rules and universal principles is all that is required, apart from the fairly simple matter of their resolute application. This worldview is intellectualist, deductive, and oriented to the possession of correct doctrine. Its tendency to degenerate into nihilism is but one symptom among many that this orientation is no longer viable. Other obvious symptoms are the conflict and violence which constitute so much of the history of the 20th and 21st centuries. The Ideological, which is common to personal as well as more broadly political strategies, involves retreat from a complex and threatening world, into an illusion of knowing which shuts down relationship and sensitivity to the world. Especially under conditions of heterogeneous world community, it becomes lethal. We should be mature enough by now to recognize that this lifeway only leads to more frustration and fanaticism, and ultimately to nihilism. Paul, in the Christian New Testament, provides an essential statement of the frustration implicit in the Ideological Worldview with his confession: "For the good that I would I do not; but the evil which I would not, that I do" (Romans 7:1). Intense and dangerous frustration is inevitable when we ignore practice by assuming that the holding of good intentions must be sufficient unto right action.

The Relational Worldview, by contrast, is focused on the quality and effectiveness of relationships as the locus of our thriving and continued, mutual growth. This is not radical individualism and a public life of negotiation and social contract, as in the natural rights tradition. Neither is it "pragmatism" insofar as this term is so often confused with relativistic instrumentalism—i.e., what works for me is good and true and beautiful.[18] Rather, in the Relational (and in the fullness of pragmatism) it is understood that the Good, the True, and the Beautiful, and the Just (GTBJ) are real, dynamic, immanent, and manifest through relationship on an ongoing basis. This is not to say that I do not have (or am not serious about) my own particular understandings of the GTBJ, but rather that I am able to see that my understandings are limited because I—and my people, my community and my tradition, my language and symbol system, in fact, everything about me!—is limited, *and, furthermore,* that I am capable of growth, actual learning, development beyond what society had accepted as "adulthood" in the past. My understanding and articulation of the GTBJ develops over time as I develop, as I am progressively able not only to formulate them intellectually, but more importantly, as I am able actually to *embody* them, to *live* them in the whole of my life rather than merely possess them in the form of the One Best Doctrine. And to say that relationship is the locus of our thriving is to say that the place where growth occurs, and the place where the GTBJ become manifest and available for my own transformation and that of others, is in a certain kind of relationship (neither in isolated individualism nor in simple deference to authority).

The main problem with the Relational historically is that it presents a developmental challenge, one which has come to be well recognized by social science.[19] It is rooted in a paradox, something abhorrent to the Ideological/Absolutistic mindset with its idolatry of the intellect. The paradox is that I am able to be fully present as my genuine self in those moments when I am simultaneously *definite* about what I stand for, what I believe and what I think should happen in deliberation about the issue before us, and at the same time *open* to the possibility of being persuaded otherwise, to the revelation of a larger or deeper understanding which may become manifest through your presence and our relating. Here is where I am most fully alive, and where we together discover the best course of action in whatever life—large or small—we share. Here civic virtue becomes possible.

The most obvious point of contrast with the Ideological Worldview, then, is that the relationalist holds the intellectual function in a very different way from that which characterizes the ideologue. In the Ideological, intellectual formulation is of supreme importance, and everything else must follow. In the Relational, the intellectual function is essential, but it is not everything, such that I am able to renounce obsession with being absolutely and exclusively correct, and be open to growth in both thought and action. This I can do without fear of hitting the proverbial "slippery slope" which descends into the quagmire of relativism and subjectivism, because I am committed to my own principles, to a trust in the dynamic and immanent reality of the GTBJ (or, in theological terms, of God), and to the life we share on this extremely fragile planet.

A powerful example of the presence of the Relational Worldview in American history can be found in the life and work of William James. Especially in his later work, he came to terms with the Ideological Worldview and broke through it to articulation of the Relational Worldview. He presents a radically empirical and process view of experience which is responsive to our continuous growth, and a pluralistic view of the world in which the variety of intellectual formulations are understood pragmatically in terms of their capacity to serve the commonly shared aspiration to move us from "foreignness" to "intimacy" in life. The sense of his relational perspective is well communicated in one of his popular essays, "On a Certain Blindness in Human Beings": "Hands off: neither the whole of truth nor the whole of good is revealed to any single observer, although each observer gains a partial superiority of insight from the peculiar position in which he stands."[20] In his lifetime and beyond, James was enormously significant in a wide variety of social and political programs, as well as in the inspiration of countless individuals through articulation of a perspective which gave voice to their own deepest intuitions. But then, with World War II and the encounter with the radical evil of the Nazi regime and the atmosphere of fear it spawned, America turned away from the Relational Worldview, drawing back into the fixed positions and absolutistic certainties of the Ideological. With this turn, James' view was foreshortened in the popular understanding to "pragmatism" in the greatly reduced sense which was equated with relativistic individualism and instrumentalism.[21]

But in our day it becomes clear that the Ideological Worldview is too rigid, too isolated, and too self-serving—too ego-oriented. The world is now too small to continue with traditionalist absolutisms and their post-traditional ideological reassertions. They become dangerous, to the extent that Leonard Swidler, one of the founders of the inter-religious and inter-cultural dialogue movement, speaks of our time as a time of "death or dialogue."[22]

Indeed, we could even say that the movement from the Ideological to the Relational worldview signals a third great period of crisis and growth of the American republic. The first crisis, of course, was that of slavery, revolving around the fact that lofty founding ideals existed alongside the exclusion of some people not only from citizenship, but even from humanity itself. With the Civil War, America nearly collapsed, and Abraham Lincoln came forward as our greatest president, rearticulating foundational principles on the broader horizon of a democracy "of, by, and for the people." The second crisis was that of suffrage, the extension of civil and political rights to all adult persons. It began with First Wave Feminism and the Suffrage Movement, and continued through the Civil Rights Movement of the sixties, culminating with the dismantling of the Jim Crow system and enactment of the Voting Rights Acts of 1964 and 1965. And now we are in the midst of the third crisis, the crisis of "second generation rights" as identified in the 1948 U.N. Universal Declaration of Human Rights. These rights are distinguished from the civil and political "first generation rights" of the U.S. Declaration of Independence and Bills of Rights, which are passive and negative injunctions against interfering with a person's autonomy. Second generation rights are economic, social, and cultural, and they are active and positive in that they require not only action to remove historic constraints against their being available to all people, but active affirmation of cultural and personal diversity and inclusion with which we become concerned in the third period of American crisis. Now American is challenged to extend and deepen its ideals of "liberty and justice for all" to embrace and celebrate otherness and genuine difference, becoming a truly pluralistic society, a society which no longer needs the cement of shared belief and a dominating ideology to hold it together, including the mindset of Western and American individualism which gave rise to first generation rights and is often—as a consequence of over-emphasis—blind to the dynamics of second generation rights.[23]

This third crisis is, of course, most difficult to describe because we are in the middle of it.[24] But I think it is helpful in terms of our understanding and ability to respond, to see that this crisis is fully global in that it involves the generalized movement beyond traditional absolutistic/ideological forms of culture, and passage through the ensuing post-traditional relativism and the surrogate worldview of modernity, as well as past threats of reactions against the latter in the form of fundamentalist and nihilistic movements. I think it is also very important—and hopeful—to note that these crises arose as a result of expansion of human consciousness and ethical horizon. Is it not possible that in the future we might regard the denial of second generation rights as we now regard slavery and the denial of suffrage, as abhorrent? The third crisis implicitly involves discovery of socialization and acculturation, as processes whereby oppressed people come to internalize the values of their oppressors. If consciousness of these age-old processes which served to structure so much of human life historically is possible, is it not possible for humans to become conscious of the limitations—and oppression—of modern values as well?

Surviving the crisis of this passage requires a great deal of us, both personally and culturally. And in this I think it helpful to understand the passage in terms of movement from the Ideological to the Relational. But even as we begin to have some experience of the liberation entailed in living the Relational Worldview, the sense in which it makes it possible to be more fully alive and present in life, and even as we begin to develop some understanding as to its meaning and dimensions, it remains very challenging. We enact struggles within ourselves and in the "culture wars" around us which can be seen as analogous to the struggles of the two previous eras of crisis. And it seems clear that our very survival is at stake.

Making the transition from the Ideological to the Relational is a little like learning to do a back dive off a diving board, requiring that we override old circuits and do something which is counterintuitive: accept vulnerability, let go of defenses that do not defend, and find strength through a position of openness which is principled, alert, and compassionate.

This, of course, is especially difficult in a time of heightened fear. But perhaps it truly is darkest before dawn, and there is still time to grow. Maybe Hegel is right: the Owl of Minerva only flies at dusk.

NOTES

1. John Dewey, *The Public and Its Problems* (Chicago: Swallow Press, 1927), p. 126.

2. Alfred North Whitehead, *Science and the Modern World* (New York: Free Press, 1925), pp. 196–197. On the significance of the public intellectual or citizenly perspective which is excluded under these conditions, see William Dean, "The Rise of the Professional Intellectual," in *The Religious Critic in American Culture* (Albany, NY: SUNY Press, 1974), pp. 19–39.

3. Note potential confusion between the "Modern Period," beginning in the 17th century, and "modernization," indicating the impact of the factors just mentioned.

4. See James Weinstein, *The Corporate Ideal and the Liberal State* (Boston: Beacon Press, 1968).

5. See Si Khan and Elizabeth Minnich, *The Fox in the Henhouse: How Privatization Threatens Democracy* (San Francisco: Berrett-Koehler, 2005).

6. For a detailed articulation of these developments, see Gordon L. Anderson, *Life, Liberty, and the Pursuit of Happiness* (St. Paul: Paragon House, 2009), and Sheldon Wolin, *Democracy Incorporated: Managed Democracy and the Specter of Inverted Totalitarianism* (Princeton, NJ: Princeton University Press, 2008).

7. Here is the root of most human problems! Someone elevates a limited or partial good to the status of *summum bonum*, refusing thereafter to consider the evidence of other partial goods or the need for further refinement in their own.

8. An example that brings this irony to a fine point, is the cost-saving measure that involved the use of inflatable dolls as extras on the set of the Angelina Jolie film, *Salt*.

9. Sometimes, when discussing this relatively recent managerial revolution with students, and the question as to whether/when "the jobs will come back," I tell them about a time not so long ago when it was not uncommon to fly on airplanes which were less than half full. It is as

though they did not notice this "inefficiency" which today would be regarded as obvious. Somehow, strange as it might seem to us today, it simply did not come into conscious awareness. We then go on to wonder if this kind of awareness, and the computer technology with which to hone it to fine calculations, does not count for a major—and permanent—portion of the U.S. employment problem. And from there we go on to wonder if tax friendliness to corporations and the rich no longer results in the "trickle down" benefits for al- in America, because it no longer corresponds with how business is actually conducted.

10. For plausible answers, see Thomas Frank, *What's the Matter With Kansas: How Conservative Won the Heart of America* (New York: Metropolitan Books, 2004) and Bryant Welch, *State of Confusion: Political Manipulation and the Assault on the American Mind* (New York: Thomas Dunne Books, 2008).

11. A brief report from China may be helpful here: my colleagues in the P.R.C. struggle with the same issue, that of the directive principle or the "brain" function of their society, except that they have just the opposite problem from that which we have in the U.S. There the Chinese Communist Party (CCP) decides and controls from the top down, and in recent times has been ruling in a way which is favorable to the people (including allowance for some capitalism within the accommodation announced by Deng Xiao Ping as a "socialist market economy"). Perhaps since June of 1989 the Party has learned to fear protest and the power of democratic claims magnified by media. And it seems likely that the party has become much more informed on effective policy formation, and undergone a kind of top-down democratizing. And it certainly is possible that they love the people more than they fear revolt. But still, Chinese people are at the mercy of a "brain" which might turn against them, and over which they have no control. But then they look at us and see a situation that is not all that different. They see blind obedience to the deeply flawed abstract principle of "free market," a principle which they see as quite obviously leading to breakdown of community, rule by the rich, degradation of character, and the ignoring of social problems. There is one big difference: Chinese people tend to see America as spiraling downward in near-fanatical adherence to its rapidly failing principle, while they see themselves spiraling upwards not just economically, but also in terms of being able to ask about the nature of Chinese vitality and formulate policy-relevant answers to the big question: "What is the China model?"

12. Maybe blindness to the dangers of corporate capitalism arises as a coincidence of intellectualism and historical circumstance. The "red scare" of the 1950s involved the fear that communism was spreading across the whole world and even seeping into American institutions. This fear, sometimes formulated as the "domino theory" in foreign policy (one would fall, falling into the next, and so on in the whole world—especially Southeast Asia) apparently provoked advocacy of the polar opposite of communism, in dogmatic assertion of what Fred Dallmayr calls "neo-liberalism" (see his *The Promise of Democracy*, p. 205). Had it not been for the underlying intellectualism and its tendency toward polar opposition, some more sophisticated thinking might have been possible—both in analysis of communism, and in response.

13. *Phaedo*, 89d, in *The Collected Dialogues of Plato*, p. 71.

14. I want to distinguish "ideology" from the sincere and committed holding of a position. I am influenced in this usage by Hannah Arendt, especially in her seminal chapter "Ideology and Terror: A Novel Form of Government," which is ch. 13 of vol. III of *The Origins of Totalitarianism* (Cleveland and New York: Meridian Books, 1958), pp. 460–479.

15. On African American spirituality and its contributions to American culture, see Peter Paris, *The Spirituality of African peoples: The Search for a Common Moral Discourse* (Minneapolis: Fortress Press, 1995).

16. For interpretation of American culture in the sixties and seventies, see my *Leaving and Returning: On America's Contribution to a World Ethic* (Lewisburg, PA: Bucknell University Press, 1989).

17. For a work on culture which is closest to my own and centered on "vision," see Karl J. Weintraub, *Visions of Culture* (Chicago: University of Chicago Press, 1966).

18. The profoundly relational quality of pragmatism is revealed in John Dewey's two simple but profoundly essential traits of democratic life: ". . . some interest held in common [within a group], and we find a certain amount of interaction and cooperative intercourse with other groups." John Dewey, *Democracy and Education* (New York: Free Press, 1966), p. 83.

19. On the significance of developmental psychology in our time, see the works of Lawrence Kohlberg, Benjamin Bloom, William Perry, Carol Gilligan, Jurgen Habermas, and Robert Keegan. See especially Habermas, "Moral Consciousness and Communicative Action," in *Moral Consciousness and Communicative Action* (Cambridge, MA: MIT Press, 2001), pp. 116–194, and Kegan, *The Evolving Self: Problem and Process in Human Development* (Cambridge, MA: Harvard University Press, 1982).

20. William James, "On a Certain Blindness in Human Beings," in John J. McDermott, ed., *The Writings of William James* (Chicago: University of Chicago Press, 1977), pp. 629–645.

21. The more generous, open, and relational worldview returned for a time in the sixties in America, but it was so largely coopted by Cold War and Viet Nam War apocalypticism, distractions of the sexual revolution, and New Age mysticism, that it was easily dismissed with the repression of the Reagan era. See my *Leaving and Returning*.

22. Leonard Swidler, "Death or Dialogue: From the Age of Monologue to the Age of Dialogue." Lecture delivered at Grand Valley State University, May 20, 1990, and *After the Absolute: The Dialogical Future of Religious Reflection* (Minneapolis: Fortress, 1990). See also, Douglas Sturm, "Crossing the Boundaries: Interreligious Dialogue and the Political Question," in *Solidarity and Suffering: Toward a Politics of Relationality* (Albany, NY: SUNY Press, 1998), pp. 181–199.

23. I am especially indebted to Henry Rosemont, one of my distinguished Confucian colleagues, for articulation of this crucial distinction between first and second generation rights, and for his explanation as to how over-emphasis on the first leads to blindness to the second, a blindness which is not benign, as, for example, when it leads to toleration of poverty. I have heard Rosemont present this articulation in several lectures and comparative philosophy or intercultural dialogue events. In print it can be found as follows: Henry Rosemont, Jr., "On Freedom and Equality," in Roger T. Ames, ed., *The Aesthetic Turn: Reading Eliot Deutsch on Comparative Philosophy* (Chicago: Open Court, 2000), pp. 115–133.

24. For helpful perspective on the third crisis as a "third time of trial" in the American civil religion, see Robert N. Bellah, "Civil Religion in America, in *Daedalus: Journal of the American Academy of Arts and Sciences*, vol. 96., no. 1 (Winter 1967), pp. 1–21.

Chapter Three

Moral Disease

The Late-Modern Condition in America

THE MODERN ECLIPSE OF AMERICA

The most distinctive legacy of our era is moral disease. This condition is, first of all, one of rejecting and even disdaining "reasonable discourse," a condition Socrates identified many centuries ago as "the worst fate a person could suffer." It is the worst because it results in the breakdown of relationships, isolation, and the endless variety of unhealthy and antirelational notions which are cooked up apart from the continuous correction and inspiration of others. Within the late-modern confusions of America, interactions are reduced to the clashing of hardened ideological positions, and the manipulations of a cynical nihilism in which there is no good or evil, only power—and which is, at worst, even more concerned with bringing others down than it is with pursuit of anyone's interest. The consequence of moral disease, both in the world and in our selves, is that it eclipses that most basic quality of a culture which is thriving: the ability of people to be present in creative mutuality, engaging a synergy of self and other, forming and maintaining bonds and ties.

In this chapter we need to investigate the historical roots of moral disease, in terms of the process by which it infects persons and communities. Such an understanding is necessary in order to talk effectively about prevention and cure. Before historical investigation, though, there is one other big point which needs to be out in the open: the moral disease of America is very hard for Americans to see, since we are living in the midst of it. But it is not so hard for people in other parts of the world to see, which is a major factor in anti-Americanism in the world at large. Many in the world are coming to understand that the problem with America is that it is the quintessential expression of the modern, the result of turning loose that package of interrelated values which constitutes modernization: scientific rationality, market economy, individualism, and consumerism.[1]

The consequences are devastating in ways that do not become apparent right away. The modern package is addictive to human beings. Vaclav Havel states the consequences of the addiction very concisely as "the general unwillingness of consumption-oriented people to sacrifice some material certainties for the sake of their own spiritual and moral integrity."[2] With modernization, human beings turn away from their traditional culture and values, and in the process they turn away from broader and deeper horizons of meaning and value altogether. Values are *reduced* to those of producing and consuming, at the same time they are *relativized,* such that all values become merely matters of individual preference, and all relationships become relationships of power and competitive advantage within an enveloping atmosphere of consumption. Under these conditions the human spirit atrophies and development is stunted. Higher aspirations and deeper intuitions as to what a human being can become, at least according to the best of traditional cultures, are not cultivated—or even noticed in the midst of reduction and relativism. We wind up with, in the words of Martin Luther King, "guided missiles but misguided men [*sic*]."[3]

The current condition of America is one in which its root values are eclipsed by the modern. But that which is eclipsed is not only original or traditional American values, values such as those represented by the Declaration of Independence, the Constitution, and the Gettysburg Address, as well as other expressions of the democratic spirit in the literary, cultural, and social activist heritage of the American republic. We can look still deeper, and see the democratic spirit in America as itself expressive of an even more fundamental source of value and energy. This source, one which appears to be the ultimate source of any human society, that crucial point upon which civilizations rise and fall, is what I have just described as *presence,* the ability and the willingness of people to be present to the world and each other in their genuineness or sincerity, giving their best energies to a shared life.[4] In the language of African American culture, we are talking about "soul" and "being real." Perhaps initial description of this quality can be most effective by contrasting it with that degradation of presence which occurs under modern conditions: that non-presence of cynicism, relationships of use, suspiciousness; the scattered consciousness of multiple-tasking and instant gratification; the cloudiness of living in virtual realities of entertainment or money or drugs; the perpetual uneasiness of materialism.

In order to avoid the death of America, we need effective awareness of its eclipse by the modern, and reappropriation of the democratic spirit, as that which both expresses and cultivates healthy human presence, the presence of thriving. But before the work of reappropriation can become in the least bit compelling, we need a more clear and complete articulation of the problem. Such an articulation, in addition to helping us cure the moral disease of our society, might also enable us to see that some in the world who hate America might be reacting to the emptiness of modernization and the resulting moral and spiritual weakness of America and other developed nations. America failed to get the message about the insufficiency and "hypocracy" of modern values from its own children in the sixties. Could it be that some of those who hate America in the new millennium represent the same voice (actually not unlike that, for example, of the SDS extremist Weatherman faction in the frustrated late sixties), as the unfortunate expression of our common humanity in protest of an inhumane culture, a culture which claims greatness but which is unwittingly suppressive, exploitative, and shallow?

CONVERSATIONAL ASIDE

In higher education, we encourage our students to include international travel and studies as an integral part of their undergraduate education. They need to discover the world in a way that is only possible with your feet on the ground. They also need to discover America, which requires—as with all real discovery—being outside of it, having your feet off the ground you have always trodden, being able to look and see from an embodied perspective which is different.

Again and again, with students returning from international studies, we hear variations of the same discovery: the people in those other places were so real and responsive, and Americans, upon return, are found to be so hidden and cynical, so distant, and overtaken by trivial and/or merely materialistic concerns. This generates a reentry crisis which is most usually expressed as a kind of depression, and sometimes as a sense that something like this depression—or suppression, or self-censorship—is actually required in order to fit in and function in American society; that it must be normalized, that we must "deal with it."[5] Sometimes, and usually with some conscious resolve and effort, students are able to sustain themselves at a higher level of presence as they reenter, and—interestingly—many of these students wind up refocusing their overall program so as to include a strong service or civic engagement dimension. But for many, discovery and depression dissolve—or become normalized—fairly quickly, and our students sink back into what they still recognize at some level as a less than healthy situation.

What I want to do in this chapter is to catch a snapshot of what our students see upon return—before normalization and disappointment set in.

TWO MODERNITIES

As Stephen Toulman points out so effectively in his book, *Cosmopolis,*[6] there were really *two* distinct starting points of the Modern Era, a humanistic one arising from the 16th-century Renaissance, and a scientific one arising from 17th-century natural philosophy and social thought. The humanistic beginning was tolerant, sympathetically interested in the variety of human lifeways, oriented to literature, skeptical about the human capacity to generate grand theories, and focused on the exercise and development of practical wisdom in the particulars of lived life. We see these qualities in Shakespeare, Montaigne, Bacon, Rabelais, and Erasmus, all of whom shared in the sentiment articulated by Aristotle in the *Nicomachean Ethics,* that "The Good has no universal form, regardless of the subject matter or situation: sound moral judgment always respects the detailed circumstances of specific kinds of cases."[7]

The second beginning of Modernity arose through Descartes, Galileo, and Hobbes, and was immediately different from the Renaissance in its orientation to abstraction, concern for theory and logical rigor, and focus on expediency. Following the example of Plato, "They limited 'rationality' to theoretical arguments that achieve a quasi-geometrical certainty or necessity."[8] As Toulman tells the story, the transition from the humanistic 16th century to the rationalistic 17th century involved the disclaiming of four kinds of practical knowledge and the elevation of four abstract kinds: from the oral to the written, the particular to the universal, the local to the general, and the timely to the timeless.[9]

The story of Modernity in the West is the story of the scientific beginning of the 17th Century progressively overshadowing the earlier humanistic beginning. This included the increasing domination of theory in philosophy, culminating in the ascendancy of the Analytic Movement in the 20th century with its attempt to match the logical rigor of science, and ideally its certainty and universality as well.[10] More broadly, overshadowing included a generalized elevation of science to the level of worldview, including the understanding that all dimensions of life should be submitted to objective knowing and quantification, and thereby to the certainty and control promised by science. This rising up of science became especially evident in the late 19th century with the emergence of the social sciences, which explicitly extended the reach of science from the natural world to the human world, and promised results of the same sort as those which followed from bringing the natural world under control through the laws of science.

We begin to see the overshadowing in the human world, including understandings of what it means to be a person, as early as the 17th century with Natural Rights Liberalism overshadowing the humanism of the

Renaissance. With Hobbes and Locke especially, the separate individual, defined in terms of their "natural rights" to extend themselves primarily in the acquisition of property, were brought to the fore and given priority status through social contract theory. Society came to be conceived as a framework of more or less civilized negotiation into which individuals enter by their consent, in order to protect their natural rights and pursue their interests. In the "Age of Reason," it was assumed that the good of society and all of its members would result automatically from an arrangement in which each individual agrees to a body of essentially negative laws or limits. These were thought to protect against the more base and violent aspects of human nature, but most essentially to free the individual to pursue their "enlightened self interest"—though the "enlightened" part was largely unaddressed, on the assumption that this was a matter for individual definition.[11]

In this paradigm, which many later came to know as "the Enlightenment mentality" and "Western individualism," relationships, community, and "the public" lose standing. The basic unit of reality becomes the isolated individual, more and more conceived on the analogy of the scientific atom, and any relationship or society is regarded as an artificial construction—or contract—made by individuals. To put it most directly, relationship and society came to be understood in terms of their *extrinsic* value only, and to be variable according to their capacity to serve the pursuit of individual interests, whatever those might be. In a great reversal from the earlier period of monarchy in which collectivity was prior, in the Modern Period the individual comes to stand supreme.[12]

The shadow of scientific rationalism began to fall across and cover not only the hierarchical Medieval world, but also an early modern relational liberalism which viewed democracy as the best form of governance and community life because it involves discussion, discovery, and a dynamic and emergent sense of truth.[13] What was most essentially lost was the understanding of humans as relational beings, beings of community and mutuality who live together in circumstances of rich and complex particularity. Lost was the *intrinsic* value of relationship, the sense in which it is the relationship of synergy between individual and communal dimensions, not isolation, which is the locus of human thriving. With increasing dominance of the scientific paradigm, including its domination in our intellectual life,[14] we lost the capacity to support the democratic spirit through the ways we think and speak, and hence also in the ways we position ourselves in relation to the world and each other.

The earlier more humanistic and more relational, and hence more democratic, understanding associated with the first beginning of modernity was replaced with concerns for abstraction, quantification, and control, and the tendency to understand relationships in terms of either absolute equality or dominance-submission. Earlier ideas of mutuality and unity in diversity began to fade or be relegated to the sidelines of modern life. Equality of difference, associated with democratic community life and friendship, came to be either too complex or too "unrealistic" to be affirmed by modern social and political theory. Instead, looking upon the social order, theoreticians were only able to see and generalize from either isolated individuals or an organic whole, in effect denying—from either side—the existence of association and relationship.[15]

Fortunately, though, the overshadowing has not (yet) been complete. The humanistic/relational worldview is still present and available to some degree and in some sectors of the culture. We see it in some educational institutions which are focused on liberal education and pedagogies of inquiry and dialogue, in some religious groups which are oriented to an immanent and dynamic sense of the Ultimate, and some public-regarding voluntary associations and political leaders who are committed to "the public" as something more than an arena for negotiation. But for the most part this alternative Western worldview has not been widely available, has been relegated to the shade of the scientific worldview.

A major milestone in awareness of this modern condition, that of there being two Western worldviews, with the scientific dominating over the humanistic/relational, came in 1959 with C. P. Snow's groundbreaking book, *The Two Cultures and the Scientific Revolution.* The distinctiveness of this work lay in bringing to fairly broad public recognition the two opposed views: "Literary intellectuals at one pole—at the other scientists, and as the most representative, the physical scientists. Between the two a gulf of mutual incomprehension—sometimes (particularly among the young) hostility and dislike, but most of all lack of understanding."[16] A more recent statement of this same awareness came through Martin Luther King in the late 1960s, with his exhortation: "We must work passionately and indefatigably to bridge the gulf between our scientific progress and our moral progress. One of the great problems of mankind is that we suffer from a poverty of the spirit which stands in glaring contrast to our scientific and technological abundance. The richer we have become materially, the poorer we have become morally and spiritually."[17]

Both Snow and King—and Toulman as well—recommend with urgency that revitalization of America and the West requires "reappropriation" of that humanistic/relational worldview which has been suppressed through the course of modernization. Obviously, after all the time which has passed since these prophetic statements were made, this is not an easy prescription. My suggestion is this cannot occur until we acknowledge that there are in fact two distinct and conflicting worldviews at work in the West, and then come to understand the dangers of the scientific worldview when it dominates unchecked by the humanistic/relational view. I think we are beginning to understand this danger in terms of the consequences of the scientific worldview in the natural world, especially in relation to environmental issues, and we are gathering awareness of the limitations of unrestrained capitalism and its inability to act on behalf of the common good, its intimate connection with managerialism as an architectonic social discipline which reduces humans to functions and procedures,[18] and its dependence on advertising and public relations which legitimate manipulation and even lying.

However, in order for the work of reappropriating the humanistic/ relational to become compelling it is also necessary to see consequences more intimately, in terms of the impact of the scientific/individualist worldview at the level of personal life (as we have, however briefly, in the previous chapter in terms of the macrocosmic dimension). Hence in the next section I turn to description of the moral and spiritual disease which occurs when the scientific worldview eclipses the humanistic/relational worldview, a disease which becomes quite widespread in the later stages of modernity. Here, at the tender level of persons and relationships, I think we see most vividly what so much of the world knows about the problems of America, and what is invisible to so many Americans.

FROM INDIVIDUALISM TO MORAL DISEASE

Beginning in the 1950s, some disturbing reports about the state of American individualism began to appear. Coincident with ever greater dominance of the post-traditional, scientific worldview, especially after World War II, Americans were found to be increasingly removed from traditional culture as "a design of motives directing the self outward to communal purposes in which alone the self can be realized and satisfied."[19] In this condition, there began to emerge the highly vulnerable and increasingly protean "other-directed" personality, a personality which is simultaneously isolated and dependent, capable of neither real intimacy nor real independence.[20] Lacking culture mediated through tradition, and isolated from community and a sense of the intrinsic value of relationship, this self was found to be increasingly empty and in "a highly suggestible and vulnerable state."[21] It began to find meaning and purpose not so much through the connections with others and the world which were provided by tradition, but more in the expectations of the immediate context in which the individual was located. Philip Cushman emphasizes the compensation aspect of defining "immediate context" in terms of acquisition and consumption: "The post World War II self thus yearns to acquire and consume as an unconscious way of compensating for what has been lost: It is empty."[22] This compensation, of course, was supported by the natural rights individualism out of which it grew, its orientation to "life, liberty, and the pursuit of property" (before Jefferson revised Locke to read "the pursuit of happiness") as "inalienable" rights.

At the same time, there emerged a new and distinctly post-traditional culture or quasi-culture to support and guide the late-modern individual. This culture is distinguished by the fact that it is not oriented, as even individualistic Western societies of the past had been, to commonly shared beliefs, but rather entirely to the liberation of the individual through scientific insight. In fact, Philip Rieff, in his monumental work on the emergence of the culture of "the therapeutic," characterizes it in terms of "the systematic hunting down and uprooting of settled convictions"[23] The post-communal, post-orthodoxy, post-traditional culture of the therapeutic is, as Zygmunt Bauman points out, essentially *liquid* in its nature,[24] or, in the terms of description we see in both Hannah Arendt and Robert Jay Lifton, protean—void of any definite and enduring form.

The post-traditional culture was/is profoundly ambiguous. On one side, this culture contributed to the postmodern uprooting of and liberation from problematic traditional convictions. It made possible identification of injustices that had not come to consciousness before, such as those of racism, sexism, and classism, as well as the many ways in which individuals place unhealthy limits on themselves and others. Also on the positive side, the therapeutic perspective supported the possibility of what is coming to be acknowledged as a critical threshold of human development: the threshold beyond which the person transcends their ego sufficiently to be able to take responsibility for their wounds and neuroses, so as not to simply displace or project them onto others as a way of maintaining the illusion of their own perfection, accepting fallibility and hence also both the need for and the possibility of growth. With emergence of the therapeutic perspective, we begin to see relatively widespread awareness of what Robert Bellah calls "knowledge of the laws of the formation of the self,"[25] as well as ability to act on this awareness.

However, the liberation orientation, as manifest in both society and individual, tended to be limited in the same way freedom in the Modern Period had been limited generally. In terms of a famous distinction made by Isaiah Berlin, it was mostly about freedom *from,* the negative side of freedom, and virtually incoherent—or completely individualistic and hence relativistic also—when it came to the positive, to the question of what freedom was *for.* Therefore, definition of freedom as removal of previous constraints, or "uprooting," tended to exacerbate emptiness, vulnerability, an indiscriminate readiness for new senses of meaning and direction, and/or naiveté about the significance of this function of a human life, a certain gullibility.

This definition of freedom left the door open to the inflowing of science, now in the form of social science, as definer of meaning and direction—as a form of culture or quasi-culture which brought the scientific paradigm into the most intimate reaches of human life. So at the same time traditional definitions of meaning and direction flowed out—or were swept out—new definitions flowed in. And since so much critical attention or "hunting down" was directed to the former, the inflowing tide of social science was not much noticed and was rapidly taken for truth itself.

Treatment of the person in the social scientific paradigm involves work on "self," as container of ego components or "drives" to be adjusted and brought under control in the service of healthy functioning through the objective knowing of therapeutic interpretation.[26] "Ego therapies," then, are severed from connection with community on the one hand, and from traditional conceptions of a deeper Self in the process of transforming that ego on the other. The therapeutic orientation took root in popular culture generally, and gave rise to a post-traditional scientific (or scientistic) priesthood of therapists, counselors, and psychologists who were trained to help people in this mode. They claimed the authority of science, though the evidence to support this claim was mixed, often contentious, sometimes internally contradictory, and often very thin. Further contributing to the problematic nature of the therapeutic was the fact that there was little ability on the part of the larger community to identify and discipline those therapists who were engaging in the highly tempting vice of "narcissistic transference,"[27] taking advantage of the vulnerability of clients/patients in order to satisfy needs of the therapist. Despite these limitations, the therapeutic orientation became established as a distinctly post-traditional orthodoxy. Along with the advertising industry and management, two parallel post-traditional extensions of the scientific worldview into the realm of human behavior, it became the default position in American society, something analogous to the established religions of traditional cultures.

But what about the disease? Let us turn from the more external qualities of vulnerability and potential for exploitation of the post-traditional, modern self, and now look directly into the emptiness from which these qualities flow. From here we need to track progression of the moral and spiritual disease which issues from that emptiness.

What gestates in the emptiness of post-traditional disconnection from the world, and what fuels moral disease, is *anger.* It is large and deep, and difficult to articulate since it is nearly synonymous with the emptiness itself. It has many faces, one of which is reaction against the inhumanity of our situation, response to the fact that the deeper dimensions of selfhood are virtually excluded from modern society, even in the popular modes of caring for the person. It is expressive of a sense of abandonment and betrayal, associated with the perception of absence of something we once had: a comfort or repose, home, and definiteness of role assignment and expectation, a sense of connection with the world and others which had been given by traditional culture—despite the fact that traditional cultures determined these based on values we now find unacceptable.

This is the kind of anger which induces the nihilistic conclusion: life is about nothing more than conflicting or coinciding interests, competition, and the power to assert and impose one's will upon others. And not only power in the physical sense. "Reality" itself comes to be understood as that interpretation which is "socially constructed" and imposed by those who have power. This conclusion requires getting past "old convictions" now seen as oppressions which counseled such old virtues as veracity, altruism, and concern for the common good, as nothing more than devices by which those in positions of domination were/are able to maintain control; as hidden expressions of ethnocentrism at best, exploitative power at worst. The new ethic of competitive social construction requires that one stop being "passive" and learn new virtues of assertiveness, maintaining a self-image of decisiveness and success, and living with a strong sense of self-generated self-esteem.

With this stepping beyond what is taken to be the illusion that there is anything more to life than interest and power, the urge is not only to impose one's will in the pursuit of self-interest, but something more: a peculiar kind of evangelism sets in, the insistence that all others submit to the nihilistic conclusion. Here arises the face of envy: the resentful wish to tear down or "deconstruct" those who still live in the enclosure of traditional culture, to *reduce* those who aspire to too much, with cynical mocking or reductive psychological diagnosis. So the conclusion about the ultimacy of power-relations is by no means benign or passive. Fueled by the anger out of which it arises, and the manic intensity of Faustian liberation, it is very different from lazy relativism and "live and let live" toleration. It presents a new kind of absolutism, an absolutism of competitive social construction,[28] the post-traditional absolutized relativism which is nihilism. The intensity and destructiveness of nihilism, its frustration over alienation from value and enchantment in life, is revealed in a chilling statement from Nietzsche: "man would sooner have the void for his purpose than be void of purpose."[29]

As disease progresses, nihilism penetrates society, relationships, and persons to such an extent that it becomes difficult to see. Here is the normalizing mentioned earlier. At the same time there is a drawing back from the actual world of complex experience. The theme here is isolation, retreat from a world that has become intolerably ambiguous, unstable, uncertain, dangerous. There are many forms of isolation (American society can be seen as a smorgasbord of options), but escape into *knowing*, especially in the form of diagnosis of the other as a common way of isolation and escape. It reflects the deep Western tendency to place knowing before being, and to understand living as essentially about application or implementation of knowing. Here we speak not of the knowing of mutuality, but of the specifically scientific knowing which *objectifies,* which sees that which is to be known through the lens of separation, fixity, materiality, and control. In American society, this kind of knowing, especially in the context of a weak sense of shared reality, becomes a primary way to exercise power, a form of Bacon's "knowledge is power." The difference is that now the power-relation is extended from the natural world to the social and interpersonal world. Knowing becomes both weapon and shield in the struggle to prevail in the highly competitive game of socially constructing reality, gaining the upper hand by having one's interpretation become the "correct" one—the one which prevails. In the aggressive knowing, truth is defined as strength of assertion; it becomes a tool with which to consolidate and wield power within a social environment whose chief feature is perpetual war of interpretation.

This kind of knowing does not recognize the reality of either relationship or personhood, and hence is profoundly confusing and destructive from a human perspective. The significance of knowing as objectification in the human world is described very clearly by Hans-Georg Gadamer:

> By understanding the other, by claiming to know him, one takes from him all justification of his own claims. The dialectic of charitable or welfare work in particular operates in this way, penetrating all relationships between men as a reflective form of the effort to dominate. The claim to understand the other person in advance performs the function of keeping the claim of the other person at a distance. . . . A person who does not accept that he is dominated by prejudices will fail to see what is shown by their light. It is like the relation between the 'I' and the 'Thou.' A person who reflects himself out of the mutuality of such a relation changes this relationship and destroys its moral bond.[30]

With the dominance of this kind of knowing, its claim to be free of all prejudice and its legitimation as a scientific diagnosis, we see systematic violation of the most basic tenet of traditional Western ethics: that the person must always be treated as a subject rather than an object, as an "end in themselves" rather than a means, as a person rather than a thing.[31]

With the nihilistic conclusion, and once the moral bond is broken, there is no inhibition against manipulation. With knowing as power, the person is reduced to whatever category they are required to represent. And at the same time the one who "knows" is further isolated from sensitivity and relationship—from the webs of mutuality, responsibility, and criticism that are necessary to human well-being. The essential cultural quality of sincerity—which, again, requires the presence of others, the relationship of mutuality, and the presumption of good faith—is eroded and weakened, as is the supporting ability to sustain belief in anything higher or deeper than the material world, stimulus-response conditioning, and power relations.

As the natural progression of disease unfolds, lying begins to be a major theme, reflecting Dostoyevsky's prophetic statement: "If God does not exist, everything is permitted." If knowing is relative not to truth but to power, and if power defines social reality, then the option of Plato's "noble lie" becomes available to all (for who is to define "nobility"?). The typical lying of our time is not only about this or that fact, but also comes in packages wrapped up as *interpretation* of persons, situations, or policies, interpretations which serve the interests of the liar. Lying of this sort is effective when people do not quite know what is going on: because they are overwhelmed or confused, because the social fabric has been so badly weakened, because the circumstances are complex and ambiguous, because people are compromised in their humanity due to chronic multiple-tasking, and/or because of prevailing emptiness and vulnerability, or because they are young. In this state, aggressive knowing can be imposed, in a dynamic not unlike that of brainwashing, through insistence backed by the threat of violence (mostly emotional violence in American society, such as anger or the threat of anger), repetition, the invocation of currently popular trends in diagnosis (for example, repressed memory of childhood sexual abuse), and other forms of manipulative preying on the vulnerability of the other. And since the confusion and uncertainty in the human world are so widespread today, we are especially vulnerable to predators, vulnerable psychologically, politically, culturally, and spiritually. Part of the difficulty is that predators are often difficult to identify (some have credentials and prestigious positions) until after their damage has been done. And awareness of this fact further weakens trust, generates suspicion, wariness, and cynicism, which together constitute the breeding ground of moral disease. Like a firestorm, it begins to feed on itself—as the individualism, with its professed concern for freedom, begins to look more like Max Weber's famous "iron cage."[32]

The combined effect of the above elements is progressive suffocation of the self—and of mutuality in both private and public life. As ego becomes ever more isolated, and in isolation ever more focused on *control* as the means of gaining and maintaining power, it becomes closed, often losing awareness of its lying, disappearing into its own construction. In the enclosure of ego, no spirit can blow through, no insight or affection from the other, no energy of friendship or of the deeper self. In isolation, and in an entropy of the ego starved of incoming energy, the person is increasingly propelled by anger alone, in its attempt to win competitive advantage and enforce its ideological conclusions—in a life which is increasingly removed from any new experience of the world or of the other. World and other become mere occasions onto which opportunistic knowing can be asserted, or from which threat can be anticipated. And this knowing comes to be closely associated with identification of the problems, pain, and negative experiences of the other, almost a *possession* of these experiences in order to establish superiority of control through the objectifying power of diagnosis, and hence the annihilation of the other to which Gadamer refers, by reducing them to their problems.

Meanwhile, simultaneous with ever greater identification of the other with their problems or the diagnosis which has been assigned to them, the one who knows develops a very distinct loss of self-transcendence and blindness to their own individuality and fallibility, isolated even to him/ herself, amazingly unconsciousness as to what she/he is being and doing. As Gadamer points out, the *prejudice* to having no prejudice within the enclosure of scientific objectivity results in a kind of hyper-awareness of others which has the consequence of keeping the purposes of the knower in the shadows, in a peculiar exemption from self-examination. In this progressively isolated condition, all manner of strange and unhealthy mental states can incubate, recalling the wisdom of those who have said that ultimately it is necessary to act in cultural good faith in order to avoid being overcome by one's own disease. [33]

At some point it ceases to be clear that there *is* a deeper self, at least in traditional terms of conscience, soul, and at least occasional self-transcending wisdom, along with ongoing need for confession, forgiveness, and intimacy. The person comes to be defined almost exclusively by ego, a package of deconstructive projects, political alliances, and superficial engagements—all swirling around in the anger, otherwise without center. And in the absence of centered selfhood, [34] the individual becomes "bad faith" (*mauvaise foi),* a malevolent agent who cannot be addressed and who cannot respond in sincerity—even though he/she often is able to perform well among those with whom alliance is found to be advantageous. [35]

As the grip of moral disease tightens, another element comes into view, and that is *blaming,* and the associated purpose of capturing the position of being *victim.* But it is not only blaming in the usual sense of off-loading onto the other that which cannot be tolerated in the self, along with inability to take responsibility for the actions of a limited self, inability to confess mistakes. Beyond this, the form of blaming that is characteristic of late-stage individualism involves the inversion of accusing the other of doing precisely what the one blaming is doing, thereby hiding one's action under the accusation. This manipulative adaptation of the isolated self serves as a way of both defense and control, maintaining a taboo against any questioning of their actions. Hence through preemptive attack, both superiority and the isolation are aggressively enforced. In its ultimate form, the degraded self will turn to accuse the other of *blaming* itself. This serves to deflect any and all criticism because, having laid down the accusation/diagnosis of the other as one who is blaming, anything they say can then be taken as a case in point—so it is always possible to invoke the old Ronald Reagan phrase, "See, there you go again," as defense against any criticism whatsoever. Now the isolation is complete.

Here, then, is the angry, post-modern individual, starving in the emptiness of its own enclosure. It can persist for some time, and it can cause great harm—before the anger finally begins to spill over all strategies of containment. Legislating their nihilistic conclusion, insisting on it with frantic, quasi-religious fervor, the individualist winds up disappearing into a cloud of confusion in the midst of multiple strategies of manipulation, engulfed by the anger, effectively "willing the void" within themselves. At this point a certain feebleness begins to be manifest, one which is often hidden with aggressive assertion and defensiveness. It is like a deep chill, something like a spiritual equivalent to hypothermia—among those who have allowed their *Qi* (vital energy) to be displaced and scattered by anger.

This is Modern individualism at the edge, and the condition of a culture at war with itself. Ironically, what I have just described can be seen as a form of the very "war of all against all" and "state of nature" from which Hobbes and other early modern champions of natural rights individualism had sought escape. The return to (or creation of) this nightmare state—sometimes known as "culture wars"—is also ironic because it obstructs the profoundly significant developmental possibilities implicit in the therapeutic perspective (which are discussed in other chapters). In fact, what we see with the syndrome I have just described is competitive individualism coming to exploit the deep insights and positive possibilities of psychology—and often feminism at the same time—as fundamental to the creative possibilities of our era. In Bellah's terms the individualist exploitation represents "pathological distortion" as against "creative possibility."[36] In the language of Alfred North Whitehead, this exemplifies the historical tendency for "great ideas [to] enter history with disgusting alliances."[37]

Modern individualism ends in nihilism, short of the full encounter with Nothingness toward which it drives. This is extremely basic and subtle. The experience of Nothingness is experience of complete lack of traditional support for any life-interpretation, *including* even that of the nihilistic conclusion. It includes the subsequent experience of a mysterious liberation associated with a sense of the presence of what some describe as the Dao, or God, or the deepest wellspring of life itself. But the experience of Nothingness is an experience most Western people are not prepared for,[38] especially given our history of heavy metaphysics, both traditional and scientific—heavy in the sense that they insist on absolutized correctness in the cognitive dimension as a function of correspondence with displaced, static principles or commandments.

Yet some wise guides to the treacherous post-traditional territory point not only to the inevitability but also to the necessity of the experience of Nothingness, as prelude to the crossing of a crucial developmental threshold which takes us beyond the emptiness of nihilism. Karl Jaspers, for example, says that "if man [*sic*] is not to be allowed to founder in the mere persistence of life, it may seem essential that in his consciousness he shall be confronted with Nothingness; he must recall his origin."[39] The key is in the word "origin," in experience of Nothingness beyond nihilism as experience of the radically ineffable source of creativity, genuine presence, and life-affirmation. But, again, most individuals do not actually come to that encounter which Jaspers and other post-traditional visionaries find so significant to the rebirth that is necessary in our time. Instead of moving beyond nihilism and *through* Nothingness, into a new affirmation, most individualists become snared within the oblivion of nihilism and the emptiness of moral disease, an emptiness which is nearly the same as the anger, an emptiness—or hollowness—which at the same time becomes full of manipulative projects.[40] They become arrested on the near-side of Nothingness, in the post-traditional world of never-ending distraction, numbing, and forms of education, psychology, and religion which baptize isolation and teach self-esteem as the highest value. In the oblivion of nihilism and the "mere persistence" of moral disease, people are unable radicalize their nihilism and hence move beyond it, unable to move forward into the Nothingness and what some call a "new nobility" of "self-existent" personhood,[41] or a "soul beyond psychology."[42] At the same time they are unable to reconnect with or reappropriate traditional values which might provide guidance, support, and traction. However, fundamentalism, as the adoption of a totalistic and absolutized ideology, is an obvious option for those who grow weary of nihilistic individualism.

NOTES

1. Evidence of others in the world becoming aware of the consequences of modernization and seeking to moderate its impact is found, for example, in Peter L. Berger and Samuel P. Huntington, eds., *Many Globalizations: Cultural Diversity in the Contemporary World* (New York: Oxford University Press, 2002).

2. Vaclav Havel, *Living in Truth,* ed. Jan Vladislav (London: Faber and Faber, 1989), p. 54.

3. Martin Luther King, Jr., *Where Do We Go From Here: Chaos or Community?* (Boston: Beacon Press, 1967), p. 172.

4. It is important for Americans to realize that, as strongly as we may feel about "democracy" as the best kind of society, it is not the only kind in which human thriving and presence occur. See Sor-hoon Tan, *Confucian Democracy: A Deweyan Reconstruction* (Albany, NY: SUNY Press, 2004). We need to be aware that the miracle and mystery of human

thriving exceeds all human capacity for containment; or perhaps we could say that the democratic spirit can be present in surprising ways and under surprising circumstances (beyond what we might see as required conditions).

5. Now *here* is an interesting thought. It is similar to a point Erich Fromm once made, in *Revolution of Hope: Toward a Humanized Technology* (New York: Harper Colophon, 1968), about our society suffering from a "chronic, low-grade schizophrenia," one which has been normalized to such an extent that few notice its presence.

6. Stephen Toulman, *Cosmopolis: The Hidden Agenda of Modernity* (Chicago: University of Chicago Press, 1990).

7. Quoted in Toulman, *Cosmopolis*, pp. 31–32.

8. *Ibid.*, p. 20.

9. *Ibid.*, pp. 30–35.

10. See Bruce Wilshire, "A Specimin Case of Professionalizing a Field of Learning: Philosophy," in *The Moral Collapse of the University* (Albany, NY: SUNY Press, 1990), pp. 99–128.

11. Exceptions to this were Mill and de Tocqueville, but in popular culture this seemed to offer little qualification to the definition of interests as both individual and material. Hence commitment to society and the values of community were increasingly eroded.

12. Of course, collectivity does not disappear. When it is no longer mediated by hierarchy, as in the Medieval Period, and when it is neglected or thought to be "automatic," as in the Modern, the principle of collectivity takes on a free-floating quality which can be extremely unstable and dangerous. The classic case of this is Rousseau's "general will," and the terror of the French Revolution. The same instability seems to turn up later with the fascist regimes of the 20th century.

13. See my "Modern History as Forgetting—and Remembering (a Reflection on the Sixties)," in *Leaving and Returning*, pp. 99–117. See also A. D. Lindsay, *The Essentials of Democracy* (Oxford: Claredon Press, 1935).

14. On the temptations of "realism" and democratic revisionism, see Henry Kariel, ed., *Frontiers of Democratic Theory* (New York: Random House, 1970).

15. Leonard Boonin, "Man and Society: An Example of Three Models," in J. Roland Pennock and John W. Chapman, eds., *Voluntary Associations*(New York: Atherton Press, 1969), pp. 69–84.

16. C. P. Snow, *The Two Cultures and the Scientific Revolution* (Cambridge: Cambridge University Press, 1959), p. 4.

17. Martin Luther King, Jr., *Where Do We Go From Here?*, p. 171.

18. See my essay, "A Humanities Response to Managerialism: Democracy, Diversity, and Liberal Education in the Shade," in *The International Journal of the Humanities*, vol. 5, 2007, pp. 95–102.

19. Philip Rieff, *The Triumph of the Therapeutic* (New York: Harper Torchbooks, 1968), p. 4. I take Rieff's book to be among the greatest on the fate of Western individualism. Other authors who are helpful in this genre are Christopher Lasch, *The Culture of Narcissism* (New York: Norton, 1979) and Philip Slater, *The Pursuit of Loneliness* (Boston: Beacon Press, 1970).

20. See David Riesman, *The Lonely Crowd* (New Haven: Yale, 19610), and Robert Jay Lifton, *The Protean Self*(New York: Basic Books, 1993).

21. Philip Cushman, "Why the Self is Empty: Toward a Historically Situated Psychology," in *American Psychologist*, May 1990, p. 600.

22. *Ibid.*

23. Rieff, *The Triumph of the Therapeutic*, p. 12.

24. Zygmunt Bauman, *Liquid Modernity* (Cambridge: Policy Press, 2000).

25. Bellah, "Religious Evolution," p. 45.

26. There have been significant exceptions, following in the tradition of R. D. Lang's *The Divided Self*(New York: Penguin, 1960). For contemporary articulations of a movement away from "drive-based" theories and toward "relational therapy," see Peter Wilberg, "Modes of Relatedness in Psychotherapy" (via his website).

27. Cushman, p. 607.

28. On the relationship between power and meaning, see Richard Stivers, *The Culture of Cynicism: American Morality in Decline* (Oxford: Blackwell, 1994), especially ch. 8, "Against the New Morality," pp. 169–181.

29. Friedrich Nietzsche, *The Genealogy of Morals*, in Francis Golffing, trans., ed., *The Birth of Tragedy and the Genealogy of Morals* (Garden City, NY: Doubleday Anchor, 1956), p. 299.

30. Hans-Georg Gadamer, *Truth and Method* (New York: Crossroad, 1988), pp. 323–324. But again note that not all social scientists objectify in this way. For a significant exception, see Robert Kegan's "constructive-developmental perspective," which "leads us to bracket every hope, save the growth of the truth," as a form of "care" which "is *not* merely another of 'my values' but [is] itself rooted in the psychological and philosophical development of the truth. It arises out of a recognition of the other's distinctness." In *The Evolving Self,* p. 296.

31. Observance of this tenet becomes especially complex in the context of human growth, where objectification of the self or ego is to some degree a necessary prerequisite to healing and growth. One must confront one's ego self as other in order for the open space to occur, and for genuine self or soul to be present. For further discussion of this point, see my *Living Philosophy,* pp. 80–83.

32. Max Weber, *The Protestant Ethic and the Spirit of Capitalism*, trans. Talcott Parsons (New York: Charles Scribner' Sons, 1958), p. 181.

33. Rieff, p. 3.

34. There is a big issue here. *Is* there a self, a genuine or centered self? Or is it more effective to speak in more Buddhist language of non-self, of any sense of self as a displacement, or in Confucian terms of a purely relational self? Addressing this could result in a long (and important) essay. For now at least, I want to say that "self," like "God," is fundamentally mysterious, and that each way of speaking has both assets and liabilities.

35. See William Barrett, *Death of the Soul* (Garden City, NY: Anchor Doubleday, 1986), especially ch. 9, "The Disappearing Self," pp. 119–141.

36. Bellah, "Religious Evolution," p. 44.

37. Alfred North Whitehead, *Adventures of Ideas* (New York: Free Press, 1933), p. 18.

38. For perspective on how it is that some sense that Western people, and perhaps Americans in particular, are most vulnerable to the nihilism which is implicit in the Modern life, see, Hans Waldenfels, *Absolute Nothingness: Foundations for Buddhist-Christian Dialogue*, trans. J. W. Heisig (New York: Paulist Press, 1980).

39. Karl Jaspers, *Man in the Modern Age* (Garden City, NY: Anchor Books, 1957), p. 193.

40. Maybe the best way to draw the crucial distinction between Nothingness and emptiness is to say that Nothingness is *open,* while emptiness is *closed.* Here I think Hannah Arendt's distinction between solitude and loneliness is helpful also; where solitude entails the openness of dialogue between me and myself, and loneliness is painful isolation.

41. Jaspers, *Man in the Modern Age,* pp. 210–217, and Vaclav Havel, "The Power of the Powerless," in *Living in Truth,* pp. 36–122.

42. Ira Progoff, *The Death and Rebirth of Psychology* (New York: Julian Press, 1956), p. 15.

Chapter Four

Nothingness and Gift

Eleven Glimpses

What could it mean to say encounter with Nothingness is necessary as doorway to revitalization, cure for moral disease, and path of transition from the traditional/absolutistic/ideological worldview to a relational/democratic worldview? Karl Jaspers says that in order to avoid "founder[ing] in the mere persistence of life" we must "recall our origin;" we must recall and reconnect with the source of life itself and the headwater from which our better moments flow, our moments of unmediated creativity, compassion, right action, and genuine presence.

The purpose of this chapter is to bring some experiential light to the potentially confusing claim about Nothingness. And for this purpose I think it could be most effective to adopt a method of *glimpses*. What follows, then, are a series of views on the experience of Nothingness and the large claims with which it is associated, including that of a new or renewed life which arises from the encounter. This method seems appropriate because the very first and most consistent thing to be said about the experience of Nothingness is that it is experience of that which is both *ineffable,* experience of that which lies beyond and prior to any speech or symbolizing, and *source*— source of guidance, calmness, confidence, insight, compassion, and vitality itself. As such, it can be *pointed to,* but it can never be captured or contained in intellectual formulation or doctrine, or even art.

1. Must "encounter with Nothingness" require the grand identity crisis of European Existentialism, as, for example, is implied in the famous first line of Albert Camus' *The Myth of Sisyphus:* "There is but one truly serious philosophical question, and that is the question of suicide"? Must it mean a complete overturning of one's life, a reorientation so total that one must either hold it off or face an entirely different life?—Or jump?

No (although in some cases . . .). Encounter with Nothingness often happens gradually, and is frequently associated with a natural process of maturation. It may begin with passing moods which have a mysteriously ontic flavor, as though we were standing—as Heidegger said—"in the draft of Being." It may come in the shock of sudden and complete loss, the stark moment of coming to live outside of the life in which we had been enfolded previously, suddenly floating naked on top of this sea of mortality. The experience of Nothingness may come with the passing of grief, with the natural sense of new life which is often found on the far side of loss, as "the God who appears when God has disappeared in the anxiety of doubt," in the words of Paul Tillich. [1]

2. Some say we must let the survivor, the one who has had intimate contact with death, become our mentor. For example, here is Robert Jay Lifton:

> They all tell us that civilization—human life itself—is threatened, dying or dead; that we must recognize this death or near-death, pursue it, record it, and enter into it if we are to learn the truth about ourselves, if we are to live. This capacity for intimacy with (and knowledge of) death in the cause of renewed life is the survivor's special quality of imagination, his [*sic*] special wisdom. But how can that wisdom be shared? Can survivors be mentors to the world? [2]

It seems the answer is mainly negative. In our society, this quality of imagination, which we perhaps see most directly in contemporary art, is so quickly diagnosed as "depression" or some other form of disfunction. It is then "treated" so as to suppress or eliminate the root awareness. This is ambiguous. On the one hand, this approach relieves pain and suffering at some level. But on the other, it deprives both society and the person of deep awareness, an awareness which may turn out to be a passing phase in a larger movement of growth. Could the survivor teach us that it is possible to be both alive and deeply aware, embracing of the full ambiguity of life, its joy and its sorrow? [3]

3. Humans are religious—there is no getting around it. We are religious in that we are beings of trust; we base our lives on something "outside" of our selves, as that which provides meaning, value, purpose. Each life contains an "ultimate concern." Our problems and struggles in life arise from the fact that out of our insecurity we place our trust in that which cannot support us, that which crumbles, abandons, or otherwise turns out to be unreliable. So we move on, and find another object of trust, hopefully one with greater reliability than the one before. And so it goes, in a developmental movement within which the sense of "God" is refined over time. If it goes well, if we do not become stuck or arrested in repetition of old patterns (Nietzsch's "eternal return"), we finally begin to experience a source of both frustration and support which is beyond our control. Alfred North Whitehead's statement about religious development at this stage is profound: "Religion . . . runs through three stages, if it evolves to its final satisfaction. It is the transition from God the void to God the enemy, and from God the enemy to God the companion."[4] In other words, moving beyond traditional Western theism, with God as giver of commandments and chooser of people(s) from *out there*, religion in the mature sense actually *begins* when the question of "God" becomes an internal, existential dynamic—"God the void," God the radically ineffable. God—in the real and existential rather than merely social sense—is first experienced as benign mystery, then as enemy which confounds and frustrates all our ego-generated efforts, and finally comes to be experienced as that radically ineffable source of insight, guidance, and energy which can be trusted—as companion.

4. Consider the photograph of the Earth from outer space. Has this image been so commodified that we can no longer contemplate what we are seeing and the perspective from which we see? What does it say about us that this incredible image, one which can be taken as the most fundamental religious symbol of our era, is so rarely spoken of? Is it somehow noticed without speech, or has it not yet found the (essentially religious) language and institutions which bring the significance of this image to effective notice through speaking the unspeakable? Awkward as this last proposition sounds, it may be the major agenda of our century, the deeper meaning—in both thought and action—behind such key terms as "sustainability," "thriving," and, more recently, "vulnerability."

Earth just *is*—in Nothingness, the void, the infinite infinitude of outer space. Beyond science of orbits and planetary systems, probabilities of fatal meteor crash, etc., it is just there/here. Encounter with Nothingness is seeing the Earth and all therein against the backdrop of the great Void of outer space. It is experience of the sheer improbability and unprecedentedness of all that is; experiencing the question, "Why is there something rather than nothing?" From this perspective we can see life on the Earth not as test or trial or condemnation (as in so much of the traditional period of human history), but as gift; we might move to appreciation of the gift quality of life, from refusal and control to celebration and even some degree of trust. In the words of one of my friends, encounter with Nothingness means approaching and living life as though it was all miracle. It is little different from the experience of abiding in wonder. The sense of it is well-spoken in the poetry of Rainer Maria Rilke, especially with the phrase "whole and against a wide sky." We come to experience Life itself, directly and unmediated by either the authority of tradition or the distractions of modern life.

5. William James wrestled mightily with depression ("melancholia" in those days) and the question as to how (or why) he could live. He articulated his experience of nihilism as determinism, as that which closes off freedom and possibility. He was speaking of both the scientific kind of determinism, which he perceived beneath the great enthusiasm which accompanied its spread in the society of his time, but also of the religious and cultural kinds which he took to be implicit in the dominant historical forms of his inheritance. Either way, the possibility of freedom was foreclosed, and along with it the possibility of ever really *doing* anything, the possibility of living a meaningful life, of contributing, changing, growing. If it is all a "block universe," then all is settled even before it begins.

James's way beyond determinism is recorded in his journal entry of April 30, 1870, a statement from which most of his later philosophical work unfolded: "My first act of free will shall be to believe in free will. . . . [N]ow I will go a step further [than suicide] with my free will, not only act with it, but believe as well; believe in my own individual reality and creative power."[5] James, out of his own experience of Nothingness, finally decided that it was up to him: to *decide* whether life has meaning, and whether our efforts can make any difference. He decided to "posit life." This enabled him to learn to trust what he took to be the most fundamental of religious experiences: "experiences of an unexpected life succeeding upon death. . . . The phenomenon is that of new ranges of life succeeding on our most despairing moments."[6] Tolerating these moments, and maintaining the faith which is implicit in his statement about them, makes it possible for us to have access to "another kind of happiness and power, based on giving up our own will and letting something higher work for us."[7] This understanding, which both required and arose from the renunciation of Western intellectualism with its insistence on absolute certainty, made it possible for James to practice, in his own unique way, religion as the continuous movement of "harmonious adjustment to an unseen order." For James, Nothingness means faithfulness to "pure experience," and "learning to think in non-conceptualized terms,"[8] which is very similar to Whitehead's "void as companion." It means responsiveness of a kind of presence which only becomes available when our efforts have been exhausted, and when we learn to "unclamp" and draw strength from the energy of pure experience which flows through the undifferentiated immediacy of life,[9] prior to the judgments, distinctions, and the many other abstractions on which we build our lives.

6. On both sides of gender identification within the feminist revolution of our era, there is speech about Nothingness. In relation to women, I point to Adrienne Rich, who speaks of the need to "go down into the darkness of the core," where we find "the something born of that nothing [which] is the beginning of our truth."[10] On the male side, I turn to Richard Tarnas's great history of the West, *The Passion of the Western Mind*, where he concludes that what is most immediately obvious about the history of the West overall is that it has been "an overwhelmingly masculine phenomenon." He goes on to say that the deepest quest of Western history had been to differentiate and achieve autonomy within the male paradigm, but that in the post-traditional world of today the challenge shifts to rediscovering and reuniting with the feminine principle as the ground of its being, and that "to achieve this reintegration of the repressed feminine, the masculine must undergo a sacrifice, an ego death."[11]

In Rich, Nothingness is (re)discovery of source after constraint is removed. In Tarnas, Nothingness involves the self-transcendence and "unflinching self-discernment" of confessing hubris and one-sidedness to the point of planetary destruction, and the emergence from this death to embrace the feminine "not [as] objectified 'other,' but rather [as] source, goal, and immanent presence."[12]

7. Nothingness is the center of mystical experience, through meditation, silent prayer, spiritual listening, contemplation. It is the "still point," the *silentium mysticum*. It is where we come to when we clear our minds and think nothing. It is the self-transcendence of *Sunyata* (Emptiness) in which we somehow stand apart from the ongoing flow of ego and the world as we ordinarily know it, in a state of non-attached awareness which is both peaceful and compassionately understanding. Out of this state, in the words of Joan Didion, we are able to "love and remain indifferent."[13]

8. Socrates is similar to James in many ways, only Socrates is more explicitly relational. For Socrates, experience of Nothingness occurs through living "the examined life," a major part of which is coming to moments of radical perplexity or "not knowing" *(aporia),* moments in which our cognitive facilities come to their limit, bringing us to a crucial edge. Experience at that edge counsels modesty about what I claim to know, greater willingness to listen to others, as well as greater distance on that ego reflex which tells me I must always pretend to know everything. It is also crucial because, for Socrates, that state of not-knowing is at the same time the state out of which we begin to have access to a different kind of knowing which comes from within (instead of from the senses), as wisdom, conscience, and authentic self. Practice of the examined life, and repeated contact with the Nothingness of *aporia,* is precisely the process through which human transformation occurs, the process through which we grow from a confused and conflicted, ego-driven being to one who truly loves wisdom *(philo-sophia).*

9. According to the Japanese Kyoto School of philosophy, the structures of modern life drive people in any society beyond all traditional metaphysics and theologies, beyond all senses of certainty and knowing how the universe is constructed and how to address the essential human problem of alienation. Modern life, in its very essence, drives people to the experience of Nothingness, an experience most cultures—especially those of the West, oriented as they have been by displaced and static first principles supervising an essentially dead world of material objects—are ill-prepared to handle. For Japanese culture, however, this experience is very familiar. Here the experience of Nothingness is stated by Keiji Nishitani, as experience of Emptiness:[14]

> Emptiness is something we are aware of as an absolute near side. It opens up more to the near side than we, in our usual consciousness, take our own self to be. It opens up, so to speak, still closer to us than what we ordinarily think of as ourselves. In other words, by turning from what we ordinarily call 'self' to the field of *Sunyata* [Emptiness, Nothingness], we become truly ourselves. . . . We take leave of the ordinary self-attachment that lurks in the essence of self-consciousness and by virtue of which we get caught in our own grasp in trying to grasp ourselves.[15]

In slightly different terms, Masao Abe describes the movement from an initially negative and fundamentally threatening experience of Nothingness or Emptiness (again, *Sunyata*) to a Great Affirmation which occurs when we are finally able to radicalize that experience of Nothingness, negate even *that* experience, and let it go. As Abe-sensei says, the mature stage of Zen is "realized only though the total negation of total negation, i.e., through a great negation or double negation," whereby "true self, therefore, is not *something* unattainable, but rather *the 'unattainable' itself.*"[16] Great Negation becomes Great Affirmation, as we move beyond objectifying (and ego) consciousness which cannot admit as experience anything that does not pass through the filter of subject-object distinction, where "I" must be known in *and by* separation, and "other" must be known as an essentially inert object.

10. The next glimpse arises from discovery of life-interpretation: first the initially startling fact that we *have* one, as distinct from the earlier, unconscious assumption that we simply know what is real—in contrast with all those others who must be wrong; and, second, that the interpretation we have is determined, contingent, one among many, unsupported by any proof, validation, or certification. We are confronted with the unavoidable fact that, as human beings, we have a "position," a view of life and a way of interpreting, a comprehensive understanding with respect to value and significance: a way of life affirmation or a worldview. And we learn that as part of our inheritance from the ideological/absolutistic era (and/or from ego consciousness) we have a strong tendency to generalize and assume that our position is best, is superior to all others. This human tendency is accentuated with Westerners through our historic need to organize our lives around both certainty in *knowing* and/or special revelation as it is given by God to a chosen group. To accept the fact that those who are other need to be not merely tolerated in their knowing which is different, to accept that our knowing is not *the* knowing, is an especially difficult developmental challenge. And it is complicated by the obvious limitations of the alternative as it is envisioned from the perspective of absolutism: relativism, the understanding that any interpretation is as good as any other, and that therefore none really matters.

So here is the dilemma: we must renounce not our tradition but rather the absolutistic claims with which it was associated in the past. We must somehow renounce absolutistic claims without thereby being severed from tradition altogether, becoming a complete relativist, an opportunistic cynic, or a nihilist—all of which, we discover, are still "positions." So one element of the stress and frustration of our era is that there is no exemption from the having of a position. And neither, it appears, is there exemption from the encounter with Nothingness. Not even "camping out" in the oblivion of nihilism can provide shelter.

If we can avoid temptations to hide from the experience of Nothingness, refusing to cross over into conscious choice and responsibility for the positions or worldviews we hold—"against a wide sky," we discover that we do not need to be *right* all the time and endlessly on the defensive. We find that life is more full and rich when we are *open* to the gift quality of life, and that we are able to tolerate the ambiguity and complexity of what is really happening—no longer needing to filter and contort what we experience according to the constraints of a dense and absolutized interpretive structure. We learn to have access to the vitality and goodness of "God the companion," beginning to learn *wu wei* (action of non-action) or the wisdom of Socratic *aporia* and "knowing nothing," or the sublimity of "it is not I who speaks but Christ who speaks through me" (Gal 2:20)—learning to live and thrive with the radical ineffability of the ultimate source of our well-being. We become capable of holding a position and an interpretation in a de-absolutized way without becoming a relativist.

Relationship becomes possible, not relationship simply as exchange and construction of social contracts, but relationship as locus of presence, discovery, and growth. We experience the relationship of mutuality in which we are able to be most fully ourselves when we are in compassionate relationship with the other, that full relationship which I have earlier described in terms of the simultaneity of openness and definiteness. We come to what I have previously called the imperative of otherness or alterity, what Richard Bernstein describes as the fundamental *Aufgabe* (task or obligation) of "cultivat[ing] the type of imagination where we are at once sensitive to the sameness of 'the Other' with ourselves *and* the radical alterity that defies and resists reduction of 'the Other' to 'the Same.'"[17] We discover "civic virtue" as care for the radiant space of our mutual thriving as beings who are both the same and different, a kind of care which is ultimately no different from our appearing in that space as who we really are, as beings who have returned from all other-worldly mysticism with the realization that our being together is the highest form of spiritual practice. Here is how we transition from the Ideological to the Relational Worldview.

11. What, then, is Nothingness? It is none other than source of everything—including our various traditions of articulation as response to this source. It is expressed as experience of Aporia, Sunyata, non-duality, the Void, non-objectification, the creative energy of the cosmos which in the past had ben mediated through culture, but which in our post-traditional environment becomes a matter of choice—and responsibility—for each person, a choice to live "the new nobility."

It is, again, life affirmation. And it is not about something "out there" in any way, but in here, more intimate to me than the self of my ego which desperately tries to obscure it or displace it in its obsession with achieving supremacy. Letting go of the ego, learning to let its endless obsessions pass by calmly without attaching to them, we discover that the Nothingness is paradoxically identical with our sincerity and genuine presence. With this last statement I recall an old Japanese Zen saying which seems a fitting conclusion to this chapter: "A dunce once went searching for fire with a lighted lantern. Had he known what fire was, he would have eaten his rice much sooner."

NOTES

1. Paul Tillich, *The Courage to Be* (New Haven: Yale University Press, 1952), p. 190.
2. Robert Jay Lifton, "The Survivor as Creator," in Rowe, ed., *Living Beyond Crisis*, p. 189.
3. For a shining example of this quality, see Hans Jonas, *The Phenomenon of Life: Towards a Philosophical Biology* (Chicago: University of Chicago Press, 2001).
4. Whitehead, *Religion in the Making* (Cleveland: Meridian Books, 1960), p. 16.
5. James, Journal entry, April 30, 1870, McDermott, ed., *The Writings of James*, 7–8
6. James, *A Pluralistic Universe*, pp. 265–66
7. *Ibid.*
8. *Ibid.*, p. 297.
9. William James, "The Gospel of Relaxation," in *Talks to Teachers on Psychology; and to Students on some of Life's Ideals* (New York: Norton, 1958), p. 144.
10. Adrienne Rich, *On Lies, Secrets, and Silence* (New York: Norton, 1979), p. 64. The essay in which this statement appears, "Women and Honor: Some Notes on Lying," is also included in my anthology, *Living Beyond Crisis*, p. 71.

11. Richard Tarnas, *The Passion of the Western Mind* (New York: Ballantine, 1991), 441, 443, 444.

12. *Ibid.*, 444.

13. Joan Didion, *Slouching Toward Bethlehem* (New York: Farrar, Straus and Giroux, 1961), p 147. For a work which is remarkably similar in its wisdom and practical value, see Madeleine L'Engle, *A Circle of Quiet* (New York: Seabury press, 1979), comparing especially p. 50.

14. Note that this usage of the term "emptiness" is different from my previous usage, in which I distinguish emptiness from Nothingness. Abe's use of the term "nihilism" is equivalent to my "emptiness."

15. Keiji Nishitani, *Religion and Nothingness* (Berkeley: University of California Press, 1982), p. 285.

16. Masao Abe, "Zen and its Elucidation," in William R. LeFleur, ed., *Zen and Western Thought* (Honolulu: University of Hawaii Press, 1985) pp. 15, 13.

17. Richard J. Bernstein, "Incommensurability and Otherness Revisited," in Eliot Deutsch, ed., *Culture and Modernity: East-West Philosophic Perspectives* (Honolulu: University of Hawaii Press, 1999), p. 99.

Part II

Relational Worldview

Chapter Five

Reappropriating Tradition

CONVERSATIONAL ASIDE

Now we must look through the eyes of Nothingness, adopt the perspective of Nothingness. We must say what is seen from this perspective, especially how it is that Relational Worldview becomes compelling. The next part of this work must address the developmental movement out of which the new worldview arises, including the crucial differentiation between experience of nihilism and Nothingness, and between healthy development and terrorist reaction. Somehow this description must participate in actual remedy for moral disease and be a practical resource for revitalization; something more than just the delivery of a better set of ideas, or—at the opposite extreme—a more complete confession. I, like other pragmatists and feminists like Elizabeth Johnson, want to write not just about the relational, but in the relational. [1]

Here is where the genre issue presses in. I look around at my peers, talk with colleagues and friends, and discover that the aspiration just described is widely shared, but so also is frustration and paralysis. It is as though everything has already been said, and the real issue is that nobody is listening. Recall, for example, the Club of Rome reports on environmental degradation in the early 1970s, which were clear, accurate, and scientifically sound—and completely ignored in the Reagan era that followed. [2] *The issue is not so much one of what needs to be said, but whether and/or when people will hear; an issue of speaking in a way which is supportive of real listening.*

Maybe the problem is even more serious. Maybe Herzog, the protagonist of Saul Bellow's great novel by the same name, was right when he said "All the ideas have been used up." And besides, the point is not ideas but how we live, not ideas but the effective engagement of transformative practice. Beyond this, there seems to be a mysterious kind of stifling, a suspicion, self-censorship, or thwarting of those who would speak on behalf of our common humanity (even—or especially?—among liberals who might otherwise support each other), a sort of suppression which seems an unavoidable element of our cultural environment and historical moment. Maybe it is the "depression" I mentioned earlier in relation to our being survivors, a subtle manifestation of moral disease, or an expression of Western guilt and paralysis. Reflecting on this, Peter Hershock's phrase, "the colonizing of consciousness"³ comes to mind: our minds, which we like to imagine as dwelling in Cartesian purity apart from the messy world, have themselves been tainted in ways we cannot see, such that what we need is an entirely new way of thinking, or a way beyond thinking—and yet not a way which renounces or fails to honor critical facilities.

I don't know how helpful it is to say these things.

Pursuing the claim that the experience of Nothingness opens onto a new way of being human, surveying the landscape from this perspective, learning how to live with self, other, and the natural world on this new ground, the first thing (chapter 5) that comes into view is the beauty of tradition, and the possibility of reappropriating elements of tradition as nutrition and guidance for life in the present. Tradition is envisioned as remedy for the modern

Only later (chapter 6) does it become clear that "tradition" is both vast and problematic, and that reappropriation must presuppose some positive values or "prejudices" in the present which provide criteria as to what we wish to reappropriate from tradition. In fact, this realization reveals our initial appreciation of tradition to have been overly universalistic, alienated from transformative practice, blind to the social and cultural constraints within which the wisdom of tradition was housed in the Traditional Period of human history, and driven by antimodernism.

Movement beyond these limitations entails discovery of positive values in modernity and in the present. We come to conscious awareness of those values in the present which serve as criteria for what it is we need to reappropriate from tradition. In fact, those values in the present—affirmation of gift quality of life, necessity of traditional wisdom, reflexive awareness, commitment to mutual growth, urge toward thriving, and identification of relatedness as locus of well-being—come to be seen as expressive of a new worldview, a new ethic and spirituality which is emerging on the planet though a very definite developmental process. This is a very large claim: I am suggesting that through the vitality of dialogue (as the inclusive term for the interdependent set of values just mentioned) we can move from moral disease to the new way of living we so urgently need. Reaching way back to the statements from Deuteronomy and Confucius at the very beginning of this book, dialogue—again, as synonym for the vitality of the present, including reappropriation of traditional wisdom—provides a lifeway through which we are able to "choose life" and "make the Way great."

Then, in chapter 7, it is important to give a concrete example of dialogue with the Other which I advocate as the medium of reappropriation and revitalization. The best way I can do this is through sharing my own experience with China.

And finally, I think it will be important to step back (in chapter 8) to explicit consideration of the relationship between dialogue and human development, dialogue as a path as well as a destination. Here it is important to integrate what has been learned in the previous chapters of Part II, as well as to give an example.

From here, we should be able to return in part III to North America with the aim of nurturing a fragile and ambitious hope, helping it toward embodiment.

From the perspective of Nothingness, the unsustainable quality of the modern life becomes clear in a starkly existential way. But also on the ground of that experience new possibilities for growth and actualization. "Reappropriating tradition" becomes possible, meaning the ability to reach in and gain access to the life-affirmation which is buried in the unconscious depths of tradition, including wisdom as to how to live, how to cultivate both self and other.

TRADITIONAL WISDOM

America is *late-modern,* wallowing in the insufficiency of the modern worldview as it breaks down. This is something which is very clear to many people in the world, though it is not at all clear to most Americans, immersed as we are in our circumstance. The way out of the unsteady late-modern condition includes reappropriation of some traditional values which had been left behind in the rush of modernity.

Why traditional values? Because traditions do more than connect people with each other and the world in ways which we now find problematic. They save people from the diseases of "morbid introspection" (James) or "infinite regress of motive" (Arendt) which come to afflict us in the late modern period. They also contain wisdom, which is something much greater than simply good ideas or procedures; wisdom is the ability to live well, with compassion, acceptance, joy, and to be present in one's genuineness. Traditions as bearers of wisdom contain pathways which cultivate the emergence of the full human being, as well as a vivid sense of ideal, and above all, an energy or spirit which we can learn to access ever more fully and continuously. Wisdom is one of those qualities that may be most vividly know in its absence, as when situations or relationships degenerate to mere application of technical knowledge or procedure, devoid of good judgment or sensitivity, let alone anything like serendipity, grace, or enchantment.

Yet I am recommending neither fundamentalism nor traditionalism. I speak of reappropriating "some" traditional values. Traditions are huge, and there is no such thing as just going back, or bringing them forward, or even "them" apart from someone's act of selecting what they take to be important from the vastness of the past, its junkyards, its museums, its random Tuesday afternoons. Besides, who would want to embrace tradition completely, given our awareness of values within traditions which are completely unacceptable to us today (racism, sexism, classism, etc.)?

We inevitably *choose* elements of tradition to reappropriate (and call "tradition") based on values/criteria we hold in the present. So it seems a matter of common sense that healthy reappropriation will be aware of what Hans-Georg Gadamer, one of the great philosophers of interpretation in the 20th century, calls "prejudices" of the present—by which he means predispositions which we can examine and regard as positive as well as negative (as distinct from the modern prejudice toward claiming freedom from all prejudice).[4]

While there are several specific prejudices which we will need to discuss later on, the first and most inclusive of these is "dialogue" itself. Reappropriation of tradition in the mode of dialogue is to say reappropriation in the companionship with others in the world who are engaged in the same process of discovery and movement beyond the limitations of the modern. Reappropriation through dialogue, then, involves the movement to a way of living which is both profoundly distinctive to the group which appropriates, at the same time it is quite friendly to others who are different, and appreciative of the common ground on which this movement beyond the problematic aspects of the modern is possible. It is pluralistic, within a commonly shared life condition.

MODERNITY, REAPPROPRIATION, AND DIALOGUE

Let me attempt to clarify this tight set of dynamics: Modernity is a problem which is commonly shared by the peoples of the Earth, a problem in that it enhances material life and degrades our humanity at the same time. I have thought about this proposition, been depressed by it, and heartened by those who have suggested rather recently that "many globalizations" are possible, that it is possible for societies to accept the benefits of modernization while moderating its dangerous aspects.[5] This possibility, though, seems to be dependent on emerging clarity as to what is problematic about the modern, a clarity I find to be well-articulated in the Vaclav Havel statement I have already cited, about the unwillingness—or inability—of humans, once they have become consumption-oriented, to act on any values other than those of their own material well-being, even those of their own moral and spiritual well-being. Is unwillingness a loss of will, a will in captivity, or a sick will? Whichever of these, we are talking about addiction, mass hypnosis—within an unsteady post-traditional quasi-culture.

It is essential to the modern condition that it involves a radical break with the traditional past. And yet it is also part of modernization that there comes, in its later phases, awareness of its insufficiency, and the need for something more than the modern itself can provide. That "more" is interpreted and sought after in a broad array of entertainments, adventures, therapies, religious affiliations, etc. The argument of those who advocate addressing this need through reappropriation of tradition—as distinct from those other ways—is, again, that tradition contains wisdom, which is to say sources of meaning, direction, and even energy—those aspects of life about which the modern/scientific worldview is mute, or which it even denies.

But the first problem with reappropriation is that the need and the desirability of traditional sources do not become evident until after the modern break with tradition and past has occurred. So we come to dilemma: we discover the need to reappropriate traditional values within a context in which tradition has become other to us.

Closely associated with the need for a distinctively human "more" to life is awareness of an imperative of growth and development: awareness that response to the insufficiencies of modern life requires that we become beings who are more alert, more responsive, and more compassionate than our ancestors had been. As a response to this imperative, reappropriation becomes the task of identifying essential sources from tradition to be integrated into the depleted present.[6] Yet, again –as in the dilemma just mentioned, finding a bridge to the otherness of that which is to be integrated is among the most difficult challenges of our era. Simply leaping into some sense of a good past with no bridge at all and with complete acceptance of that past is one way of understanding fundamentalism—which is closely related to fascism, in its repudiation of the present through assertion against it of doctrinal and ethical rigidity associated with another time, whether past or future. With this move, that which is reappropriated is incapable of identifying sources of goodness in the present which it can nurture. Instead it judges the modern and postmodern to be utterly lost, and sooner or later counsels holy war against life in the present, reminding us that healthy reappropriation entails the engagement of positive values in the present. But this brings us back to dilemma: we cannot experience revitalization in the present without reconnection with the past, and yet we cannot make the connection without identifying what is vital in the present.

Impossible as it may seem, however, there are cases where reappropriation of traditional sources appears to be healthy and effective, where some have been able to meet the dilemma of our needing something essential from that which we had earlier rejected. Some do seem to have been able to move past the modern alienation from tradition, to a situation where a bridge is opened up so that sources from tradition are able to flow into and revitalize life in the present. As an example, I cite Third Epoch Confucianism.[7] Here the vision of Confucius, and those who came after him in ancient times as his immediate interpreters, is reconsidered (and often retranslated) and brought to bear on issues of living today. Acknowledging the complexities and improbabilities of reappropriation, one Third Epoch Confucian referred to the analogy of that species of bird which, according to the laws of physics, is unable to fly—and yet which does fly nonetheless![8] As evidence of the vitality of Confucian reappropriation, I cite two examples, both of which address the relationship between the historical tradition of Confucianism and modernity, and, more specifically, the relationship between Confucianism and democracy. First, Chenyang Li, in his *The Tao Encounters the West,* argues that Confucianism and democracy "are not compatible within a single value system," that both are needed, and that "the harmony model" at the core of Chinese culture makes it possible to embrace both (despite incompatability), resulting in the survival of Confucianism along with a form of democracy which is "more socially responsive and responsible" [than Western-style democracy].[9] Second, Sor-hoon Tan, in her *Confucian Democracy,* argues that development of a Confucian democracy is both possible and desirable, and "requires not only reconstruction of Confucianism, it also requires reconstruction of democracy," and has the advantage of providing "a politics that avoids authoritarianism without neglecting the joint realization of a common good in free discussion."[10]

Now is not the time to discuss the content of the reappropriated Confucianism (that will come soon), but only to point to it as a case to exemplify the possibility of reappropriation—that it can fly. Here I will only share one strong hunch as to how this can happen, in the form of a statement of Confucius which is cited rather often by Third Epoch Confucians: "It is the human being who is able to make the Way great, not the Way that can make the human being great."[11] Perhaps this is a clue about how the relationship between past and present can occur in other traditions as well, in such a way that reappropriation which honors both past and present becomes possible. We will need to come back to this clue later on, and the enlarged order of choice and responsibility which it implies.

For now, though, I want to return to dialogue, and suggest that this term itself contains an answer to the question: it indicates the healthy (as distinct from doctrinal—or ideological) form of relationship with the traditional past, as well as the healthy or mature form of relationship with the modern present—at the center of which is relationship with the other. For at the center of this particular kind of relationship we are open to meeting the other as other, at the same time as we are also able to be present in our own full definiteness, and able to share discovery and growth together. This is very different from three other kinds of encounter with which we are familiar: (1) the encounter of "incommensurability," in which foreignness prohibits any real meeting, only exchange, (2) the dominance-submission relations of both traditional and contemporary societies, and (3) the constricted, competitive relations of power and exchange as they issue from modern western natural rights individualism. In dialogue—whether with persons or with tradition—something else happens: we can draw from the other without losing our self, and we can be fully present without diminishing or exploiting the other. We are beyond the push-pull world of Newtonian physics and the natural rights individualism with which it is associated, to something like synergetic relationship. Together we come to both simultaneous affirmation and an open space of possibility between us, a space out of which solutions to mutually shared problems sometimes appear as though by magic.

This possibility returns us to the imperative of growth, and to the difficult fact that the dynamics of postmodern consciousness and dialogical relationship are *ambitious*—requiring a great deal of us, including forms of growth which are very hard to imagine until they have actually occurred—until they actually fly. Elizabeth Johnson indicates what is entailed in this taking wing:

> . . . the goal is the flourishing of all beings in their uniqueness and interrelation—both sexes, all races and social groups, all creatures in the universe. This calls for a new model of relationship, neither a hierarchical one that requires an over-under structure, nor a univocal one that reduces all to a given norm. The model is rather inclusive, celebratory of difference, circular, feminist—we reach for words. . . . Neither heteronomy (exclusive other-directedness) nor autonomy in a closed egocentric sense but a model of relational independence, freedom in relation, full related selfhood becomes the ideal.[12]

But, as Daniel Yankelovich and others have noted, not many have developed the self-knowledge or maturity on which this ideal depends.[13] The enormity of what is required of us, both developmentally and in terms of transition from one cultural paradigm to another, leads many to either passive despair or to aggressive and manipulative assertion of their "socially constructed" view of reality. And many alternate back and forth between the two, within the nihilistic temper of our time. Yet if we avoid the temptation to nihilism with its reduction of all relationships to those of interest and power, and if we remain sincere, the sense of possibility remains—and is, in fact, quite manifest in some sectors of society—for example in American higher education.[14]

From another angle of vision, perhaps the experience of dialogue is not as rare as it may seem. Maybe the problem is that our intellectual tradition and our theorists have failed to provide articulation of this kind of relationship, ways of pointing to it, reminding of its importance, communicating its inspirational quality. This is suggested in a powerful way in a report from one of the principal participants in the world deliberations which led to creation of the Earth Charter, J. Ronald Engel. He speaks of participants *experiencing* democracy as a way of relating that "can outrun the thinking of democratic theorists who insist that ethics are relative and that people of diverse cultures cannot agree on a vision and a standard of the common good."[15] Again, the theme is that of our being able to *do* something which we cannot quite think, something that *happens* in our better moments.[16] And this raises, again, the question as to the adequacy of our inherited ways of thinking, interpreting, prioritizing, the issue of worldview and its adequacy to our best experiences. It appears that there are ways of living and relating, including those which are indicated by the words "dialogue" and "democratic pluralism," which have not been comprehended, supported, or given priority by the dominant ways of speaking and theorizing, ways which have been eclipsed and hidden in remote subtraditions of Western culture, eclipsed by the dominant ways of thinking which have been either hierarchical or atomistic, collectivist or individualist, socialist or capitalist. Elizabeth Minnich speaks with eloquence about the developmental challenge of democratic pluralism:

> Democratic pluralism, on the face of it a fine position, cannot be espoused in today's world as if all we had to do was choose it. To achieve a truly egalitarian pluralism conceptually and politically, it is necessary for all groups to achieve self-knowledge, developed from within rather than imposed from without. . . . [We need] to think much more subtly and to live and work with more complexity and fineness of feeling and comprehension, taste and judgment. We begin again to create ways of thinking that support democracy rather than undermining it."[17]

This point brings us back to the matter of prejudices, along with the clue from Confucius about humans "making the Way great," which implies that our valuing in the present could be a matter of active *choice*, rather than merely a detached and passive observation, a matter of prescription and not only description, and ultimately a matter of appreciating what it means to be human. Gadamer supports this possibility with his insistence that we get past what he calls the Enlightenment "prejudice against prejudice,"[18] and the associated assumption that the detached, transparent, *and passive* observer is both possible and desirable. In Minnich's terms, which I take to be quite compatible with those of Confucius, we can "*create* ways of thinking," choose them and cultivate them.

With this in mind, I want to report that after many decades of experience with inter-cultural and inter-religious dialogue, as well as with liberal education and democratic political life, I have come to awareness of some very positive "prejudices" of our time, ones which support vital rather than doctrinaire reappropriation, and the possibility of creative dialogue—and hence also the possibility of surviving the modern. And I need to say that I am very serious about "reporting;" that these are values and ways of thinking we are creating/choosing together, not the inventions of an isolated thinker. They are "prejudices" which perhaps reveal that dialogue is a possibility in our world to a degree which is not acknowledged by the dominant ways of thinking. In the next chapter it will be important to speak at some length about these elements of pre-understanding which indicate the vitality of life in the present, or what it might mean for "the human to make the Way great." Here I will only introduce them very briefly:

1. Affirmation of the gift quality of life, and related significance of natality, the human capacity for creating ex nihilo, being bearers of the new.
2. The necessity of reappropriating wisdom from traditions, specifically wisdom having to do with meaning, value, life-direction, and cultivation of the human being—wisdom as to what it means *for humans* to affirm life as a gift.
3. Reflexivity, indicating the developed capacity for self-awareness, predicated upon awareness of the limitations of one's own self and tradition, and the ability to acknowledge mistakes. This includes acknowledgment of the limits of any human interpretation, and the ineffability of that which is ultimate.
4. Commitment to growth/maturity, and a vision of the adult person as capable of both intimacy and independence, both the openness and the definiteness which are necessary to dialogue. This includes understanding that the life-interpretation of both persons and communities develop over time, within a life-long transformative process. It also includes commitment to practice as the necessary cultivation of growth.
5. Urge toward flourishing or thriving, as the state of well-being which is characterized by maximum diversity within a unified whole, a state in which diversity and unity are in harmonious or synergetic relation, a state which is "sustainable."

6. Identification of relationality as the space in which human beings exhibit the qualities of thriving or flourishing, and "democracy" or "pluralism" as that social/political/cultural form which is oriented to relationality.

My suggestion is that these understandings constitute the ground of definiteness in the present from which dialogue with the traditional past and healthy reappropriation become possible, at the same time—and again with apology for the sometimes vexing complexity of communication in our time—they can be seen as *results* of that dialogue, as *capacities* which develop through practice of dialogue. To complicate one step further, I also think they together constitute or at least point in the direction of a new world ethic and spirituality which are emerging in our time, which is also to say a new way of thinking and ordering experience, one which is both more "developed" and more supportive of dialogue, democracy, and the thriving of all life, including the natural world. They point to the emergence of a post-modern, relational worldview.

Here, then, is the underlying claim: that a new worldview and way of living, including a new ethic and spirituality, is *available*. It is one which is genuinely pluralistic, truly valuing of difference while at the same time finding unity in the deep commonality of our all being children of the same mother Earth. Yet this worldview cannot simply be delivered as some new intellectual formulation, doctrine, or power point presentation. This is because of both its developmental aspect and its relational-pluralistic quality.

POSTMODERN CRITIQUE AND RETURN OF WISDOM

From a Western perspective, the root experience of traditional cultures can be understood as offering ways of moving beyond or (in more Chinese terms) harmonizing the several antinomies which seem inherent in the human condition itself: the one and the many, the individual and the collective, free will and determinism, effort and acceptance, the absolute and the relative, similarity and difference, the objective and the subjective, and unity and diversity. Traditional cultures, as we have learned in the post-traditional 20th century, resolved or went "beyond" these antinomies in ways that involved racism, sexism, and classism, and other notions of superiority based on factors other than merit or wisdom. They filled and ordered the space between the otherwise irreconcilable antinomies with values and meanings which were determined by structures of dominance and submission. In doing this they seem—especially from the perspective of the postmodern liberation movements and the struggle for second generation rights—to have eclipsed the very root experiences from which they arose initially in the Axial Period, such experiences as: the beauty and goodness of all life, the dignity of the human, the possibility of just and harmonious community, and the coincidence of wisdom and compassion. We have to wonder, along the lines of what is known as "perennial philosophy," whether wisdom itself was eclipsed and suffocated by the traditions that arose on top of the original wisdom. Here may be the underlying tragedy of the traditional period which does not become evident until it ends—again, that its development, from a very early moment, suffocated the genius with which it began in the Axial Age. And at the same time we have to wonder whether the postmodernist critique will throw out the proverbial baby with the bath, whether the wisdom which is hidden in the wings of tradition will be lost in the descent into a pre-civilized or uncivilized state of clash and nihilism and terror, a state in which no one wins and everyone loses.

Another possibility is that postmodernist critique actually releases wisdom from its containment in tradition, at the same time it also generates movement beyond critique to clarity about what is positive both at the base of tradition and in modernity. This, of course, can only happen as postmodern critique begins to appreciate that which it might not otherwise notice because it is standing on it, namely reasonableness, the principle of its presence in all people, and the assumption that a better world can be created through increased communication and cooperation. What I am getting at is that with the new ethic and spirituality we now have the possibility of "going beyond" in ways that are much more egalitarian and pluralistic, ways which avoid resolutions requiring authoritarianism, fundamentalism, or other forms of simply *submitting* to those with "higher" knowledge or status, ways which entail "the renunciation, not of one's own tradition and national past, but of the binding authority and universal validity which tradition and past have always claimed."[19] (Arendt). Through dialogue in the context of reappropriation there is plenty of room for all to be humble, and to correct against—to borrow some helpful language from the Confucian tradition—authoritativeness which becomes authoritarian. For we are speaking of a *relational* ideal, not an ideal of monarchical and patriarchical domination. We are also speaking of a worldview oriented to *practice* and a developmental ideal which knows no final plateau, or any human exemption from its discipline. And in reappropriation through dialogue we have a way of addressing what I have previously referred to as the chief imperative of our time, that of choosing a new way of life, and the three subsidiary imperatives of growth/maturity, encounter with the other, and transformative practice. But, above all, through the new ethic and spirituality, we have the possibility that wisdom, which is no different from compassion, can reenter the world and be active here.

AMERICAN TRADITION AND DEMOCRATIC SPIRIT

All of the above is necessary background to any serious attempt to reappropriate the democratic spirit as it has been and still is present in the American tradition—and in other traditions as well. It was necessary to go all the way to world ethic and spirituality in order to say this, to invoke the project of revitalization. This is so because any articulation of the American spirit (or any other) which is not understood to be a local version of world spirit becomes either useless or dangerous. All that has been said above also requires that this work on the democratic spirit in America must be conducted in dialogue with life in the present, both in America and in other parts of the world, with others who are pursuing the same postmodern work of overcoming the modern and reappropriating elements of tradition. For here is the higher loyalty: as great as the American past can be, it is my neighbors in the global present, those with whom I live and struggle with the overwhelming issues of today, to whom my deepest allegiance is due. For it is with them that we will live or die, thrive or languish. This, of course, includes my American neighbors, for whom I have particular affection—even if some of them are not yet as global as we need them to be.

My claim is that the democratic spirit has been present in the American tradition and is *still* present in America today. It can be a vital resource not only for Americans but for the whole world, and yet the releasing of this vitality requires the multidimensional dialogue of which I speak. My best analogy on this point is the Jack Pine, that species of pine tree which requires the heat of fire in order for its seed to open and give forth new life. It is on the horizon of this possibility of revitalization through dialogue and reappropriation that we can find inspiration in the words of that American prophet of democracy, Walt Whitman: "We have frequently printed the word Democracy, yet I cannot too often repeat that it is a word the real gist of which still sleeps. . . . [Its] history has yet to be enacted."[20]

From what we know of the democratic spirit, it seems clear that it requires the fire of our response, our conscious choice, in order for it to be manifest. This is complex, paradoxical, and mentally (and spiritually) challenging, but the issue is clear from our side: we must respond, and exercise some degree of free will. The democratic spirit, in this sense at least, seems similar to the Way in Confucianism, in that it is paradoxically and profoundly dependent on the human. And this connection, within the grand world dialogue of our time, takes us back to William James, who spoke of "the Will to Believe" as a positive kind of social construction, of "cases where a fact cannot come at all unless a preliminary faith exists in its coming."[21] Whether the democratic spirit is present on the Earth—or not—ultimately depends on the hearts of people like you and me.

What we need, then, is exercise in willing to believe, along with friends in America and China and all parts of the world who struggle to remain awake through the modern dream and postmodern reactions to the discovery of its insufficiency. I seek to learn with and through these friends, while at the same time locating and sharing the democratic spirit as it is still to be found and nurtured in America—both in the textures of life in the present, and in the history from which it flows. For here is the path of revitalization and reignition America so urgently needs, a path we can only walk when we walk with others.

The root question of our time is the question as to whether it is possible for human beings, in all of our similarity and difference, to continue living on the Earth at all, recalling the Hebrew scripture cited at the very beginning of our conversation: "I have set before you life and death, blessing and curse; therefore choose life." My thesis is that the word "dialogue" is expressive of positive response to this choice, and of the possibility of a form of life which values thriving over and above—and more deeply then—the accumulation of material wealth, healthy relationship and community over individual glorification, and spiritual presence over victories of ego competition. And I suggest that there are resources for this way of living in the democratic spirit of America, as well as in the vision of the sincere person in Chinese Confucianism, and, in fact, in all of the historic traditions—despite what on some days appears as overwhelming evidence that the societies which gave birth to these traditions are now completely lost in their own versions of the modern degradation and confusion.

Ultimately, then, we are inquiring into the conditions under which life is given us, and into what it therefore means to live in faithfulness to the gift quality of life. We can do this from America and help others in the process, even as they can help us as they do the same.

CONVERSATIONAL ASIDE

I want to distinguish more finely the view that is emerging through this inquiry from the most visible orientation in the philosophy and cultural theory of the West in the early 21st century.

"Postmodernism" is a relativistic sibling to absolutistic fundamentalism. It is not just an esoteric academic specialization, but a generalized cultural mood which is reflected (sometimes refracted) through the lenses of scholars who, for all their sophistication, can be astonishingly naive. I find the mood in question to be quite poignantly articulated by Arendt, when she remarked that "When Europe in all earnest began to prescribe its 'laws' to all other continents, it so happened that she herself had already lost her belief in

them."[22] *Others have spoken along similar lines, in terms of a Western "failure of nerve" (Sidney Hook), "incredulity toward metanarratives" (Jean Francois Lyotard), and even "self loathing."*[23] *The mood is that of one who is experiencing irreversible decline following upon some decisive though unspecified break with original vitality, an underlying attitude of pessimism and wariness tinged with "irony," as covert expression of complicity in the break. It is a species of guilt.*

An essay by Richard Rorty, in which he distinguishes between private and public orientations to philosophy and declares his strong preference for the former and equally strong suspicion of the latter, provides a way to see more deeply into the limitations and dangers of postmodernism.[24] *Rorty argues against Jurgen Habermas's judgment that Nietzsche, Heidegger, Derrida, and "the [postmodern] philosophy of consciousness" movement they represent are "symptomatic of cultural exhaustion." Against Habermas, Rorty asserts that these philosophers signify not exhaustion but vitality; that they are not bad public philosophers but good private philosophers. He praises what he takes to be their purely private orientation, as "the ironists' quest for ever deeper irony and ever more ineffable sublimity."*[25] *He then goes on, despite what he says at the beginning of the essay about his intention to show how these two forms "complement rather than oppose each other," to associate Habermas's concern with democracy and the public— and, by implication if not direct argument,* anyone's *concern with a commonly shared life beyond immediate and strictly contingent circumstances—with "German-style 'social theory.'" By this Rorty means that Habermas's theory is liable to becoming fascist, as a result of his intoxication with the idea of "Something Larger."*[26]

Rorty, like others associated with postmodernism, remains modern—and even hyper-modern. Not only is his definition of freedom entirely private and negative, as we have just seen, but he is also intellectualist. As an intellectualist he drives all questions to the antinomies of reason, to either-or choices. Among these are public-private (per above), and also the mind-body dichotomy bequeathed by Descartes at the beginning of the Modern Period. For Rorty, there is no possibility on the far side of opposition between a mind which would necessarily become hegemonic and imperialistic if it went public with claims about a common good, and a body which is forever contained within its local frame of contingency and incommensurability with all other such containments. Despite his hope to unmask cruelty and humiliation, and his openness to philosophy as effective/pragmatic cultural criticism, Rorty's prior and underlying intellectualism deprives his hope of wings. The sentiments he wishes to affirm are not recommended, except through personal disclosure. He fails to locate or enter the public as a relational dimension which has claims beyond combinations of personal/ private preference.

Rorty does not come through with the "complementarity" he promises at the beginning of his essay. Everything remains private, an entirely relative and subjective matter of what one happens to love and appreciate.[27] *There is no sign of reason in the service of cultivating the human, no hint of identifying relationship and community as locus of vitality, no commitment to reason contributing to our thriving together on an endangered planet. With Rorty, postmodernism is not all that different from the world of Locke, Hobbes, and the modernity of natural rights individualism, except that fear of fascism replaces naïve and unwittingly hegemonic faith in the common good and metaphysical order. It seems that, as is so often the case in human life, postmodernism winds up inviting the very thing it fears. It comes to an unstable and dangerous relativism. In its zeal to get past the false and hegemonic reasoning of the past, postmodernism denies the possibility of a reformed and more developed embodiment of reason of the sort which is recommended by such figures as Habermas, Stephen Toulmin, Alison Jaggar,*[28] *and Tu Weiming.*

As distinct from Rorty and the postmodernist mood, I posit life,[29] *a commonly shared life founded on the reality of relationships, a life which quite paradoxically includes and thrives on real differences. This life was initially constituted on a global scale very imperfectly (like America itself), by the modern western intervention spreading modernism all over the planet, via what we have come to understand as the negative values of the modern (again, materialism, hyper-individualism, consumerism). More recently, the modern and essentially Western positing of life has reflected the urgent need to articulate the positive values of the modern, and expand and reform this deeply problematic common heritage through inclusion of cultures and values as other ways of positing life which it had excluded previously. The emergent understanding of a shared life centers on relationality and transformation; is responsive to local wisdom, emotional and spiritual dimensions, feminine and ecological values, and it posits a life in which acts of compassion resonate with the deepest source of reality, opening a channel through which thriving occurs.*

Yes, but all of the above is not metaphysical assertion so much as it is choice, a hope, an affirmative response to the gift quality of life in the midst of Nothingness. And yet it is empirically based, and shared by many people and movements on the planet, a palpable hope which can be nurtured. In this sense it is more like what Confucius had in mind when he said "the human makes the way great" than it is like Rorty's choice to stay private. Yet how could it be advocated in a world of difference and conflict, a partially collapsed world of indifference to all values but those of maximizing individual interest, and a postmodernist world in which the slide through relativism opens onto the hell of nihilism?

NOTES

1. See Richard Poirier, "Why Do Pragmatists Want to Be Like Poets?," in Morris Dickstein, ed., *The Revival of Pragmatism: New Essays on Social Thought, Law, and Culture* (Durham: Duke University Press, 1999), pp. 347–361.

2. Donella H. Meadows, *The Limits to Growth* (New York: Signet, 1972).

3. Peter D. Hershock, *Reinventing the Wheel: A Buddhist Response to the Information Age* (Albany, NY: SUNY Press, 2001), p. 272.

4. Gadamer, *Truth and Method*, pp. 239–240. For indication of the linkage between the hermeneutical revolution of the 20th century and the contemporary dialogue movement, see David Tracy, *Plurality and Ambiguity: Hermeneutics, Religion, Hope* (San Francisco: Harper & Row, 1989).

5. Again, see Peter L. Berger and Samuel P. Huntington, eds., *Many Globalizations,* and also *Multiple Modernities, Daedalus,* 129/1 (Winter 2000).

6. There are two other (not mutually exclusive) ways of speaking about and finding resources for integration and revitalization of a humanly problematic postmodern present. The first is in terms of dimensions of our humanity which were repressed in the traditional period, chiefly, the feminine, the prehistoric, the Eastern, and the right brain. See my *Leaving and Returning* for discussion of these. The second is in terms of contemporary social scientific visions of human development, and life-span development to which I have previously referred.

7. Members of this group who write in English include Tu Weiming, Henry Rosemont, Peimin Ni, Sor-hoon Tan, Roger Ames, Chenyang Li, David Hall, and Yaming An.

8. This has been attributed to Joel J. Kupperman, who is author of *Learning from Asian Philosophy* (New York: Oxford University Press, 1999).

9. Chenyang Li, *The Tao Encounters the West: Explorations in Comparative Philosophy* (Albany, NY: SUNY Press, 1999), pp. 5, 191, 192.

10. Sor-hoon Tan, *Confucian Democracy,* pp. 9, 12.

11. Confucius, *The Analects of Confucius,* 15/29, trans Roger T. Ames and Henry Rosemont, Jr. (New York Ballantine, 1998), p. 190.

12. Elizabeth Johnson, *She Who Is: The Mystery of God in Feminist Theological Discourse* (New York: Crossroad, 1993), pp. 32, 68.

13. See Daniel Yankelovich, *The Magic of Dialogue: Transforming Conflict into Cooperation* (New York: Simon & Schuster, 1999), p. 17.

14. See chapter 12.

15. J. Ronald Engel, "The Earth Charter as a New Covenant for Democracy," in *Just Ecological Integrity: The Ethics of Maintaining Planetary Life,* ed., Peter Miller and Laura Westra (New York: Rowman & Littlefield, 2002), pp. 48–49.

16. This crucial dynamic recalls John Dewey's point about the public in modern times being primarily an intellectual problem. It also brings into high relief a point that some postmodern philosophers bring up, about the necessary priority of *the ethical* (as distinct from the traditional priority of the metaphysical and the epistemological) in our times, for example, Richard Bernstein, Sissela Bok, and Immanuel Levinas.

17. Elizabeth Minnich, *Transforming Knowledge* (Philadelphia: Temple University Press, 1990), p. 184.

18. Gadamer, *Truth and Method,* pp. 239–240.

19. Hannah Arendt, "Karl Jaspers: Citizen of the World?," in *Men in Dark Times* (New York: Harcourt, Brace & World, 1968), p. 84. In Rowe, ed., *Living Beyond Crisis,* pp. 253–54.

20. Walt Whitman, *Democratic Vistas,* ed. Ed Folsom (Iowa City: University of Iowa Press, 2010), p. 37.

21. James, "The Will to Believe," in *The Writings of William James,* p. 731.

22. Arendt, "Karl Jaspers: Citizen of the World?," p. 252.

23. Christopher Caldwell, *Reflections on the Revolution in Europe: Immigration, Islam and the West* (New York: Anchor Books, 2009), pp. 82–84.

24. Richard Rorty, "Habermas, Derrida, and Philosophy," in *Truth and Progress: Philosophical Papers* (Cambridge: Cambridge University Press, 1998), pp. 307–326.

25. *Ibid.*, p. 310.

26. *Ibid.*, p. 326.

27. See Rorty's autobiographical essay, "Trotsky and the Wild Orchids," in *Philosophy and Social Hope* (London: Penguin Books, 1999), pp. 3–20.

28. See especially her "Love and Emotion in Feminist Epistemology," in *Inquiry* (Oslo: Scandinavian University Press, 1989).

29. The allusion here to James is quite intentional. See chapter 11, "Pragmatism Revisited."

Chapter Six

Dialogue as Democratic Possibility

Reappropriating the Modern

THE EMERGENCE OF DIALOGUE

Recent times have been marked by critical awareness of the limitations of the modern and the secular, and a return of religion, spirituality, and tradition. Fundamentalism, with its urge to shut down individual choice and *go back,* is not the only expression of this return—and movement beyond. There are forms of post-traditional culture which push forward, some of which see the relativism and associated ethical and political breakdown of the late modern period as preparation for stepping across a developmental (or even evolutionary) threshold, into a new stage of human life and culture, one which is not only conducive to our surviving in these times and those that lie ahead, but to our thriving as well. These forms of post-traditional culture share with fundamentalism acknowledgment of the deeply problematic nature of the modern, and affirmation of the necessity of traditional resources to the human spirit. But the forms of post-traditional culture of which I speak are also profoundly different from fundamentalism: in their trust of the individual, their recognition of the gift character of life on the Earth, and in their cultivation of a spirituality which is commonly shared among all humans—one which paradoxically values and even enhances our particular/ local/embodied differences. For these forms, "return" is fully embraced as a dimension of the present.

All this, of course, is a long story, and one which contains an utterly crucial distinction for our journey into an uncertain future—between those cultural forms which honor and cultivate the person, and those which insist on order through authoritarian imposition from above. Mention of this distinction seems a fitting prelude to a chapter on one of those forms of post-traditional culture which is friendly to religion and tradition without being fundamentalist, the one associated with the word "Dialogue."

The thesis of this chapter is that the Intercultural Dialogue Movement (ICDM) is a medium through which a new ethic, spirituality, and vision of human maturity are finding their ways into our commonly shared life on the planet as a whole. The ICDM, as constitutive of a new worldview and our best hope for the future, offers us the opportunity to grow into a way of life in which we can solve the riddle of unity and diversity which marks our time, into a way in which unity is given substance and integrity through diversity, and in which diversity finds the kind of discipline which makes real growth possible.

In 2001 the ICDM came to greater visibility when the United Nations General Assembly declared that year as the Year of Dialogue Among Civilizations.[1] Here, and in the ICDM generally, dialogue has been associated with a new global paradigm based on positive valuation of diversity: "Dialogue is a proper instrument to achieve a new paradigm of global relations. Dialogue is a first step in providing a sense of belonging, for by communicating and listening we take the first step toward recognizing our own commonality. . . . The key to a new paradigm of global relations is to overcome the misunderstanding that diversity is a synonym for enmity."[2] We can add that, within the ICDM dialogue is seen as a way of conflict resolution, community building, and democratic participation. It is seen as a way that is capable of solving real and urgent problems with moral authority. Though dialogue may sound unrealistic and romantic initially, its authority is understood to arise from the strength of its contact with both persons and communities, the sense in which it is recognized as the best choice in the direction of thriving and hope for the human future, its resonance with truth, love, democracy, and what Martin Luther called "other preservation . . . [as] the first law of life."[3]

Despite the tragedy of 9/11 and the War on Terror which followed shortly after the U.N. declaration, the ICDM has continued to gather strength. The term "dialogue" has entered the vocabulary of foreign policy, corporate negotiation, and public (and even private) life generally. As a key term of our era, many like to use it, since it carries a vaguely positive connotation—and an array of even more vague and various definitions (we should not be surprised to see a small, energy-efficient car named "Dialogue" soon!). However, in the specific usage of the ICDM, dialogue has been understood to indicate a distinct alternative to two other obvious and unacceptable options for the human future: the homogenized globalization of Western-style modernization,[4] and the ongoing and ever more destructive "clash of civilizations."[5] These, of course, are variations on the "Catch 22" choice between a relativism that reduces us all to a least common denominator (and hence is absolutistic in its own way), and absolutisms which will fight to the death in order to escape relativism and impose their interpretation. In contrast to these two unacceptable possibilities, we who have shared the vocation of the ICDM have envisioned a world that is neither absolutistic nor relativistic, but *pluralistic*, and likewise, a world in which unity and diversity support and enhance each other rather than constituting an either-or choice. We have been working for dialogue as the constitutional principle of world community, and also as a developmental challenge for each one of us.

In presenting dialogue and its association with democratic possibility, my appeal is not to abstract theory construction but to the actual *experience* and *practice* of dialogue. For dialogue is more like an event than an idea or a doctrine; it is more like a place than an abstraction, as, for example, in Hannah Arendt's reference to as "the shining brilliance of the public realm."[6] My aim is to be faithful to the experience of a creative open space in which others and ourselves appear both distinctly and in relation, in an atmosphere of liberation, possibility, and often surprising solutions to real problems and conflicts.

There are many descriptions of dialogue, many connections between dialogue and the world's traditions, many ways in which we can understand dialogue as vital to the future of the human race. My purpose in venturing the description which follows in this chapter is to make it possible for people to see and connect with a certain stream of possibility and development which is already at work in the world and perhaps unnoticed in our own lives as well.

After description in the next section, I will then step back in a third part, to think about implications and prospects.

SIX QUALITIES OF DIALOGUE

In my understanding of dialogue, there are six interdependent qualities, the same six I mentioned briefly by way of preview in the previous chapter. These at the same time constitute components of the emerging ethic/ spirituality/maturity, ones which are both necessary for and cultivated by the practice of dialogue. They can also be seen as expressions of the vitality of life in the present, and at the same time as expressions (or "reappropriations") of what is positive in modernity.

The six qualities are: Affirmation of Gift, Reappropriation of Tradition, Commitment to Growth/Maturity, Reflexivity, Urge Toward Flourishing, and Relationship as Locus. In what follows I will relate awareness of these qualities and components to actual experiences of the ICDM in the past twenty years or so.

1. Affirmation of Gift

One of the most important discoveries of the post-traditional 20th century is that of the Axial movement of humankind all across the Earth in the first millennium BCE, in which the oneness of existence was experienced and later articulated in the form of the great traditions.[7] It was also discovered that one of the attributes of those great traditions was that they had been Earth and life-denying, essentially oriented to *getting out,* to life in this world as a problematic place we must pass through or escape in order to arrive at another, better world.[8] In the post-traditional 20th century, we began to encounter the legacy of this orientation in the shape of a very limited and largely ruined Earth.

Dialogue opens up as a possibility and is grounded in the decision to turn away from this ago-old orientation, in the willingness to "choose life." It abides in maintaining awareness of the gift quality of life. It is in this sense that the photograph of the Earth from outer space can be taken as the chief religious symbol of our time. The Earth and everything upon it is experienced as miraculous, against the backdrop of the abyss of outer space, in a state of wonder and appreciation that there is "something rather than nothing."[9]

2. Reappropriation of Tradition

We come to discover that secularism and the claims of the scientific worldview (including its expressions as social science) are not sufficient to the human spirit. We also discover the larger body of who we are, the sense in which body, the life we em-body, includes tradition. I cannot be everything, and my capacity to respond to the gift quality of life depends on clarity about the nature of the gift: life is given, within conditions, one of which is that we are inseparably one with the particularity of our circumstance—including our being expressions of one tradition or another.

Reappropriation of tradition has been most dramatically evident to me in China and with Chinese Third Epoch Confucians. When I first started traveling to China in the mid-1990's after *Rediscovering the West* had been published in translation there, the philosophy departments to which I was invited were mostly engaged in Western philosophy, mostly Modern and Analytical. But some were interested in the central suggestion of my book that encounter with the other makes it possible to see and gain access to the genius of one's own tradition, as well as in reports about the value of classical Chinese philosophy for Western people. In a few years, by the late 1990s, the situation had changed dramatically, to the point where classical Chinese philosophy was no longer seen as a part of the pre-May Fourth [1919] Movement past that must be left behind: as impossibly vague and/or naïve, or as merely a matter of antiquarian value—good for decoration only.

Rather, dialogue with Chinese philosophers has centered on overcoming the limitations of the modern worldview as it has been imposed on so much of the planet, including attention to such dynamics as those of "reappropriation" and comparative philosophy.[10] In fact, dialogue has developed to the point where there is growing expectation among Chinese colleagues that, in the words of Peimin Ni, "Confucian philosophy is what we should count on for recovery from the materialized and alienated world and for the revitalization of humanity."[11] It is understood that this philosophy is inseparable from *both* Chinese tradition and post-traditional dialogue.

There has been a reciprocal process in my own life: the effect of contact with other cultures has led me to reappropriation of my own tradition that is deeper and more solid than what I had before, more fully practical and alive, more secure from the distractions of consumer society.

I remember an especially vivid moment of dialogue when I suddenly discovered the beauty and profundity of Socrates at a deeper level. I was speaking with a Daoist about how one can discern the promptings of the Dao from within one's own experience, how one can distinguish those genuine promptings from one's own desire or fear. I found myself saying that the "inner voice" or "divine sign" of Socrates never told him what to do, but only warned him about what not to do when he was about to make a bad decision. This insight led to an opening where I could see the paradox of simultaneity between self and the divine shining through Socrates in a way that had enormous practical significance for my own development. No need to wait for "God's word" to come from a mountaintop or the great beyond, or *anywhere* displaced from the self; and yet no need to worry about possible perversions of this most ambitious spirituality, because God can be trusted to speak through caution and what later Western culture called "conscience." "Atman is Brahman" is an effective articulation for many Hindu people (and others), and Socrates' radical affirmation of freedom and human creativity was/is for me.

Getting to the place from which this kind of revaluing and reappropriation can occur has involved a journey—across the broad and barren plains of post-traditional secularism in which I was raised (as though there *were no* human spirit), and past temptations to deflect either into fundamentalist involvement in a particular tradition (or cult), or into universalist meandering in the great museum of the world's traditions. But I have been fortunate to have reminders from members of my tradition who have gone before, such as Alfred North Whitehead when he said "definiteness is the soul of actuality."[12] More to the point, I have received this crucial learning through the discipline of dialogue itself. One way to put it is in terms of a basic paradox of our post-traditional journey: the nectar of universality is only available through the particular, including the humble (and humbling) practice of a definite tradition.

Yet in our time the very existence of traditions is threatened by the tight and tenuous interdependence of peoples and ecosystems, the homogenizing force of global capitalism, and the eclipse of traditions by the scientific worldview. In this context, Kofi Annan, Secretary-General of the United Nations, gives a practical argument for the importance of dialogue as it inherently involves reappropriation of traditions: "it helps us draw on the deeper, ancient roots cultures and civilizations to find what unites us across all boundaries, and shows us that the past can provide signposts to unity just as easily as to enmity."[13] Dialogue and comparative study are of immediate and practical value in giving us access to the wisdom of the great traditions in the present, and, in the complexity of our situation, there is a sense in which the wisdom at the root of the great traditions can be even *more* powerfully available to us today than it was for most of our ancestors, after so many of the traditional structures of mediation and orthodoxy have melted under the heat of modern and post-modern historical consciousness and critique.

Along with availability, we discover through genuine dialogue that definiteness and openness need not be opposed; in fact, the expansiveness that is so desirable as a human experience—that nectar of universality—is only available when we are definite in/as "the soul of actuality," while our own authentic definiteness becomes vividly available to us when we are open to the other. This is why Tu Weiming, one of the great masters of dialogue in our era, says: "Many kinds of 'thick descriptions' from a variety of spiritual traditions will have to be presented. We depend on the concrete manifestations of general principles to live a meaningful life in the world. The need for dialogue between civilizations is obvious."[14] Reappropriation of tradition on the post-traditional landscape is necessary in order for those "concrete manifestations" to be present.

3. Reflexivity

The choosing of healthy reappropriation is not fundamentalism; it does not retreat from life in the present, in the attempt to deny and get back to the Traditional Period; it is not rigid with assertion of unquestionable and absolute judgment. Healthy reappropriation is encouraged by dialogue which contains within it an essential hermeneutical awareness.

Reflexivity is the developed capacity for self-transcendence, becoming aware that I inevitably represent a tradition and have a life-interpretation—rather than simply playing these things out as the unconscious given, the unreflective "way things are." Once a little distance has occurred (distance, yes, that *can* put us on the "slippery slope" toward relativism, but by no means necessarily), we begin to move into a whole new order of choice and responsibility. Distance on "self" means we are liberated from defensiveness and the ego's absurd pretense to perfection, free to be honest about our vulnerability and limitations, free to enter the movement from ego consciousness to reality consciousness that John Hick and others see as central to all of the great traditions. [15] Distance on tradition means we are able to exercise what Robert Bellah calls "responsibility for choice of symbol system," [16] to appreciate that all traditions are limited by culture and society—such that each points to the Ultimate while none is ultimate in itself.

I have seen the emergence of this hermeneutical awareness most purely in the dialogue with my students, for whom it is a fundamental aspect of a liberal education. They seem to learn this awareness most effectively through feminist critique, which is possible, in the words of Elizabeth Minnich, because of "the human gift of reflexive thought" and "the liberatory quality of reflexive thinking." [17] Reflexivity makes it possible to "particularize what was [falsely] universal" and hence "open ourselves to greater diversity." [18] Similarly, Elizabeth Johnson, in an approach she identifies as "somewhat analogous to inter-religious dialogue," engages "a feminist hermeneutic." [19] Based on the understanding that "there has been no timeless speech about God" and that "words about God are cultural creatures," [20] she criticizes and reforms the classical tradition in light of the experience and the practice of "the emancipation of women toward human flourishing." [21] Again, hermeneutical awareness opens the door for us to be more fully faithful to our finest experiences.

In more formal dialogue settings, the 2000 Jewish Christian Dialogue program entitled "Old Boundaries, New Boundaries—Taking the Next Step" was especially clear on the significance of reflexivity. Rabbi Irving Greenberg emphasized the necessity of knowing one's limits, and that this reflexive knowing is in fact a precondition for the maintenance of one's own position in a plural world. He was eloquent:

> . . . the deepest truth is that we hold on to our absolutes in pluralism only if we know the limits of our position. My truth cannot and does not cover all people, all possibilities, all times, because God wants others to contribute. We need the checks and balances to prevent the spinning out of control of our individual positions. This is why our dialogue is so vital and so necessary. We are embarked on one of the great moral adventures of all time: to give up triumphalism, to accept that it is God's will that will be done, to accept that we are only servants and agents, to know that we have not been the sole vehicles of God's love or the redemption that is coming. It is this generation's calling to undertake this task for the sake of redeeming suffering humanity. [22]

Reflexivity—as the developmental ground of any genuine pluralism—indicates a capacity to reflect on or *see* one's self/tradition, as though from another location, a post-traditional place from which we can respond to both the limitations and the greatness/gift of our tradition/self, along with our most complete experiences of being alive.

4. Commitment to Growth/Maturity

Reflexivity and growth/maturity go hand in hand: as implied in discussion of
the previous quality, dialogue entails the kind of distance from both self and
tradition associated with healthy growth. However, there is much distance in
our time—even homelessness as a major theme—so that the distance of
healthy growth needs to be distinguished carefully from the other forms.
Healthy growth makes it possible for us to affirm life as a gift, to appropriate
resources of tradition effectively, without denial of life in the present (by
escape into either an idealized traditional past or an ideology for the future),
exercise reflexivity, maintain healthy growth, contribute to thriving of others
and self, and be at home in relationality—again, the interdependence of the
six qualities.

To say we must grow is first of all to say—maybe especially to
Westerners—that we must move beyond fixed systems and static
understandings of the absolute and transcendent, which have themselves
been absolutized in the form of dogma, intellectualism, and patriarchy. This
means we must learn to affirm process and immanence, "ongoing creation,"
both in ourselves and in the larger world, maybe even theologically in terms
of "God's" ways of relating to the world.

Growth means pattern of movement, and a way of distinguishing the
healthy motion from those that are cancerous or otherwise dangerous—either
by kind, or direction, or by failure of a part to move in an otherwise dynamic
system. I think that since Gail Sheehy's groundbreaking 1976 book,
Passages: Predictable Crises of Adult Life, [23] the conversation that has
evolved about "life-span development" and the fullness of human growth
(beyond age 21!) is one of the most distinctive intellectual breakthroughs of
our period. Here I can only briefly point to two voices that show the intimate
connection between dialogue and the healthy pattern of growth—into an
expanded vision of human maturity:

First, William Fowler, in his influential *Stages of Faith,* [24] describes his
fifth stage, beyond the dichotomizing logic of the fourth, as conjunctive and
dialogical: "In dialogical knowing the multiplex structure of the world is
invited to disclose itself. In a mutual 'speaking' and 'hearing,' knower and
known converse in an I-Thou relationship," on the understanding that "truth
is more multidimensional and organically interdependent than most theories
or accounts of truth can grasp." [25] Development and maturity through this
stage "implies no lack of commitment to one's own truth," but rather "radical
openness to the truth of the other [which] stems precisely from its confidence
in the reality mediated by its own tradition and in the awareness that that
reality overspills its mediation." [26] My understanding at any point in life is

limited, and yet my understanding grows, becomes deeper, more clear, and more effective over time. This is quite the reverse of the previous paradigm which favored understanding that is absolute and unchanging.

The second voice is that, again, of Elizabeth Johnson. She too speaks of growth beyond dichotomizing logic, and its association with the limited male ideal and definition of maturity as nonrelational autonomy: "What is slowly coming to light is a new construal of the notion of the person, neither as a [male] self-encapsulated ego nor a [female] diffuse self denied, but selfhood on the model of relational autonomy."[27] Hence "Oppositional, either-or thinking, which is endemic to the androcentric construction of reality, dissolves into a new paradigm of both-and," and the vision of "the coinherence of autonomy and mutuality as constitutive of the mature person."[28]

Whether in the language of social science, feminism, or that which is more specific to intercultural dialogue, the point seems common—and twofold: first, humans (especially Western humans) must mature past a way of thinking and relating that is oppositional, generative of dichotomy and forced choice which denies and does violence to the complexity of real life. This older way or stage may be described as that of male-domination, or of the Western atomistic individualism, or of intellectualism. Second, we begin to develop into a new stage in which we become capable of what we cannot quite articulate. It involves living beyond the dichotomizing mentality, *living* the paradox of autonomy and mutuality, male and female, definiteness and openness, West and the rest, universal and particular, global and local. In dialogue we experience moments in which we are fully present in our genuineness, our maturity. It is as though our deep or authentic self is able to shine through the clouds of ego that otherwise subdue and obstruct. This self-evidently good experience occurs at the very same moment when we are attentive and open to the other—in dialogue.

5. Urge to Flourishing

The word "flourishing" enters the vocabulary of the dialogue movement (often with "thriving" as a synonym). For example, Tu Weiming, evaluating the Western Enlightenment, says it was "detrimental to human flourishing" because of its anthropocentric self-assertion.[29] Clearly this usage of the word "flourishing" is broader than the practices and definitions of any particular society, such as to open the possibility of this sort of cross-cultural criticism. J. Ronald Engel, one of the framers of the Earth Charter speaks of "the flourishing of all life": "If there is one overarching moral and practical priority for the Earth Charter it is the radical democratic imperative of forming a global compact among all citizens to engage in individual and collective moral deliberation for the sake of the flourishing of all life."[30] Here the reference is not only broader than any particular society, but planetary in scope.

"Flourishing" reveals the ways in which the intercultural dialogue movement overlaps the environmental movement (as we have already seen its overlap with some forms of feminism and social science). It connotes awareness and support of vital ecosystems in which humans cohabitate in a natural order of harmonious interdependence. This vision of well-being goes beyond the materialistic and atomistic modern notions of both capitalism and communism; it echoes the traditional visions of well-being, as Greek *Eudaimonia* and Chinese *Xing Fu*, and ideal community as envisioned by *Datong* and *Polis*.

Arising out of the post-traditional period in which humans are no longer embraced and supervised by metaphysical authority, we can distinguish the orientation to thriving from Nietzsche's "will to power." The Nietzschian response in the West to the absence of metaphysical context, and the resulting nihilism, arises from the individual will and its social constructivist assertion. The flourishing orientation is also post-traditional, but moves through and past the negativity of nihilism ("negating negation," in the language of the Kyoto School) to conscious affirmation of post-traditional life as liberation and gift, and develops toward greater awareness of the conditions under which gift is given. Sometimes associated with "survivors' wisdom,"[31] the flourishing response opens onto an ethic of care[32] and a reappropriation of democracy (rather than resignation to the war of all against all). Reporting on the dialogue process that resulted in the Earth Charter, J. Ronald Engel speaks of participants *experiencing* democracy as a way of relating that is beyond the thinking of democratic theorists, and involves appreciation of "gifts that outrun what we can see or understand," leading the Earth Charter to take "the radical democratic posture that underneath all these different interpretations there is a natural religious piety we all can share and a common covenant we can all make with the ultimately reliable powers of life."[33]

Clearly this vision of flourishing as democracy is deeper than the broadly accepted "procedural democracy" associated with the globalization of free markets, representative government, and constitutional rights. Not to deny the preferability of this type of political system over many others, Engel points out that merely procedural definitions of democracy fail to provide space for genuine citizenship and a vision of the common good—they do not result in or lead toward flourishing. The Earth-affirming vision of democracy is decidedly religious: it locates and specifies our human well-being within the harmonious interdependence of the many peoples, species, and geographies of this planet. To flourish is to live on and celebrate the whole planet, at the same time we rest and work in our local niche, simultaneously global and local.

6. Relationality as Locus

Flourishing identifies interdependence within the ecology of Earth as our home, and leads to awareness that "world civilization will become a universal moral democracy, or perish,"[34] and the religious significance of our faithfulness to the Earth as what William James calls "the common mother."[35] Relationality as Locus, as a separate sixth quality, goes a crucial step further to specify the meaning of interdependence for humans. "Flourishing," like affirmation of gift, can be vague and romantic without specification as to how and where. For humans, full experience of flourishing arises not from detached appreciation of interdependence, but rather from the midst of rigorous engagement with the other who becomes mysteriously both more other and more same in that moment of meeting. At the same time both self and other come into bright distinctiveness, the space between opens up as a space of possibility, creativity, and freedom—as locus of the ultimate, even as temple or holy place, the space in or out of which the divine appears, the new, and the "unexpected life" to which James refers. Here is both the place and the activity in (or through) which we are most faithful to the gift of life that is given to us. Hence this sixth quality, with its crucial specification, identifies dialogue as a religious *practice.*

The distinctively human interdependence is neither the isolation of atomistic individualism nor is it co-dependence, but rather the simultaneity of independence and intimacy—in what Peter Hershock speaks of, from a Buddhist perspective, as "truly liberating intimacy."[36] It is not exchange or social contract or construction, but rather that way of being to which Jesus points when he says that he is present when two or more are gathered in his name,[37] or Confucius when he asks: "Am I not one among the people of this world? If not them, with whom should I associate?"[38] Dialogue, for humans, *is* democracy—and pluralism—in that it entails openness to truth appearing through and with the other, and in that truth is understood as manifest in a kind of relationship rather than as correspondence with a reality that is external to encounter. The distinctively human form of interdependence is beyond competition and the assumption that all association must be ordered by the law of dominance and submission.

In traditional religious language, this sixth quality can be spoken of in terms of the fullness of return: the broadly shared sense that the truly enlightened being is not the one who leaves, or who retreats from the world into his/her own mystical purity, but the one who comes back from (or *in*—or *as*) the enlightenment experience out of love/compassion/service/

stewardship—and this not as "sacrifice," but as the fullness (or maturity) of enlightenment itself. In more contemporary terms: coming out of the nihilism—and the relativism that swirls around it—which many take to be inherent to modern and "post-modern" life,[39] and understanding this as a sort of leaving, then awareness of relatedness as locus of the ultimate for humans can be seen as return ("beyond the post-modern"). One very clear example of this sentiment and awareness is Karl Jaspers—in radical distinction from the "leaving" of Nietzsche—when he says (in what we could call the returning spirit) that personal ties are the only source of hope for a "new and trustworthy objectivity."[40] Relatedness with the other is both our salvation and our service; it is locus of our thriving.

AMERICA AND NEW WORLDVIEW

America is in a position to model dialogue by honoring the intimate connection between dialogue and her own founding principles and aspirations. But in recent times the United States has been deeply involved with the two negative possibilities I mentioned at the beginning of this chapter: globalization through the universal imposition of a single way of life, and the collapse of civilizations into cycles of fear and terror, kill or be killed—the war of all against all on a global scale.

It is essential that the world turn away from escalating barbarism, and return to those delicate webs of relationship that were being woven by the intercultural dialogue movement prior to 9/11/01. And in order for this to happen it is essential that America back away from its fear and temptation to rely solely on the "hard power" of the military and economics, that it might be re-inspired by what I am calling founding principles and aspirations. Otherwise, a terrible irony is about to occur: the nation that offers most as a model for a world community of unity and diversity, a world of dialogue and democracy, will not be available because it will have been seized by those very forces from which it *could* help protect the rest of the world. The world needs America to return; America needs America to return. The world needs an America that is more persuasive than forceful.

America, once thought of as the land of ongoing revolution, needs a revolving back (*re-volare*) to most basic commitments and purposes: those of freedom in community, equality of opportunity and difference, due process, and public discourse. But in order to have access to these as anything more than advertising slogans, America must engage reflexivity and confess its limitations also, the shortcomings and contradictions of its history and present moment. This essential humility becomes possible in the relationship of dialogue. It will not only allow America to reappropriate and be reinspired by its own informing vision, but also to grow through access to insight from dialogue partners from other parts of the planet. Indeed, it may be that the deep paradox of our global era is that none of us can be whole and complete unless/until we open ourselves to the other, a time in which cultivation of "global memory" becomes a necessity. Perhaps this paradox makes it possible to see Engel's "democratic imperative" in a different light.

The central argument of this chapter is that through this paradoxical process a new worldview is emerging, one that is both particular and universal, one that involves the magnificent pluralism Professor Tu refers to with the phrase "the globalization of local knowledge." Indeed, the American relational liberal perspective from which this chapter is written is itself an expression of the kind of local knowledge that becomes available through dialogue,[41] as well as testimony to the connection between dialogue and democracy.

Looking at the stream of possibility from which the six qualities in this essay flow, and after discussion of the qualities separately, two things become evident: First, Affirmation of Gift and Relatedness as Locus are different from the other four qualities. The first quality, Affirmation of Gift, supported by philosophies of life—or return—is the headwater of the new ethic/spirituality/maturity, its source. Flowing out of the root experience of Nothingness as the "recalling of our origin," everything else follows from this, as specification of how the gift is given, and as developed capacity actually to *live* the gift (not just to think about it, make art about it, sing about it, but to fully embody it). Relatedness as locus, the last quality, points to the fullness of actual human living. If the gift quality of life is the opening and wellspring of the new ethic/spirituality/maturity, then relatedness as locus is the inclusive quality (in something like the relationship between transcendence and immanence in process thought[42]).

Second, the stream of emerging ethic/spirituality/maturity may be stronger than it seems at first, less a philosopher's dream and more a real power in the world. One testimony of strength is the way in which the intercultural dialogue overlaps and is interwoven with other powerful movements of our time: especially, as we have seen, with feminism, the environmental movement, pragmatism, and comparative studies.

I conclude with appeal to this strength and persuasiveness, which at some moments appears to have a life of its own, a kind of historical momentum, and at other moments can be seen as absolutely dependent on our sincere effort, our openness to encounter and growth, our commitment to community and cooperation, and, finally—overall, our "will[ingness] to believe" in William James' terms,[43] to believe that dialogue might win over the more obvious forces of cynicism and despair. In this spirit it seems fitting to end with John Dewey, who invites us to join a movement that began long ago, one that is continuous with what I have referred to as the shared vocation of dialogue. He identifies the center of this movement in terms of a faith we share commonly as human beings, one which is quite friendly to those more particular, local, and individual faiths through which we are manifest in our uniqueness.

> The things in civilization we most prize are not of ourselves. They exist by the grace of the doings and sufferings of the continuous human community in which we are a link. Ours is the responsibility of conserving, transmitting, rectifying and expanding the heritage of values we have received that those who come after us may receive it more solid and secure, more widely accessible and more generously shared than we have received it. Here are all the elements for a religious faith that shall not be confined to sect, class, or race. Such a faith has always been implicitly the common faith of mankind.[44]

CONVERSATIONAL ASIDE: REAPPROPRIATING THE MODERN

Six qualities are discovered to be present in the world dialogue of our era. They are understood to be elements of an emerging world ethic and spirituality.

Do they not also represent reappropriation of modern/Enlightenment values, as they are in the process of being criticized and transformed through the dialogical encounter between cultures? Tu Weiming points out that the values of the Enlightenment are already global, and that our best hope is to broaden and deepen these values through dialogue:

> *The possibility of a radically different ethic or a new value system separate from and independent of the enlightenment mentality is neither realistic nor authentic. It may even appear to be either cynical or hypercritical. We need to explore the spiritual resources that may help us to broaden the scope of the Enlightenment project, deepen its moral sensitivity, and if necessary creatively transform its genetic constraints in order to fully realize its potential as a world view for the human community as a whole.[45]*

It is not enough to critique the modern and advocate the value of traditional wisdom. It is necessary to go a step beyond critique to identify positive values in the modern and Enlightenment project. For the modern was not only loss and falling away. Even though the 17th century values of abstraction and mastery came to the fore, the earlier 16th century values of embodiment, appreciation, and focus on practice remain and resurface in our time— through the dialogue movement, higher education, feminism, the environmental movement, etc. The positive modern values of democracy/ pluralism/diversity, the integrity of individual experience, and the possibility of growth are present and strong, and they caution us against romanticizing tradition. We need to remember that, despite the amazing riches we discover in the traditions, the experience of most people living within the traditional past was antithetical to the best values of the modern (which we so often assume, and so infrequently notice, again, like the ground which is directly under our feet): they lived in a hierarchy of fixed roles, mediated truth, and life-determination according to conditions of birth. The riches and wisdom of traditional cultures as we know them today were available to very few people in the traditional period.

And again, the modern is not only about loss, as Huston Smith and other 20th-century critics often claim. There is value to the modern which is more than just alternative to collapse and barbarism. Here I am suggesting, as Whitman, Habermas, and others have before, that the Enlightenment project has not yet been tried, and that now is the time.

Back to dialogue, considering it from the vantage point of what has just been said: dialogue is not only between traditions in the present, but also between the modern present and the traditional past. As with dialogue generally, each side is illuminated, refined, and energized in the encounter. The traditions, now aware of the flaws in their history, come forward with their best gifts and deepest treasures for life in the present. The modern does likewise, revealing that just in the same way that traditions are not impossibly polluted with racism/classism/sexism, so also the Enlightenment is not all about crude individualism and an economic ideology which legislates materialism and selfishness in ways which finally call forth Thomas Hobbes's Leviathan, as the inevitable dictatorship of a world in which "life is nasty, brutish, and short." Enlightenment values, as they are broadened and deepened, can support dialogue and a very different world future than that which is envisioned by either fundamentalism/terrorism or modernism unrestrained.

NOTES

1. For the broader history of this movement, see chapter 9.
2. Giandomenico Picco, ed., *Crossing the Divide: Dialogue Among Civilizations* (So. Orange, NJ: Seton Hall University School of Diplomacy and International Relations, 2001), pp. 37, 39.
3. King, *Where Do We Go From Here?*, p. 180.
4. Francis Fukuyama, *The End of History and the Last Man* (New York: Free Press, 1992).
5. Samuel Huntington, *The Clash of Civilizations and the Remaking of World Order* (New York: Simon & Schuster, 1996).
6. Hannah Arendt, *The Human Condition*, especially chapter 2, "The Public and the Private Realm."
7. See Karl Jaspers, *The Origin and Goal of History* (New Haven: Yale University Press, 1953), Hannah Arendt, "Karl Japers: Citizen of the World,?" pp. 81–94.
8. Bellah, "Religious Evolution," p. 22.

9. For profound reflection on the religious and cultural implications of gift, see Calvin O. Schrag, *God as Otherwise Than Being: Toward a Semantics of the Gift* (Evanston, IL: Northwestern University Press, 2002).

10. For me, the most creative loci of comparative philosophy are the Society for Asian and Comparative Philosophy, the Claremont Center for Process Studies, and The Institute of Philosophy at the Shanghai Academy of Social Sciences.

11. Peimin Ni, *On Confucius* (Belmont, CA: Wadsworth, 2001), p. 9.

12. Alfred North Whitehead, *Process and Reality* (New York: Free Press, 1969), p. 304.

13. Kofi Annon, untitled address at Seton Hall University's School of Diplomacy and International Relations, February 5, 2001. See www.un.org/Dialogue/pr/sgsm7705.htm

14. Tu Weiming, in Peimin Ni and Stephen Rowe, *Wandering: Brush and Pen in Philosophical Reflection* (Shanghai and Chicago: Dongfang and Art Media Resources, 2002), p. 3.

15. John Hick, *A Christian Theology of Religions* (Louisville: Westminster John Knox Press, 1995), p. 18.

16. Bellah, "Religious Evolution," p. 42.

17. Minnich, *Transforming Knowledge*, p. 30.

18. *Ibid.*, p. 184.

19. Elizabeth Johnson, *She Who Is: The Mystery of God in Feminist Theological Discourse* (New York: Crossroad, 1993), p. 9.

20. *Ibid.*, p. 6.

21. *Ibid.*, p. 30.

22. Irving Greenberg, "Covenantal Pluralism," in *Journal of Ecumenical Studies*, 34:3, Summer 1997, p. 435.

23. Gail Sheehy, *Passages: Predictable Crises of Adult Life* (New York: Dutton, 1974).

24. James W. Fowler, *Stages of Faith: The Psychology of Human Development and the Quest for Meaning* (San Francisco: Harper & Row).

25. *Ibid*, pp. 185–86.

26. *Ibid.*,, pp. 186–87.

27. Elizabeth Johnson, *She Who Is*, p. 226.

28. *Ibid.*, pp. 69, 68.

29. Tu Weiming, "Implications of the Rise of 'Confucian' East Asia," p. 202.

30. J. Ronald Engel, "The Earth Charter as a New Covenant for Democracy," p. 48.

31. Robert Jay Lifton, "Survivor as Creator," in *Living Beyond Crisis*, pp. 178–192.

32. See Nel Noddings, *Caring: A Feminine Approach to Ethics and Moral Education* (Berkeley: University of California Press, 1984). Note the similarity between a feminist care ethic and a relational liberal ethic. See my *Leaving and Returning*, on an ethic of faithfulness to the "creating form of association," pp. 103–104, 134, 148.

33. Engel, pp 48–49.

34. *Ibid.*, p. 44.

35. James, *A Pluralistic Universe*, p. 128.

36. Hershock, *Reinventing the Wheel*, p. 287.

37. Matthew 18:20.

38. Confucius, *Analects* 18.6, *The Analects of Confucius*, pp. 214–215.

39. On the American nihilism as it is reflected in philosophy, see Bruce Wilshire, *Fashionable Nihilism: A Critique of Analytical Philosophy* (Albany: SUNY Press, 2002), and John McCumber, *Time in the Ditch: American Philosophy in the McCarthy Era* (Evanston, IL: Northwestern University press, 2001).

40. Karl Jaspers, *Man in the Modern Age*, trans. Eden and Cedar Paul (Garden City, NY: Anchor Books, 1957), p. 26.

41. I have attempted to articulate "post-liberal liberalism" in previous work: for example, in *Rediscovering the West* (Albany, NY: SUNY Press, 1994), pp. 8-9, "Toward a Postliberal Liberalism: James Luther Adams and the Need for a Theory of Relational Meaning," in *American Journal of Philosophy and Theology*, vol. 17, no. 1, January 1996, pp. 51–70, and "Cultivating Mutual Growth: A Socratic Approach to the Post 9-11 World," in *Harvard Yenching Academic Series*, vol.. 3 (Beijing: SDX Press, 2003). The term is awkward, especially

when popular views associate liberalism with—and even often blame it for—everything problematic: from atomistic individualism on one side, to communism on the other. These views reflect the conundrum of Western politics and culture in our time, and the urgent need to envision a way of life that affirms individual and communal dimensions simultaneously. In my view, it is part of the tragedy (and irony) of the West that it overlooks the fact that this is precisely the genius of that relational ideal which is at the heart of liberalism. I use the term "Postliberal," and, more recently, "Relational Liberalism," then in a way that is analogous to "Third Epoch Confucianism" as it is represented in this essay, to indicate: (a) a tradition that has been rejected and in some ways lost or terminated, (b) one that later reappears as part of the "reappropriation" process I discuss in this essay, and (c) a particular tradition that is being revived *and shaped* through the ICDM.

42. See Whitehead, *Process and Reality.*

43. James, "The Will to Believe," in *The Writings of William James*, pp. 717–735.

44. Dewey, *A Common Faith* (New Haven: Yale University Press, 1934), p. 87.

45. Tu Weiming, "Toward the Possibility of a Global Community," in Lawrence Hamilton, ed., *Ethics, Religion and Biodiversity* (Cambridge: The White Horse Press, 1993), pp. 71–72.

Chapter Seven

What We Can Learn from/with China

THE MYSTERY OF CHINESE VITALITY

I have found among Chinese people, a certain vitality or zest, a willingness to be present in sincerity; maybe it comes down to confidence or optimism. Coming from America, the contrast is striking, especially in China's relative absence of cynicism and suspicion. There is also in China a generosity and a willingness to distinguish between the actions of governments and relationships between people. And there is a will to work, to engage with the world, and a sense of pride that is reflected in the saying that "to become Chinese is an accomplishment."

Perhaps these are the qualities of a society ascending. Perhaps they are expressive of China's experience with modernization, first with the long period of imperialist humiliation, then through the attempt to modernize in the wake of the May 4 (1919) Movement, followed by the crazed intensity of Mao's Cultural Revolution, and into the current phase of Deng Xiaoping's "socialist market economy." Maybe "Chineseness" has somehow endured all this, or perhaps Chinese society has been so scorched by the fire of modernization that now, like a forest which has been burned, the culture returns more strongly than before. Or perhaps there is something inherent in Chinese culture that allows it to withstand and adapt modernity to its own purposes.[1] Or maybe Chinese people are basking in a sense that history is finally shining on their side and that their time has come.

I don't know. The true nature of "the China model," the secret to China's amazing rise to power in the late 20th and early 21st centuries, remains elusive.

But let us not romanticize—or exoticize, or orientalize. My friends and colleagues often lament the tendency of Chinese people to become "money animals," and to convert wholesale to the life of consumerism. And they are often critical of the Party's efforts to counteract the impact of capitalism through reintroduction of Confucian values of "harmony" in education and popular media.

Again, I do not know. And neither do I know the degree to which the Third Epoch Confucians with whom I have been associated actually represent what is happening in/with China, or have significant influence on its direction. I do know, however, that this relatively small school of thought and partner in the vocation of reappropriation does reflect what I have discovered to be the best qualities of Chinese society. And I know as well that dialogue with them has been extremely rich and productive in terms of the efforts of many Western people to exercise the vocation of moving beyond the limitations of the modern through the reintroduction of traditional wisdom and awakening to those values of modernity we do not want to go "out with the bath" of postmodernist critique.

This response, I think, has been evident in the conversation of this book to this point, through a variety of references and comments. In this chapter we need to meet Third Epoch Confucianism (TEC) head on. So I will present a very brief synopsis of the Confucianism which is offered by this school of thought, followed by some reflections on its implications for the effort to reappropriate the democratic spirit in America.

CONFUCIAN VISION

From my American perspective, the Third Epoch reappropriation of Confucianism can be organized in three primary themes: the good society, cultivation of the person, and global/pluralistic humanity. I will speak briefly of each.

1. The Good Society

The Third Epoch reappropriation of Confucianism envisions a society of persons as centers of relationship, relationships that are intrinsically necessary to our humanity, and a society of harmony in which each accepts commitment to the common good as basic to identity. In addition, the ideal society is understood as a process of growth, in which both individuals and community come more and more to embody *ren*, the essential quality of human-heartedness, and *cheng,* that mode of being through which we are able to manifest both our own integrity and the deepest energy of the cosmos, or heaven *(tian)*. According to Tu Weiming, this process is supported by "The Confucian faith in the betterment of the human condition through self-effort, commitment to family as the basic unit of society and to family ethics as the foundation of social stability, trust in the intrinsic value of moral education, self-reliance, work, mutual aid, and a sense of organic unity with an ever-extending network of relationships."[2]

This vision of the good society is often articulated by Third Epoch Confucians in contrast with—and as alternative to—the dominant Western Enlightenment or liberal paradigm. Where the West envisions the rational, autonomous individual defined by their rights and interests, Confucianism envisions relational persons defined by duties. The two views are more deeply contrasted when they are seen as expressions of fundamentally different metaphysical views, or worldviews: the Chinese, in contrast to the Western, is "process oriented rather than substance oriented, immanent rather than transcendent, person-making rather than rule-following, and aesthetic rather than mediated through abstraction."[3] To unpack this statement a little: the classical Chinese worldview is oriented to ongoing developmental flow, rather than completed objects; alert to the ultimately creative energy in the immediacy of life, rather than that which is displaced and unchanging; concerned with cultivation rather than command, and guided by a vision of humanity and well-being rather than the attempt to make the actual correspond with an ideal which stands over against it through control.

Despite these fundamental differences, Confucianism is often presented as compatible with democracy, and in dialogue with historical periods or schools of thought in the West that are exceptions to the Western worldview described above. Henry Rosemont, for example, speaks of the compatibility between Confucianism and genuine democracy, as distinct from the more prevalent understanding of democracy as a procedural system that protects individuals so they may pursue personal preference. In a genuine democracy, "the desired would not be equated with the desirable, and democratic political participation—being a citizen—would involve engaging in collective dialogue about the appropriate means for achieving agreed-upon ends."[4] Tu, making the connection with an earlier period in Western history which was more supportive of genuine democracy, and more compatible with Confucian values as well, says that "the openness of the [Western] 18th century may provide a better guide for the dialogue of civilizations than the exclusivity of the 19th century and most of the 20th century."[5] Here he is referring to the earlier, Renaissance-based origin of modernity to which Toulmin refers also (see chapter 2).

Also despite radical differences between Confucianism reinvisioned and the dominant tradition in the West, it is important to notice that some Third Epoch Confucians articulate Confucianism by a very friendly comparison with two subtraditions within the West: pragmatism[6] and process philosophy.[7] The fact that pragmatism and process philosophy—plus the early Enlightenment values to which Tu and Toulmin refer—are themselves quite compatible suggests that there is perhaps a single subtradition in the

West that is different from the dominant worldview described above, [8] and at the same time similar in some basic respects to the subtradition of Confucian and Chinese culture that Third Epoch Confucians bring to availability. Tu indicates this deep compatibility in vision of the good society, even in relation to minimal or "liberal" conceptions of democracy: "Those who are attuned to the Confucian message inevitably discover that Confucian personality ideals (the authentic person, the worthy, or the sage) can be realized more fully in a liberal democratic society than in either a traditional imperial dictatorship or a modern authoritarian regime."[9] How much *more* compatibility could there be with the more fully democratic society that is envisioned by pragmatism, process philosophy, and the early Enlightenment?

2. Cultivation of the Person

Third Epoch Confucianism reminds us of what all of the historic traditions had known, and what is at the center of the great forgetting which gives rise to the modern moral disease: that the adult or fully formed human being requires cultivation, discipline, a process of transformation and culmination. It cannot happen by commandment alone. Tu Weiming and Ni Peimin emphasize reappropriation of *Xue*, a broad and wholistic sense of education aimed at cultivating the whole person—including not only the cognitive aspect, but emotional, ethical, and spiritual aspects as well.

In recent work, Ni Peimin has moved to the thesis that Confucianism has been misunderstood because it has been "philosophized," interpreted dimly through the assumptions of Western philosophy and culture, including that of intellectualism or the priority of theory over practice. Proper understanding of Confucianism, according to Ni, requires "the *gongfu* approach"—seeing Confucianism as a system of "how" rather than "what," as instruction about how to live and move toward full maturity. From this perspective, "treating [Confucianism] as a descriptive theory about what the world is, what a person is, and what our moral duties are would be a gross misreading."[10]

Ni goes on to say that the central practice or *gongfu* of Confucianism is *cheng,* usually translated as sincerity or integrity. This is the cardinal virtue not because it is morally correct in the sense of following a commandment or rule (though it is this also), but because it is the mode of being through which humans can gain access to the deeper energies of both themselves and the universe or heaven *(tian).*[11] This access makes it possible for humans to mature to the point of becoming co-creators, beings who are capable of participating directly in the ongoing formation of the world, in a partnership between heaven, earth, and the human. Another way to make this last point is to quote Confucius on how, at age seventy he was able to "give my heart-

and-mind free rein without overstepping the boundaries."[12] Confucius had become so thoroughly transformed that there was no longer any tension between what he desired and the mandate of heaven (*tian ming*).

For Confucianism "self" is essentially a "center of relationships" and "a dynamic process of spiritual development."[13] The *gongfu*, then, is fundamentally relational: human transformation occurs not through withdrawing into mystical detachment from the world, but right in the midst of everyday life. Living with sincerity (*cheng*) and practicing *shu* (taking the heart of another as analogous to one's own) *is* the root practice through which we can become *ren* persons, human hearted or fully human, fully sincere. Though this practice may sound mundane or merely "social" at first, it is actually founded on identification of a point of coincidence between the secular and the sacred.[14] And Tu Weiming points out that there certainly is a transcendent dimension to Confucianism. He says that "the transformative act of continuously excelling and surpassing one's experience . . . is predicated on a transcendent vision that ontologically we are infinitely better and therefore more worthy than we actually are." Hence *Shu* is motivated by the "transcending perspective" that humans are capable of forming "a trinity with Heaven and Earth."[15] It is through *cheng* and *shu* that connection with the deeper energy of reality is actualized, maintained, and expanded.

Confucianism is founded upon a fundamental vision of human cultivation and transformation in life generally, and also on a method that is both persuasive to the person and beneficial to society. It is centered, above all, on the irreducibly relational quality of human beings.

3. Global/Pluralistic Humanity

Tu Weiming, who has served on the Group of Eminent Persons for the United Nations Year of Dialogue Among Civilizations (2001), has advocated "the globalization of local knowledge."[16] This could be one of the key phrases of our era. What Tu means by it is that many life ways are universalizable, that universalizing or "globalizing" is inevitable, and that this does not necessarily entail the arrogance of thinking our way is the right way for all people. The problem in the past is that Westerner thinkers, backed up by military and economic power and an inordinate need to feel superior, imposed their local knowledge on the world. But now that which had been falsely universalized is seen in its local character, and discovered *not* to be superior to other forms of local knowledge. Tu accounts for much of the turmoil in the world today with this understanding: "In the global context, what some of the most brilliant minds in the modern West assumed to be self-evidently true has turned out to be parochial, a form of local knowledge that has, significantly, lost much of its local appeal."[17] The key awareness of the inevitability of globalizing and the dangers of universalizing opens the door for a new era and a new paradigm of dialogue: "we learn to become global citizens by working through rather than departing from our ethnicity, gender, language, land, age, and faith. Fruitful mutuality is built upon basic trust that commitment to the well-being of our roots need not be xenophobic or exclusive. Indeed, it is the global significance of local knowledge that compels us to be engaged in the dialogue of civilizations."[18]

Within this understanding of the context of reappropriation, Confucianism is presented as especially friendly to dialogue, in fact as dialogical in its nature. This goes back to its essential relationality, but is also grounded in its valuing of learning and continuing growth throughout life, not only in the cognitive dimension, but in ethics and character as well. It is only a small step from this deeply held cultural value of lifelong learning to "hav[ing] not only the willingness and courage to understand the 'radical otherness' rooted in different axial-age civilizations, but the wisdom to transform a teaching culture into a learning culture as a way to elevate our self-knowledge from local to global concerns."[19] This elevation is possible in Confucianism because just as the borders between self and family, family and community, and community and nation are permeable, so Confucian culture itself is comfortable moving into a world culture where others can be treated as family.

The key to the paradigm of dialogue, as envisioned by Confucianism, with its deep appreciation of plurality and diversity, is openness to the other in mutual commitment to growth and lifelong learning. Indeed, at one point Tu Weiming says that education should be the civil religion of society.[20]

CHINESE-AMERICAN DIALOGUE

Reappropriation and dialogue, as reciprocal and continuous, are hardly separable: they are two aspects of a single process, two aspects of relationship. For reappropriation without dialogue becomes assertion of superiority (or, sometimes in the post-traditional West, of that which is merely the opposite: assertion of guilt and inferiority, one form of which is refusal to go beyond postmodernist critique/reduction), while dialogue without reappropriation loses depth and substance, becomes mere inclusion, the sort of toleration that really does not care, the "whatever" relativism of modernized societies which degrades everyone.

Beyond the obvious values of the Neo-Confucian reappropriation for all people, I would like to reflect on a few of its implications for Americans in particular:

First, Third Epoch Confucianism can help us be aware of the significance of the task of reappropriation itself: as against the shallow and relativistic materialism of modern life, it is necessary to gain access to the wisdom and inspiration contained in tradition—while avoiding absolutistic assertions of "tradition" in fundamentalism. This, as we have seen, is a complex undertaking. Some might say that Third Epoch Confucianism looks more like understandings that are shared in the present by a certain kind of (post-modern) person and cultural-religious orientation that we find represented in all parts of the Earth—that it is closer to the hermeneutical awareness and positive prejudices of dialogue in the present I have described in other chapters than it is to historical Confucianism. From this perspective, the dialogical/hermeneutical awareness orientation, like the fundamentalist orientation, can be seen as a potential arising out of many or nearly all traditions. If this is so, we should be grateful for the strength and visibility of the Confucian reappropriation, both in itself and as a model of what we might find through engagement with other traditions. But at this point it is important to avoid being seduced by another kind of universalizing, this time the kind that celebrates the hermeneutical awareness without engagement in a particular tradition, thereby becoming a shallow and merely aesthetic universalism, one that is detached from the critical element of transformation/growth through continuous practice.[21]

In terms of America and the West, contact with Third Epoch Confucianism can remind us of the real meaning of democracy, and the distance between the genuinely democratic and the thin "liberal" or procedural political form that is prevalent today—one that is often considered to be synonymous with capitalism. In response, we might reexamine the early Greek and Native American origins of democracy, the possibilities of the early Enlightenment period to which Tu and Toulmin refer, the democratic communities of that time, the democracy of the American founders, and the vital democratic communities of our own time. The fact that we Westerners have so easily accepted this version of democracy and failed to be more diligent in reappropriating the many instances of genuine democracy in our history is testimony, I think, to the guilt and the self-destructive tendencies of Western culture at this time, as well as to the limitations of our cultural-philosophical language. Dialogue with Confucianism can help Westerners be more confident in affirming what is best in the modern western project, and to take seriously the worldwide vocation that Tu Weiming describes as "broadening and deepening" of the Enlightenment through dialogue with other cultures.

Returning to the observation about Western intellectualism, a bias that has caused Western interpreters (and those from other parts of the world who have been schooled in Western thought) to miss the subtle and utterly basic point of the priority of practice in Confucianism, I think Confucianism can help Westerners understand the limitations of the worldview we have inherited. It may be that the Confucian willingness to forego defensiveness and be forthright about its own inherited limitations and liabilities[22] makes it possible for Westerners to do the same. Perhaps we can understand in the dialogue with Confucians—beyond both defensive arrogance and pathetic guilt—the constraints on life that arise from our Western worldview, and value our own internal movements of critique and reform, such as pragmatism and process philosophy—and we should add feminist philosophy as well—which have come to be valued by Chinese philosophers also.[23] Confucianism can help us think beyond those qualities of Western thought that have constrained and constricted, that have worked against human maturity and democratic life.

We can be helped as well in the understanding that the issue of "worldview" is not simply a matter of substituting one theory for another, but rather includes attending to the place and function of theory or the cognitive dimension in relation to the living of a full and vibrant life. Here is where the Confucian emphasis on *gongfu* rather than correctness of doctrine can be extremely helpful. The critique of Western logocentrism is not only critique of limited and/or distorted metaphysical orientation, but of concern with "correctness" and compliance in the cognitive dimension to the detriment of the primary job to be done: the transformation of human beings from self-centered and isolated individuals to mature persons capable of both independence and intimacy, definiteness and openness, self-care and commitment. In relation to this primary task (again, *aufgabe)*, rightness of thought is somewhat relative, and it brings back the ancient Western concern with *phronesis,* the crucial kind of judgment that cannot occur through mere application of external rules, procedures, or pre-established formulas, but only through mature and enlightened awareness of what is right in particular situations.

In this regard, contact with Confucianism can help us revisit and reappropriate our magnificent tradition of liberal education, with its central concern for *trans*formation rather than mere *in*formation. We could start by re-encountering Socrates alongside Confucius, and come to a new appreciation as to how practice of "the examined life" brings us to "knowing nothing," and how this state *(aporia)* is the opening within the self through which a deeper energy and wisdom begin to flow—in the direction of a cultivated or transformed state very similar to that which Confucius points to when he speaks about being able to follow his heart's desire without transgressing the Way.

Also related to the priority of *gongfu,* Confucians can help us see more deeply into the richness of our own tradition, including one of the central and most complex statements on the Christian side of Western culture: "love thy neighbor as thyself." Perhaps this is not only a commandment, a rule to be followed, but also advice as to how we can find the real and reliable vitality in life—parallel to *shu*, and *cheng* as the way to care simultaneously for self and other.

In relation to the third point above regarding the Confucian vision of a pluralistic world, the contact with and the example of this vision could help Americans get past the great unsteadiness of the present which causes us to flip flop back and forth between arrogance and self-deprecation. The arrogance is quite evident in the world today, but I want to again suggest that its opposite is also a major factor in the ineffectiveness of America: guilt over having failed to live up to its extremely high ideals, guilt over association with the Western colonization, fear of any "globalization" or advocacy of American ideals in the world being just more false and hegemonic universalizing. In order to be effective and faithful world citizens, we need to grow beyond flip-flop. This is the issue Daniel Yankelovich addresses when he says "Doing dialogue takes special skills that most Americans do not yet possess."[24]

Returning to the question of Americans being able to overcome those modern values which are shallow and dangerous, and to the way in which dialogue presents the possibility of deliverance, Third Epoch Confucianism is a strong example of how reappropriation of tradition can provide depth and guidance for life in the present. It does this not through drawing back, but rather through moving in a shared life with people from other cultures who are radically other in cultural heritage, and yet similar in their wish for the flourishing of life on this planet. There is in this a double allegiance: both to a particular tradition, and at the same time to Earth as "common mother." This way of dialogue cannot be understood by those who have not experienced it because it involves paradox: it is through relationship with the other that I come into fullness of self. Here, again, is the crucial developmental point.

Another aspect of dialogue as it is manifest in Third Epoch Confucianism—and perhaps the most important aspect of all—is that it comes to be about something more than the retrieval and interpretation of *ideas*, more than simply an exchange of intellectual content. This, of course, is very difficult to discuss in the language of traditional academic work (hence the book project Ni and I undertook). It is a discussion that requires the admitting of the empirical to the territory of philosophical and religious inquiry. In this I stand with my American pragmatic mentor, William James when he said this movement is crucial to the future: "Let empiricism once become associated with religion, as hitherto, through some strange misunderstanding, it has been associated with irreligion, and I believe that a new era of religion as well as philosophy will be ready to begin."[25] Peimin Ni makes a closely related point when he tells his English language readers that "In Confucianism experience and practice are necessary for understanding."[26] Could it be that the new era which James foresees is precisely what we experience in the dialogue with Third Epoch Confucianism?

Beyond the realm of ideas, dialogue is more fundamentally about gaining access to an energy and a way of being present than to anything that can be objectified as a thought or a system of ideas. In moments of actual dialogue, and in the broader activity as it is continued in teaching and scholarship, an energy becomes available, or we find *ourselves* becoming available, present, and genuinely so (*cheng*). It is extremely important to describe in useful ways how this happens, how dialogue itself can becomes a *gongfu* and an awakening from the modern disease which is a sort of stupor, or what T. S. Eliot calls "whimpering." How *do* people wake up from that stupor to live with zest and vitality in the world of modern decadence and fragments of many traditions? What is it about dialogue that makes this possible? Here is the empirical agenda of philosophy and religion that William James thought so necessary to the revival of Western culture.[27]

In terms of the findings of this chapter, the center of the revitalization through dialogue that appears to be a magical waking up is the paradox we have already discussed. Let me state it in a different way here: that access to the energy of our being present on the Earth in our commonly shared humanity only becomes accessible as we both penetrate to the depth of our particular traditions and somehow step beyond them at the same time—into dialogue. Or, to say it the other way around, we are present in the mode of dialogue when we are able to both share the glory and confess the limitations of our particular traditions at the same time as we are able to truly listen to the other.[28] In this mode of relationship, the universal and the particular are no longer opposed, as they have been in so much of Western history, as they have been *forced* to be by the dominant forms of Western thought. Rather, we discover through the experience of genuine relationship with others in the world that the universal is only available in and through the depth of the particular, and the particular is only authentic and vitalizing when it is in dialogue with the other. Here, perhaps, is the essential wisdom of the post-traditional period. Here also is one way of seeing the significance of "the globalization of local knowledge," it's necessary and intimate connection with dialogue, and the sense in which it is a profound manifestation of our common humanity. Through the way of being which is both expressed and evoked by this phrase, we may be able to move beyond modern and postmodern limitations, into a future in which unity and diversity are no longer at war.

NOTES

1. Some have suggested that the cultural orientation which is implicit in postmodernity is radically antithetical to that of traditional Western culture, yet quite compatible with traditional Chinese culture. See, for a very clear and persuasive statement of this suggestion, David L. Hall, "Modern China and the Postmodern West," in Eliot Deutsch, ed., *Culture and Modernity: East-West Philosophic Perspectives* (Honolulu: University of Hawaii Press, 1991), pp. 50–70.

2. Tu, "Implications of the Rise of 'Confucian' East Asia," p. 211.

3. Peimin Ni, "Reading Zhongyong as a Gongfu Instruction: Comments on Focusing the Familiar, in *Dao:A Journal of Comparative Philosophy June 2004, vol. III, no. 2*, p. 189.

4. Henry Rosemont, Jr., A *Chinese Mirror: Moral Reflections on Political Economy and Society* (La Salle, IL: Open Court, 1991), p. 93.

5. Tu, "Implications," 198.

6. Sor-hoon Tan, *Confucian Democracy, and* David L. Hall and Roger T. Ames, *The Democracy of the Dead: Dewey, Confucius, and the Hope for Democracy in China* (Chicago: Open Court, 1999).

7. Roger Ames and David Hall, *Focusing the Familiar: A Translation and Philosophical Interpretation of the Zhongyong* (Honolulu: U. of Hawaii press, 2001).

8. See my *Leaving and Returning* for discussion of this subtradition, and its availability in America for a time in the sixties and early seventies.

9. Tu, "Implications," p. 212.

10. Peimin Ni, "Kung Fu for Philosophers," in "Opinionator" column of *New York Times,* Dec 8, 2010.

11. For crucial discussion of the "double role" of *cheng,* see Peimin Ni, "Reading *Zhongyong as a Gongfu Instruction*, pp. 196, 200. See also Yanming An, *The Idea of Cheng (Sincerity/Reality)*, (New York: Global Scholarly Publications, 2005).

12. Confucius, *Analects 2.4, in The Analects of Confucius*, p. 77.

13. Tu Weiming, *Confucian Thought: Selfhood as Creative Transformation* (Albany, NY: SUNY Press, 1985), p. 113.

14. Herbert Fingarette, *Confucius: The Secular as Sacred* (Long Grove, IL: Waveland Press, 1972).

15. *Ibid.,* pp. 136–137.

16. Tu, "Implications," pp. 209–210.

17. *Ibid.,* 198.

18. *Ibid.,* 209–210.

19. *Ibid.,* 209.

20. *Ibid.,* 206.

21. I have thought about this problematic aspect of universalism in *Living Philosophy.*

22. There are two limitations in particular that one hears quite often in the dialogue with TEC: that Confucianism lacks external standards for the evaluation of conduct and is hence vulnerable to distortion by those with power, and that it lacks social and political structures for democracy. Both are rooted in reliance on qualities of character—or heart—which can only be judged by those who are highly developed. It should be noted that this is the point where interpreters frequently see complementarily between East and West: the East has wisdom about cultivation of the fully human person, though it is lacking in external structures which would contain and cultivate full humanity, while the West has democratic structures of constitution and community life, though it is lacking in development of persons who are "in the maturity of their faculties" (J. S. Mill).

23. See Chenyang Li, ed., *The Sage and the Second Sex* (Chicago: Open Court, 2000), an anthology which brings dialogue between the various meanings of Confucianism and feminism into high relief.

24. Daniel Yankelovich, *The Magic of Dialogue: Transforming Conflict into Cooperation* (New York: Simon & Schuster, 1999), p. 17.

25. James, *A Pluralistic Universe*, p. 270.

26. Ni, *On Confucius*, p. 2.

27. For examples of what I mean by empirically oriented philosophy, see Philip Hallie, *Lest Innocent Blood Be Shed* (New York: Harper & Row, 1979) and Etty Hillesum, *An Interrupted Life: The Diaries of Etty Hillesum 1941–1043*. Trans. Arno Pomerans (New York: Washington Square Press, 1981).

28. Perhaps dialogue suggests a way in which *ti* and *yong,* key terms in the Chinese discourse of modernization, can be related. Perhaps *ti* (body, or sometimes tradition) corresponds to "local knowledge," while *yong* (function, or sometimes the modern) corresponds to "globalization." For complete discussion of these terms and their possible relations, see Tong Shijun, *The Dialectics of Modernization: Habermas and the Chinese Discourse of Modernization* (Sydney: Wild Peony, 2000).

Chapter Eight

Dialogue, Development, and Pluralism

Dialogue both requires and generates the kind of human development which is needed in order to move beyond the moral disease of the modern, and into a relational/democratic world. It could be helpful now to look deeper into the dynamics through which the capacity for dialogue becomes possible, into the opening of horizons, the discovery, and the learning by which people move beyond both the ideological/absolutistic and the nihilistic/relativistic stages of our era—into what it is that happens when the improbable bird of dialogue actually takes off and flies, into what we learn as we come to trust that bird and fly with it.

There is fairly broad acknowledgment of a developmental process which brings us to a level of maturity beyond what had been accepted as "adulthood" in the past. In terms of articulation of this process, we have substantial resources in the social sciences, some of which I have referred to previously.[1] It involves a process which can be spoken of in terms of developing the self-transcendence through which it becomes possible to acknowledge limitations of ego self, and to be open to growth and learning with others. In this chapter I would like to describe much the same process in the language of the humanities, as a cultural and political movement to dialogue and democratic pluralism.

THREE PLURALISMS

Dialogue is essentially *pluralistic,* which is to say that at its heart it values otherness. But "pluralism," like the key terms of any era, has many meanings, as well as what Whitehead calls some "disgusting alliances" as a result of people exploiting the term for purposes quite antithetical to it. In fact, we can see, both in American history and in current efforts to be inclusive and supportive of diversity, three distinct meanings of pluralism, each with differing degrees of intensity in its affirmation of otherness:

Toleration, Universality, and *Dialogue.* These meanings correspond with the developmental movement from the absolutistic/ideological, through the relativistic/nihilistic, and to the democratic/relational worldview.

The first is *Toleration:* Here affirmation of otherness and mutuality is weak, in an ethic of "live and let live." At the founding of the United States most churches reflected their European background by assuming establishment, that one of them would become the state church. When it became apparent that this would not happen, that no one church would prevail, "separation of church and state" became an agreeable option, since it meant—whatever else it might have meant—that no *other* church would prevail. Meanwhile, many of the founders, heavily influenced by French Deism and the spirit of what later became American Transcendentalism, took a more or less condescending view of the various (Judeo-Christian) religions and denominations, effectively saying that any of them could be good enough (i.e., that the Deist/Transcendentalist perspective is superior). Therefore "the great separation" and toleration. This attitude reveals that pluralism as toleration hides a sense of superiority in the dominant group, the superiority of which is presupposed as the basis on which the tolerating occurs. We see this today, for example, in the toleration of social science which often "appreciates diversity" while presupposing the correctness of its approach for all people and all social problems. In this view there is really no valuing of otherness or relationality beyond expediency. It remains covertly absolutistic.

A second meaning of pluralism is *Universality.* In this view it is assumed that, despite obvious differences on the surface, the various traditions share either a common origin or a common depth, and that pluralism must be grounded on a sameness of belief or metaphysical orientation. A most prominent example of the common origin approach is that which focuses on the Axial Age, which we have discussed before: the understanding that all of the great traditions arose out of the same historical period in response to a fundamental shift in human consciousness, a shift from animism and polytheism to a unitary and dualistic sense of reality. Examples of the common depth approach are William James's metaphors of apparently separate trees on a field commingling in their roots, or seemingly isolated islands being held together by the ocean bottom, Aldous Huxley's "perennial philosophy," Huston Smith's "forgotten truth," and Joseph Campbell's "power of myth."[2] Here the thesis is that at the depth of the great traditions, beneath differences on the surface, is amazing similarity in visions of the cosmos and the commonly shared experience of mystical realization.

The universalist approach has been extremely effective in bringing people out of the colonial era in which Westerners assumed the superiority of their culture and religion, and into recognition and appreciation of other cultures. It has also been inspiring, a profoundly significant wake up call for modern people to broader horizons of possibility, an aid in awakening from the slumber of modern materialism, consumption, and competition. However, the universalist orientation also contains a limitation which can be hard to see until the initial inspiration begins to wear off. Its mutuality of sameness causes universalism to slip away from engagement—both with others, and with the particularities of practice within any one tradition, into abstracted appreciation, away from the religious into the aesthetic, away from the hard work of transformation—a commonality shared by the traditions which runs deeper than any metaphysical agreements they might share. It becomes admiration without engagement, and hence a species of consumption. While it does represent critical perspective on the limitations of the modern, and some movement beyond it in terms of awareness that an alternative might exist, it remains relativistic.

CONVERSATIONAL ASIDE

It is important to emphasize the developmental realization—which marks the limit of the universalist stage—as to the necessity of practice, of the fact that the great traditions, whatever else they have in common, are essentially oriented to transformation, and that modes of practice are at their centers.

Once, with a group of students, we underscored the significance of this realization with a joke: it is as though it is discovered in the universalist stage that there are many ways to get to Pittsburg—from LA or Paris; you can even get there from Grand Rapids or Singapore! The problem is that, in the thrall of this discovery and admiration of its possibilities, no one is actually going to Pittsburg. All actual travel ceases in the midst of excitement about the possibilities.

A third meaning of pluralism and developmental stage is *dialogue,* or what is sometimes called "deep pluralism."[3] Only here is mutuality essential, rather than a derivative or instrumental value; only here do we find fully positive response to the imperative of otherness and difference. We have discussed at length the dynamics of this mutuality and the paradox at the center of true dialogue: that openness only occurs when it is co-present with definiteness. Likewise, movement into the dialogue stage entails discovery of the necessity of particularity to transformative practice, to the actual growth, and development we need. However, the way of particularity which is necessary to dialogue is not one which is outside or apart from universalism (as it is with fundamentalism), but simultaneous with it. In order to understand this crucial and challenging point effectively, we need to be clear about reappropriation, particularity, and practice.

Living pluralism at the level of intensity consistent with the maturity which is capable of dialogue requires that we survive and learn the lessons of loss we have discussed earlier in relation to the thesis which is shared by Hannah Arendt, Martin Luther King, Huston Smith, and others: that the unity of humankind at present is primarily negative, and that a significant dimension of the way beyond the modern condition consists in (going all the way back to Arendt's statement in the Introduction to our conversation) "renunciation not of one's own tradition and national past, but of the binding authority and universal validity which tradition and past have always claimed." We must survive the experience of loss and negativity, and learn the lesson of Nothingness and the affirmation that follows, the "positing of life." For we have become aware in the 20th Century, through both individualism/secularism and collectivist/fundamentalist reaction, that humans need something more and quite different from material gratification and emotional stimulation. We need *spirit,* and the adventure of our transformation together on/with this planet. We find this in tradition, along with grounding, rootedness, a crucial sense of orientation in the cosmos, as well as specific directives as to practice. We need the definiteness and discipline of "tradition" as the home of human beings, and as shelter from antinomy and crazy-making contradiction (we need it, at the very least, as something definite against which to disagree and push off). We need "religion" as *re-legiare,* that which ties or binds back to what is ultimately important in life. The problem in post-traditional times is that tradition ceases to function as it did before, once we have stood outside of it and discovered that "our" tradition is one among many such containers of human life, and that any particular tradition is flawed and tainted with problematic values and actions. We must confess the contingency of our tradition, and at the same time acknowledge the integrity of other traditions. Challenging as it is to maintain connection with tradition under these circumstances, and tempting as it may be to give up on the possibility and value of this connection altogether, we still need the definiteness of tradition, in much the same way that muscle in the body needs tendon to connect it with bone—and make it possible for any coordinated effort to occur, anything beyond muscle flapping absurdly, disconnectedly, dangerously clashing—like a fish with teeth on the deck of a boat. But reappropriation of tradition as a matter of conscious choice (and responsibility) is very new to the human race. The enormity of this is accentuated when we realize that fundamentalism is not authentic reappropriation, and that authentic reappropriation *includes* the universalist stage out of which it arises.

DIALOGUE AND/AS PRACTICE

The key to it is that in order for pluralism to be genuine, it requires reappropriation of particularity to the level of *practice*. Going back to the great realization of the universalist stage of pluralism, we discover wisdom at the core of each of the great traditions, and that all of humankind has access to an incredible resource and possibility for moving beyond the spiritual emptiness and clashing of our period. And it must be said again, especially among Western people, that this possibility is not limited to the intellectual dimension, not only a matter of better or different ideas. To say "wisdom" is indeed to indicate some ideational content, or some content that can be partially communicated in the form of ideas. But that alone is a superficial understanding of wisdom, as well as one that can easily lead to the idolatry of the intellect which is typical of the West. More basically, in our time we have rediscovered that wisdom is more profoundly about effective cultivation, and hence about the transmission or communication of an *energy*; wisdom is a matter of spirit and the whole person, only one component of which is mind. The distinctive mark of effective practice and the energy which flows through it is that it causes both persons and communities to become radiant with genuineness or presence, and that this essential quality is expressed as compassion, appreciation, freedom, and self-transcendence. Wisdom is not about metaphysics, but about that unnamable energy or presence which makes transformation—and, as Socrates says, "every other blessing"[4] — possible.

Awareness of the significance of practice and transformation through the reappropriation of traditional resources brings us to the paradox that marks the distinction between the universalist and dialogue stages: that the preciousness of wisdom which we speak about in universalist terms only becomes available as something more than ideas, images, and emotions through engagement with the depth of a particular tradition. Wisdom as wisdom is not accessible through the universalist consciousness alone (though it is *vivid* here in a *certain*, limited sense—as, for example, in some movies of our era), but only through movement beyond that consciousness and into a new and humble immersion in particularity (again, one which is quite distinct from fundamentalism).

Here is the developmental challenge of our second axial transition, and the challenge of the reappropriation of tradition. Let me state the paradox as directly as I can: the irreducible particularity of transformative practice is the commonality upon which a trustworthy future can be built.

The possibility of tradition as resource in the present, then, requires going past the dilemma quality of our post-traditional and post-modern time, one that is inscribed as the antinomy between abstracted universality and incommensurable particularity. And this requires journey through the phase of the universalist consciousness, a phase that is necessary in order to get to reappropriation and the renewed particularity of the dialogue stage, and hence to full pluralism. This entails awareness of the dangers implicit in universalism, especially in its tendency to reduce all cultural and religious dynamics to those of aesthetics, and, more specifically, to beauty as mere intensity. Moving beyond antinomy, then—and beyond the clash between individualist/relativist and collectivist/absolutist positions as well—requires both reverence for universality and the discipline of particularity. "Dialogue" indicates that mode of relationship in which this is possible, a mode which is constituted by encounter with the other who shares awareness of the limitations of the modern condition and the will to live beyond it in a shared world, the other who adopts the relationship of dialogue as a commonly shared element of practice. This element of dialogue (corresponding to the universal dimension) is discovered to be essential to further growth and deep engagement within one's own tradition, as well as to peaceful and fruitful living with the unavoidable other who is now transformed from enemy to companion, maybe even friend.

Certainly there is a wide range of ways in which people achieve this level of particularity, including some which involve individuals or groups drawing on elements of several traditions. So by "reappropriation of particularity" we cannot mean this in a narrow or exclusive way, or in a way which is pure of syncretism; we cannot speak against choosing among elements of several traditions, or even construction of "new" traditions.

To be as specific as possible about the significance of connecting with "tradition," reappropriation entails three components: a vision of the deep dimensions of human experience, an understanding of the problem or challenge of human life and its remedy, and a corresponding transformative discipline as a live alternative to the limitations of the modern worldview.

But let us not fall away from the fully paradoxical nature of dialogue by now overemphasizing particularity, or minimize the danger of disappearing into the isolation of "incommensurability," one form of which is fundamentalism. For the mature phase of pluralism, dialogue is necessary as an essential co-practice, parallel and in a creative tension with a reappropriated traditional practice. The appeal to dialogue as a commonly shared practice is no different from the claim that we share a common problem in the limitations of the modern, as well as the need of transformation—or at least cultivation beyond what is given by nature and whatever training we receive.

Ultimately the necessity and the persuasiveness of dialogue to the maturity which the future requires is rooted not only in negativity, crisis, and loss—as Arendt, Smith, and others say, in their recognition of true radical insufficiency of the modern. It is also rooted, beyond the experience of

Nothingness, in the gift quality of life and the imperative of otherness which is especially distinctive of our time. Hannah Arendt, again, is helpful on this point: two of the most general conditions within which the gift of life is given to humans are plurality and natality. The first, she articulates as "the paradoxical plurality of beings who are the same in that we are different," and it requires that we honor difference insofar as we honor life itself, to see it and live it as locus of our thriving. The second is natality, the capacity of all humans to give birth to what which is new. Natality indicates what is so compelling about difference and the fully dialogical relationship, as source of novelty, adventure, learning, disclosure, and ongoing growth. It is the space in which I am able to appear in my own uniqueness and integrity. Certainly not all instances of dialogue or forms of pluralism are grounded in the purity of gift and the conditions through which it is given, but awareness of that root provides us with a guiding aspiration and a case to be made to those who are hesitant about entering the potentially threatening encounter with those who are different, as well as a criterion by which to evaluate our lives and communities.

HUSTON SMITH AS EXAMPLE

It might be helpful to conclude this chapter with an example of what these dynamics can mean in lived life. Fortunately, we have one in Huston Smith, the great comparative religionist of the 20th century. He is, of course, is one of the towering figures of what I have called the universalist phase of movement through post-traditional confusion. He discovered and articulated the deep similarities in metaphysical perspective among the great traditions, and made the singularity of "the traditional worldview" or "forgotten truth" available to post-traditional people through especially clear and accessible contrast between the traditional and the modern scientist worldview which "we have unwittingly slipped into."[5] This contrast, along with his distinctions between Traditional, Modern, and Post-Modern worldviews, have been extremely helpful to many people,[6] and there is no doubt that Smith's *The Religions of Man* (1958)[7] will remain as one of the classics of our time, on the order of William James's *The Varieties of Religious Experience* (1904).

What is less well known about Smith and his work is his engagement with practice and reappropriation of traditional resources within what I have identified as the developmental stage which opens up after universalism, the stage of new particularity and dialogue. He may be even more appropriately the hero of this stage than he is of the one that preceded it. It is significant that Smith's work, which led to the groundbreaking *The Religions of Man* arose from travel and actual practice within the various traditions, and speaking from that experience of practice rather than from an abstracted, purely universalist perch; much of the power and integrity of his writing arises from this quality of his being grounded in practice. Smith's engagement of practice, however, is in a distinctly post-traditional context, which is to say an engagement which is able to go beyond the universalist orientation without losing universality, and able to reappropriate particularity without becoming a fundamentalist. Smith is most distinguished in his capacity to navigate the paradox of particularity and universality.[8]

Speaking about how reappropriation is possible within the dialogical relationship,[9] Smith tells of being "strongly attracted to Hinduism because of it doctrine of universal salvation."[10] In this association, he identifies with the *jnana yoga* tradition of knowledge as one of the four paths to God, and speaks about how his inherited Greek philosophy is transformed through the dialogue with Hinduism[11]—to the point where he is quite comfortable referring to his vocation as that of a *"jnana* yogin philosopher," and saying that "the project [of seeing Western philosophy as a great world religion] would never have occurred to me had I not encountered India; it is from her that my controlling paradigm is lifted."[12] Clearly it is through this encounter that Smith was able to reappropriate and revitalize his tradition and practice of Western philosophy.

But he is not an apologist for either Hinduism or Western philosophy. Throughout his work he goes beyond both aesthetic universalism and fundamentalist particularism to encourage connection with one (or more) of the great traditions in its particularity within the frame of practice. Here he exhibits a remarkable faith in human commonality, including faith that particularity will not come to be expressed as fundamentalism or jihad. How? I think the spirit and the implication of Smith's recommendations—the genius of them—are summed up in the section which was added to one of the later editions of *The World's Religions.* He says that "If one of the wisdom traditions claims us, we begin by listening to it," and goes on to speak of the importance of listening not only to our own traditions but also to the faith of others, saying that "understanding is the only place where peace can find a home. . . . For understanding brings respect, and respect prepares the way for a higher capacity which is love."[13]

Here Smith points to that higher capacity we so urgently need by way of human development. It is virtually the same as mystical knowing which is "a fourth kind of knowing that rises above sensations, images, and concepts, all three."[14] This is that active wisdom which is at the center of the great traditions, and only accessible through the particularity of practice. Here is the sense in which reappropriation is most compelling, and the paradox of universality and particularity most vivid.

CONVERSATIONAL ASIDE

There are two crucial topics which keep coming up, and about which I must say a bit more: paradox in general, and the paradox of relationality (and self) in particular:

    About Paradox:

    Paradox is gateway to that which is vital in life. This is very old news from the perspective of the great traditions. But it was lost in the West as the hubris of reason and intellectualism set in. By intellectualism I mean that orientation in which intellectual resolution is assumed to be the necessary prerequisite to acting—and living.[15] *Some think this alienation from paradox, and along with it alienation from the capacity to tolerate and appreciate and be effective within the complex textures of lived life, set in very early in the West, with preference for Aristotle's* Metaphysics, *with its identification of first principles and thereafter proceeding by deduction, as over against the embodied life of his* Ethics *and* Politics *which require judgment in the particulars* (phronesis). *The essential point is that learning to honor and move within paradox has become a major developmental challenge for most Western people. It requires going beyond the antinomies around which most of Western culture has come to turn: between rationalism and empiricism, classicism and romanticism, individual and community, scientism and irrationalism, and now universalism and particularism—and the accompanying requirement, under the assumption that correctness requires intellectual resolution and must lie on one side or the other, that we take up a position of rigid defense. The problem with this orientation, as we see so clearly today, is that it leads to ideological standoff, political "gridlock," and dangerous alienation from what is actually happening in real life. As William James reminds us, "the return to life" is not, first of all, an intellectual resolution, but an act:*

> *The return to life can't come about by talking. It is an* act; *to make you return to life, I must set an example for your imitation, I must deafen you to talk, or to the importance of talk, by showing you, as Bergson does, that the concepts we talk with are made for purposes of* practice *and not for purposes of insight. Or I must* point, *point to the mere* that *of life, and you by inner sympathy must fill out the* what *for yourselves. . . . [A]n* intellectual *answer to the intellectualist's difficulties will never come.*[16]

Our healthy and vital relationships teach us to honor paradox and go beyond antinomy most effectively. More than any school, these relationships teach us to be at home on a landscape which includes complexity, uncertainty, and ambiguity, a richer world in which we can be comfortable moving in shades of meaning and nuance, capable of far greater responsiveness and appreciation than if we define ourselves as ideologues (almost robots) in service of that which the intellect must first certify as absolutely true. Ruth Nanda Anshen, one of the great articulators of the relational worldview, and editor of several anthologies in which voices of this subtradition are brought together, speaks of our needing to live "beyond the logic of dichotomy":

> Our Judeo-Christian and Greco-Roman heritage, our Hellenistic tradition, has compelled us to think in exclusive categories. But our experience challenges us to recognize a totality much richer and far more complex than the average observer could have suspected—a totality which compels him [sic] to think in ways which the logic of dichotomy denies. We are summoned to revise fundamentally our ordinary ways of conceiving experience, and thus, by expanding our vision and by accepting those forms of thought which also include non-exclusive categories, the mind is then able to grasp what it was incapable of grasping or accepting before. [17]

Beyond the logic of dichotomy lies the complex territory of actual relationships, each with their own ambiguity and possibility. We need to learn to be alert in the midst of their ambiguities, faithful to their possibilities, and attuned to the availability of the open space out of which genuineness and inspiration occur. We need an ethic of faithfulness to those times and spaces and practices through which mutuality and genuine presence occur.

About Paradox, Selfhood, and Relationality:

The Bible—and other world scripture—encourage us to become like children, and like lilies and ravens and other forms of life which "neither toil nor reap." They are fully present in pre-reflective consciousness, fully definite. And somehow the one who can be this way in adult life without sacrificing responsibility becomes an open channel through which the deepest wellspring of life becomes manifest directly.

What, then, is the most effective way of conceiving of "self" and developing toward this enlarged sense of adulthood? The dominant Western conception of substantial self, of self as object or bundle of rights and interests, is problematic because it defines self out of the vital paradox of encounter or relationality in which Genuine Self or self as subject appears. Frustrated with this "liberal" or Natural Rights conception, some turn to Buddhist non-self, emphasizing the completely illusory and transient nature of "self." But this can be a problematic conception as well, for the same reason from the opposite extreme; once again, the self is located outside of mutuality. Therefore some move on to the Confucian relational self. But this as well can mislead, if it is taken as dissolution of self into world, into self as constituted entirely of roles and rites, the multitude of personas and functions through which each of us appear. Each of these conceptions can miss the appearance of Genuine Self in a certain kind of relationship which is paradoxical in its essence.

Yet by the same token, each of these basic conceptions of self can be highly effective as correctives, as particular ways of pointing particular people in the direction of genuineness and the locus of human presence.[18] *For example, Peter Hershock, speaking to Western people from the Ch'an Buddhist tradition recommends that we cultivate a "truly liberating intimacy:" "... a new kind of intimacy. Pursued in the spirit of expressing a truly liberating character—a character constituted not by the drawing of clear and controlled boundaries, but by their erasure."*[19] *Experience of interdependence and Buddhist at-oneness could be the corrective Western and American people need—enabling us to move beyond seeing both self and other as isolated object, and relationship as mere exchange. On the other hand, perhaps the (pre-natural rights) Western vision of the dignity and irreducibility of each person could be helpful to Asian societies struggling with human rights.*

Seen this way, each of these correctives aims at enabling the person to abide in Nothingness, which is to appreciate and thrive within paradox, exercising practical wisdom or appropriateness on one side or the other as is called for by the situation and the moment. But, again, this developmentally most ambitious capacity does not just happen, or happen through our wishing it could happen, but only out of sustained and conscious practice, out of cultivation of capacities which may be innate as possibility within all humans, but capacities which only become actual in that second act of creation through which humans become creators.

NOTES

1. Especially Habermas and his interpretation/appropriation of Kohlberg and the tradition of linking moral development to cognitive development. See Robert Apatow, *The Spiritual Art of Dialogue* (Rochester, VT: Inner Traditions, 1998), on how dialogue exercises and develops the highest mental functions.

2. Aldous Huxley; *The Perennial Philosophy* (New York: Harper Colophon 1944), Smith, *Forgotten Truth,* Joseph Campbell, *The Power of Myth* (New York: Bantam, 1972).

3. David Ray Griffin, ed., *Deep Religious Pluralism* (Louisville, KY: John Knox Press, 2005).

4. Socrates, *Apology,* 30b, in *The Collected Dialogues of Plato,* p. 16.

5. Smith, *Why Religion Matters,* 24.

6. *Ibid.* Also see Huston Smith, *Beyond the Post-Modern Mind* (New York: Crossroad, 1982).

7. This is the original title of the book published in 1958 by the New American Library (New York: Mentor Books) which, after many subsequent editions, is now published under the title of *The World's Religions: Our Great Wisdom Traditions* by HarperSanFrancisco.

8. In terms of Smith's crossing the threshold between what I am calling the universalist and dialogue stages, and for evidence that he himself saw this as a crucial moment in his own development, see Henry Rosemont and Huston Smith, *Is There a Universal Grammar of Religion?* (Chicago: Open Court, 2008), pp. 65–66, where he speaks of Islam having "the greatest impact on me next to Christianity" in that it enabled him to "solve a paradox that I had been unable to solve myself, namely believing in the parity of the eight traditions on the one hand, and believing in unity on the other." Is this not precisely the paradox of particularity and universality?

9. Smith has said he is "not much interested" in "dialogue." See Rosemont and Smith, *Is There a Universal Grammar of Religion?*, pp. 50, 67–69. It seems clear, though, that Smith and I attribute different meanings to that crucial word. Perhaps a better word here, in terms of Smith's perspective, would be "reappropriation." It is significant that in *Universal Grammar* Rosemont, Smith's partner in the dialogue of that book, does advocate "dialogue," and specifies that it is most fruitfully focused not on metaphysics and theologies, but on *practice*— in ways which are remarkably consistent with my own approach.

10. Smith, *Why Religion Matters*, p. 269.

11. See especially Huston Smith, "Western Philosophy as a Great Religion," in *Huston Smith: Essays on World Religion*. ed. M. Darrol Bryant (New York: paragon House, 1992).

12. *Ibid.,* p. 210. I see no contradiction between this statement and what he said about Islam having "the greatest impact on me next to Christianity," but rather testimony to his own development in ways which are consistent with the movement described in the previous chapter,

13. Huston Smith, *The Illustrated World's Religions* (San Francisco: HarperSanFrancisco, 1991), p. 249.

14. "Is There a Perennial Philosophy?," p. 556.

15. James goes so far as to warn against what he calls "vicious intellectualism." See *A Pluralistic Universe, 224-226*. On the problem of assuming the priority of epistemology in philosophy, see also Sissela Bok, *Lying: Moral Choice in Public and Private Life* (New York: Vintage, 1978).

16. James, *A Pluralistic Universe*, p. 260.

17. Ruth Nanda Anshen, "World Perspectives: What This Series Means," in Werner Heisenberg, *Physics and Beyond: Encounters and Conversations* (New York: Harper & Row, 1971), p. xvi.

18. Perhaps something analogous can be said of metaphysical claims: that each claim can be seen as responsive to and even corrective of the superstitions or idolatries of a particular time and place.

19. Hershock, *Reinventing the Wheel*, p. 287.

Part III

Reviving Civic Virtue

Chapter Nine

A Liberal Confession

CONVERSATIONAL ASIDE

Stepping back from the now completed Part II, I see that in the broadest sense it is a dialogue between tradition and modernity. Both are problematic—not only the modern. And both contain positive elements which, when they meet in the vitality of the present, can be conducive to thriving. Perhaps especially as a Westerner, I am shy to celebrate what is positive about the modern, to step out of the cocoon of postmodernist critique. But I am persuaded to do so—more by Tu Weiming, Sor-hoon Tan, and Amartya Sen and other non-Western voices than by colleagues in the West; more by direct experience than by theory or academic convention.

We return, then, to America, after intercultural dialogue, China, and thinking about worldview, reappropriation of tradition, and human development in the post-traditional era. How can we cure American moral disease, and turn away from impending death?—as T.S. Eliot said, either with a bang or a whimper. I think our best possibility is to follow the thread of development which has been experienced and revealed through dialogue: from moral disease, nihilism, and fundamentalism to encounter with Nothingness, universalism, and reappropriation of transformative practice. And, having discovered this movement in the broader world context, we can see it at work in America as well, as a way of reviving civic virtue and growing into the democratic promise.

In this chapter, I tell the story of return as it has occurred close to my own immediate experience, through a half century of pursuing the possibility that the world can teach us much more than competitiveness and the kind of self-esteem which requires isolation and superficial self-understanding. It is a story of pursuing the possibility that practice of civic virtue brings us to our genuine selfhood at the same time it creates a world in which others are able to do the same.

In chapter 10, "American Clash and Revival," we return to America to consider the fibers out of which "the American experiment" has been woven and their current state of array, including the dynamics of individualism, collectivism, and the paradox upon which America has rested from the beginning, the paradox of E Pluribus Unum, *the many and the one, diversity and unity, particularity and universality. Here I want to pursue the thesis that through the intercultural dialogue of our era—and, in America, concerns with diversity and second generation rights—we discover that a new or revived universalism is available, though only genuinely so when we reconnect with and reappropriate the particularity of a specific historical tradition. Further, reappropriating the meaning of America in this context, I want to suggest that the paradox of universality and particularity has been the genius of American history and culture, and America's gift to the world in the post-traditional period—as well as the way out of the post-modernist morass. This paradox is a way to understand and reappropriate that which has been and could still be great about America. It is centered on relationality or mutuality, on America's manifestation of the democratic spirit.*

Next (in chapter 11) it will be important to revisit pragmatism in light of reappropriation, pragmatism as it is taken to be America's most distinctive cultural and philosophical orientation, and the root of America's contribution to the array of the world's traditions.

The following chapter (12) is "Democratic Life, American Hope: A Meditation on the Practical Turn." Here I want to look more closely at the dynamics of healthy practice in more personal terms. For, again, the essential paradox just mentioned remains a frustration and a series of vexing antinomies—variations on abstracted (though often beautiful) universality versus incommensurable particularities—until we finally take the action of engaging a particular practice. Reappropriation must reach this level. The key to living paradox as doorway to vitality (as distinct from what it does to us when it is held in mind alone), the solution to the riddle it presents, is practice. *Here, I think, is the complete and authentic meaning of James's claim that "the return to life is an* act."

By "practice" in contemporary, post-traditional times I mean the consciously chosen discipline of transformation through which we are able to mature into the fully adult human life form, and thereby move beyond the moral disease of modern life. I am suggesting, from the perspective of the dangerous insufficiency of modern life and the imperative of growth which it contains, that we can see a common ground among the world's great traditions, the center of the wisdom which they share: the fact that mature or full humanity does not simply unfold out of the natural process the way it appears to do with other life forms, but rather requires an intervention, the cultivation of a "second nature" which is the job of culture in its highest function. So I discuss the dynamics of practice and of our choosing one which is sufficient to our thriving, developing into the state of well-being or maturity. In broad cultural terms, I am suggesting that we need a praxiological *revolution in the 21st century to follow the hermeneutical revolution of the 20th. And, again, this engagement with the discipline of a particular tradition is that which makes it possible to participate in and benefit from the universal or global tradition which becomes available in our time—the world culture which Hannah Arendt and others have been pointing to throughout the conversation of this book.*

Finally, in the concluding chapter (13), I want to share reappropriation of my own particular tradition, that of liberal education, as a specifically Western and distinctively American discipline of transformation. Here I especially want to encourage my fellow Americans to see liberal education as transformative practice, as democratic practice, and to appreciate its actual and potential function in democratic life, its variety, value, and availability as a resource for almost all Americans.

My most basic point is that America is still in a position to provide a model, to lead in the exercise of civic virtue as energizing of both person and society. There are, as most of us know, so many aspects to this vocation that it is overwhelming—most obvious of which is addressing global warming and the other issues of global interdependence, along with the profound changes in value and allocation this necessarily entails. If, however, necessary changes are made in the context of developmental movement through and beyond the limitations of the modern, and in relation to the emergence of a global ethic which is relational and democratic, then the changes which are required could take on a decidedly different face. The face of the future could be one of partnership rather than terror, cooperation rather than loss, adventure rather than collapse.

Which face prevails as the face of the future depends very largely on what Americans do now, more than most Americans realize. If Americans choose to draw back from the world in defensive protectionism, and relate in exceptionalism and aggressive assertion of privilege, America will soon be lost—an enormous loss to the whole world. It will become increasingly vulnerable to the attacks not only of bombs and other terrorist acts, but perhaps even more vulnerable to the resentment and distain of the rest of the world—and fearful reactions from within which bring on the very thing which is feared. For "America" is not now and never has been a small proposition. It will either succeed greatly or fail dramatically. Everything about America—its founding, its history and ideals, its relationships with the rest of the world—all these point to this either—or dilemma in the present global era. Each of us, within our own life-situation and unique circumstance, must decide for life out of our own consciousness, and without guarantee that others will do the same or that our choosing will make any difference, must define our part and take action.

This may be the greatest challenge that has ever faced human consciousness on this planet, and it is not at all clear that we are up to it. It is clear, though, and more so every day, that this moment of challenge and choice will very soon pass away—into either Yes, or No.

A NEARLY FORGOTTEN SUBTRADITION

It is necessary to give some more full statement of my own location, of the particularity and local circumstance from which I speak. I want to do this in the form of a confession—largely of failure, but also of an enduring hope.

And I want to be clear right at the beginning that I am and have been a liberal. *However,* I have not understood this to be the same as the Western Natural Rights Liberalism of Hobbes and Locke—the competitive and isolated individualism with which the word "liberalism" is so often identified today. Rather, I have spoken and acted from a Western subtradition that is variously referred to as Socratic, civic republicanism, renaissance humanism, the early modern democratic thought arising from the left wing of the Protestant Reformation, the Jeffersonian experience of self-governing communities, American pragmatism, relational feminism and the tradition of progressive education.

The subtradition I represent has mostly been lost in the rush of modernization, including the "realism" of democratic theorists. It, above all, is centered on a certain *experience*: the experience of bringing our views on whatever problem/issue is at hand into deliberation with the views of others, and discovering that this kind of relationship between differing persons and views can yield insight and wisdom beyond what any of us can gather in isolation. Further, the crucial experience is one of our being able, in deliberative relationship, not only to find solutions to problems/issues, but also to be/become more fully who we are—more sincere and more authentic, more fully present in our genuineness—than is possible in private. In this tradition, the public or the open space of our encounter is understood to be religiously significant, as the locus of integrity, discovery, and possibility (and more, according to some religions). Here the common good is experienced as greater and different than the sum of our private goods. Thus "civic virtue" (in a public of any size—possibly even with myself, and certainly between two or more) is among the highest virtues—with truthfulness, commitment, and service among the essential subsidiary virtues. And in terms of worldview, this subtradition entails an understanding that there are non-relative values such as Justice and Truth, that each of us is limited in our perception of them, and that they are revealed on an ongoing basis in the process of our struggling together to create a better world.

Clarity about this subtradition will, of course, take some explaining. But perhaps this thumbnail sketch is sufficient by way of introduction to the story of what I have lived through in the past four decades or so, to my confession; and hopefully sufficient also by way of disclaimer about what I mean and don't mean by "liberalism." Maybe the best term for the subtradition I represent would be "relational liberalism."

In terms of confession, Reinhold Niebuhr, one of the great figures in American relational liberalism, well describes the limitations of liberals as foolish and sentimental "children of light":

> The children of darkness are evil because they know no law beyond the self. They are wise, though evil, because they understand the power of self-interest. The children of light are virtuous because they have some conception of a higher law than their own will. They are usually foolish because they do not know the power of self-will. They underestimate the peril of anarchy in both the national and the international community. Modern democratic civilization is, in short, sentimental rather than cynical. [1]

Perhaps this is confession enough. But no. There are important details in the grey zone between light and darkness, and since the time of Niebuhr's writing in 1945 there has been significant movement beyond the postmodern dilemma of either sentimentality or cynicism.

FROM SIXTIES ACTIVISM TO LIBERAL EDUCATION

American activism in the 1960s began with great liberal optimism and ambition. Out of the aridness and paranoia of the 1950s, something quite improbable happened: a democratic fever spread across the land. Martin Luther King, Jr. proclaimed "Now is the time to make real the promise of democracy," John F. Kennedy said "Now the trumpet [of democracy] sounds again." We liberals pursued this mission with great energy in several strands of activist engagement: in community organization, the Civil Rights Movement, and in relation to the issue of poverty. Much activity and real change occurred, through the empowerment of marginal communities to claim their rights, desegregation and the de-legalization of the Jim Crow system, and through efforts to bring to light and address a heretofore hidden culture of poverty. But then came the war in Vietnam, and a gathering sense of disjunction between the rhetoric of "mak[ing] real the promise" in America on the one hand, and the realities of resource allocation to an

impossible war in Southeast Asia on the other. Democratic activism for a
more just America began to turn toward antiwar activism, and to be
dominated by a sense of betrayal by the government that had so recently
seemed to be on our side.[2]

Meanwhile, in the summer of 1966, when Martin Luther King, Jr.
attempted to bring the Civil Rights Movement North to Chicago, discovery
occurred. We found that even those in positions of power were unable to act
in relation to the real issues. We discovered *institutionalized* racism, as
distinct from the racial problems and unjust local practices on which the
earlier and essentially southern Civil Rights Movement had been predicated.
Other strands of liberal activism came to analogous discovery: that we had
been overly-optimistic—or "sentimental"—about the possibilities of
democratic social change, and that the forces governing the society were far
more complex and distant than we had thought—and imbued with very
problematic values. We encountered "The System," "The Establishment,"
"The Military-Industrial Complex." At the same time the issues became vast:
racism, sexism, unsustainable environmental policies, nuclear proliferation,
corporate domination, Third World liberation. Discovery of massive
obstacle, coupled with deep disappointment, Cold War terror, and frustration
with the war in Viet Nam, led many to moods of apocalypse, and to some
desperate attempts, such as those of the S.D.S. Weatherman faction, to
strategies designed to make people Wake Up to the newly discovered
realities. In a time of fracture, when the earlier activist coalition came apart
and spun off many different strategies and approaches, the group with which
I was associated, one that had been closely tied with the Chicago Freedom
Movement, the Urban Training Center, and the University of Chicago
deliberated intensely for some months about what to do next. We finally
came to the conclusion that the failures of the earlier activism were so severe
that any serious liberal response would require us to think in terms of a
second period of Reconstruction. For us, reconstruction involved
revitalization of the independent sector, the rich tradition of voluntary
associations acting for the common good that was so impressive to Alexis de
Tocqueville and other observers of "the American experiment" as the very
heart and core of American democracy. We founded The Commons: An
Institute of the Independent Sector for this purpose, with financial support
from progressive foundations and national church judicatories, and
intellectual support from Hannah Arendt among others. We began to identify
and reach out to projects that were significant in themselves and that also
could serve as models to support and inspire associational activity more
broadly—including, for example, Citizens for Local Democracy in New
York, groups in Oyster Bay, N.Y., Arlington Heights, Illinois, and Santa
Cruz that were pressing Fourteenth Amendment suits against municipalities
that were unwilling to provide low income housing even for those working in

their own service sector, and the Rouse Corporation, which was building the new city of Columbia, Maryland and committed to a vision of the good city as structured in a way that is friendly to associational life.

Our efforts gradually diminished—as other voices of protest against the System were proclaiming "revolution for the hell of it" and "burn, baby, burn," and we began to go our separate ways. There were two factors in this. The first was continuing discovery of the depth of the real issues, which more and more appeared to be *cultural,* underneath and woven into established structures of the society. With colleagues in The Commons, we found that the truths we stated in our rationale about why it is hard for citizens to act applied to ourselves as well: that citizens and their associations are disenfranchised by big business on one side and big government on the other, by the private determination of public policy, and by their lack of technological capacity and specialized expertise. So were we.

The second factor was consciousness. This, in some ways, was simply a more intense form of the first factor, but it was also different in that it drew a line right through the middle of the liberal community. How to explain this? In 1969 Pogo said, "We have met the enemy and he is us," and the Beatles sang "You say you want a revolution. You better change your mind instead." And in 1971 Robin Morgan, who had been engaged with sixties activism and later became one of the founding voices of Second Wave Feminism, proclaimed: "the personal is the political."[3] Among liberals, a term that described many people in American society in the 1960s and its overall tone, there developed the broad understanding that our real problems lay beyond the reach of social action and legislation, in the values or "consciousness" of the people—in the culture, but even deeper somehow, in the hearts of the people. Out of this understanding there unfolded an amazingly broad array of groups and programs to facilitate the change.

CONVERSATIONAL ASIDE

It seems impossible to communicate just how different things were then, how foreign the culture of America in the sixties and seventies is to what we know now. As part of the cultural shifts of subsequent times, these decades were interpreted in such a way as to set them aside, to wallpaper them over with clichés and past media images. This makes the insights and discoveries of those times inaccessible, which is especially frustrating because they are so pertinent to addressing the issues before us today.

I have a friend of about my age who lived through the Cultural Revolution in China—between 1966 and 1976. We talk about the remarkable similarities as well as differences in our experience on opposite sides of the planet in that

*time. After one conversation, sitting in a park in Shanghai with a huge statue
of Mao overlooking, I recalled the spring and summer of 1968 in Chicago:
riots on the West Side after King was assassinated in April, needing
documents to get past National Guard checkpoints to go to my work at the
Urban Training Center on Halstead, past jeeps covered in barbed wire and
heavily armed, very nervous soldiers. Several days later, in an attempt at a
memorial service in Grant Park by remnants of the Chicago Freedom
Movement, we felt a throbbing noise in the distance, down the lakeshore
toward Hammond. It turned out to be a line of maybe five big Army
helicopters—coming up the Lake, two of them settling down to a few hundred
feet over Grant Park, stealing the dignity of this last meeting, whipping it
into an event of confusion, frustration, and anger.*

*There are many stories. Sitting with my friend in Shanghai, I also recalled
a couple of encounters with the subversives unit of the Chicago Police
Dept—the Red Squad, as it was known (curiously similar and different from
the "Red Guard" of China) which appeared to be absolutely committed to
defense against absolute threat, all the while absolutely refusing any
thought—as though acting purely by organistic reflex, an absurd muscle of
self- preservation on a sea of chaos.*

*Then the Democratic National Convention was set for the summer of
1968, also in Chicago. In May, a reporter from one of the city's major
newspapers decided to write a several-installment exposé on the Police
Department, making known what some of us knew quite well, and possibly
staving off the inevitable confrontation. She asked a small group of us who
had been committed to democratic social change to help with the research.
But then she disappeared at just the last moment before publication—
vanished, gone, and never, to my knowledge, heard from again.*

*After this, I and several friends who had also done research for this
reporter left the city. We were aware of both the Police Department and also
the more radical elements of an activist movement that was beginning to turn
toward violence, toward what Norman Mailer in his* Armies of the Night,
*called a "lust for apocalypse"—as another muscle flapping disconnected on
the same sea of chaos. We felt completely powerless—on top of exhaustion
and despair. I recall watching the inevitable"police riot," as it was later
officially identified, unfold on a very fuzzy tv in the Adirondacks, worlds
colliding—at the same time the whole planet, including its "youth protests,"
were becoming visible from cameras in outer space, seeing the unity and
interdependence of it all, protests against those who refused to see the
necessity for change that seemed to us so utterly obvious.*

*It truly was an apocalyptic time, with the Cold War terror of nuclear
annihilation always in the background of social unrest, plus the atrocities of
Vietnam. I look back with amazement at the degree to which we were
traumatized, and wonder about what we lost in the process of surviving that*

time. On that Shanghai bench I suddenly recalled a remark by Helen Caldicott, President of Physicians for Social Responsibility in that time: After looking at a world map with push-pins representing nuclear weapons, she stepped back and said something quite uncharacteristic of a scientist: "How could it be we are still here? Could it be the grace of God?"

Some ex-liberals, as well as some of us who chose to stay on the increasingly unsteady ship of liberalism and democratic social change, began to see consciousness as an issue within liberalism itself. Another great 20th-century liberal, James Luther Adams, said that liberalism needed a fundamental transformation, and that essential to transformation was liberalism's historic neglect of "the disciplines of the inner life," "neglect [of] the deeper levels of both the human consciousness and of reality itself," and its need of a more full-bodied articulation of "the will to mutuality."[4] His statements are consistent with what I reported above about the late sixties perception of the kind of change we need being deeper than politics and legislation, at the level of basic values and culture itself. We felt the need to become beings who are more alert, more compassionate, and more fully relational than our ancestors had been. It was not only The System that needed change, but we also. This latter awareness entailed a deep erosion of confidence.

Given the severity of the issue, and its enormous distance from regular structures of political life, it is not surprising that many who would have identified themselves as liberal in the past either withdrew from public life or changed their focus. A large number of us who remained committed to liberal ideals decided that education, and the American tradition of citizens who are not only trained for jobs but also educated as critical thinkers and lifelong learners, was the most effective context for the pursuit of our democratic vocation, as a space in which the necessary changes in value could be cultivated. The university was receptive, still open to addressing the underlying issues. It was a very different place from what it has become (partially as expression of liberal failure) after being paralyzed by the "culture wars" that followed, the resulting politicization of everything in identity politics, and the subsequent domination of most universities by the corporate/managerial mindset.

My own search for a home and a place from which I could contribute led me to Michigan and an ambitious attempt to provide quality liberal education in a distinctly public context. I went from graduate school at the University of Chicago (and various part-time teaching positions) to William James College of the Grand Valley State Colleges (a "cluster college," on the Oxford model, where distinctions between units were not those of subject matter but of approaches to education. Here, at what later came to great success as Grand Valley State University, we attempted to re-energize traditional Western values of liberal education for contemporary students who were also concerned about formation of their vocations, with the help of the American traditions of pragmatism and progressive education, and the Jamesian spirit of zestful living. We contributed to the education of several generations of students, many of whom have gone on to positions of exemplary leadership in voluntary associations, education, government, and business. The integrity of who our students become has inspired many of us to sustain hard work for decades, in a public institution which is distinguished in its across the board commitment to liberal education. Through the strenuous engagement with students we have learned more deeply how liberal education can be a transformative practice through which the mature and fully formed human being can develop.[5] And we came to deeper and more articulate awareness of the intimate connection between liberal education and democracy, where democracy is understood as a vision of unity in diversity within a society in which we are all learning and growing through practice of the arts of critical thinking and civic virtue, within what used to be called "the action-reflection model."

CONVERSATIONAL ASIDE

At William James College, beginning in 1971, we were free to start over. We did away with tenure, rank, and the traditional grading system, and we included students as full voting members of policy and decision-making committees. Instead of organizing ourselves around the traditional disciplines, we took our structure from the world, organizing the curriculum into programs: Social Relations, Arts and Media, Administration and Information Management, Urban and Environmental Studies, and Synoptic, the latter being oriented to integration and development of the citizenly or generalist perspective. Courses were focused on problems and issues in the world and our efforts to address them, both as citizens and as persons whose worklife was centered on having a vocation rather than merely a job. Taking our pedagogy from the earlier Progressive Education Movement of the 1930s, we worked with individualized study plans, relied on written faculty evaluation rather than grades, and emphasized experiential learning in both classroom and internships. From our namesake, we took the integration of theory and practice as our overriding concern, and the possibility of changing both person and world for the better as our central article of faith.

We searched for new values.[6] Out of experience with what Karl Jaspers has referred to as "personal ties" ("as the only source of a new and trustworthy objectivity"—chapter 1), and especially with articulation from the feminist movement, we began to develop a conception of the whole person: as one who is neither independent to the point of being incapable of intimacy (like most traditional males), nor dependent to the point of not having a differentiated self (like most traditional females), but rather one in whom these two dimensions can coinhere. We sought to reconnect with and reintegrate that which has been repressed—and suppressed, and oppressed in the historical period. Variously spoken of as the feminine, the right brain, the Eastern sensibility, and the prehistoric or archaic mind, we sought to integrate this repressed dimension into a new and harmonious unity of the whole person. We worked very earnestly to get beyond the old dominance-submission ordering which favored the masculine, the left brain, the Occidental, and the modern/scientific mind, and to a paradigm of person and relationship in which the two aspects can each be present in harmonious simultaneity. And we constructed communities which were explicitly designed to get beyond the problematic values of competitive individualism and shallow materialism. Despite disappointment and frustration of previous efforts in the 1960's, we were still "saving the world," now through development of a vision of human maturity and healthy community. Activist energy did not disappear in 1968, but went underground.

Between 1971 and 1982, we had some vibrant years, some dramatic successes.[7] But then the culture began to change in ways that were very difficult to perceive at first: we had too many students who were attracted to our "ungraded" system for the wrong reasons, some faculty began to show signs of fatigue and cynicism, and in the classroom the assumption of the self-motivated, self-starting, well-prepared student on whom our pedagogy depended turned out—on some days—to be naive (leaving us with the terrible either-or of talking about personal experience apart from resources which would challenge and enrich, or slipping into a thinly disguised form of the traditional lecture format). In the midst of economic hard times in the late seventies, cultural shifts represented by the election of Ronald Reagan, and disturbing signs of failure from within, William James College was closed and folded into a reorganized, "traditional" state college model in 1982. Many of us took some satisfaction in that the folding involved incorporation of many of our methods and pedagogies in the new GVSU structure. But it was a very different time and place by then, literally a different culture.

WAVES OF DISCOVERY AND CHALLENGE

In an era of "rapid social change," the later decades of the 20th century saw wave after wave of discovery and challenge to the liberal vision. I want to mention four, the last of which offers the possibility of revitalization.

The first is Reaganism. It would be hard to over-emphasize the sea change that occurred in 1981 with the Presidency of Ronald Reagan. America had had enough of ambiguity, experimentalism, consciousness, and the sheer drama of the two previous decades. Out of the wish to sweep away the perceived looseness and deep questioning of the sixties and seventies,[8] Reagan was elected to preside over a new traditionalism. The fact that this orientation took as its representative of "tradition" a person who was actually a Hollywood star from romantic cowboy movies of the 1950s says a great deal. With The Moral Majority and large corporations out front, America came to identify "tradition" with "trickle-down economics" of empowering the rich, and individualism modeled on market activity in a capitalist society. As a consequence of this view, a fundamental change in American society and policy-orientation occurred: no longer was the public good seen as prior to private interest, but with Reaganism the relationship was reversed—the "invisible hand" of Adam Smith's *laissez faire* individualism became doctrine: the public good would result automatically from individuals pursuing their private interests.

This was extremely discouraging to liberals, and frightening. It was frightening because the American people bought into this orientation that seemed so obviously constricted and even mean-spirited, insisting, against the obvious facts, that all people were playing on a level field, free of constraints such as those of race or gender or class. Maybe more deeply it was also frightening because Reaganism so clearly constituted a denial of the facts of life as we had come to know them: the facts of global interdependence, limited resources, ecological consequences, economic redistribution, military insanity, and Third World development and liberation—each of which cried out for immediate action, and each of which had been demonstrated by scientific studies such as those of The Club of Rome. Liberalism was not able to stand up to the massive consensus of the Reagan era, but rather tended to withdraw further into "consciousness," cultural change, and often into the life of cynical critique. And with withdrawing came diaspora, a scattering and loss of focus and discipline, and a generalized pessimism about public life.

The second wave of discovery and challenge came in the 1990s, as liberalism returned in diminished form with Clinton and multiculturalism. With multiculturalism, the need for cultural change was specified as *inclusion*: the need to empower, entitle, or provide Affirmative Action for those groups that had been excluded from access to equal opportunity in the past. Guided by a vague notion of the desirability of a society of unity in diversity, this movement also stressed the importance of sensitivity to otherness, and a willingness to learn and grow through interaction with those who are different.

But vagueness was a problem. With the ideal of the common good having been articulated so generally as to consist in little more than inclusion itself, and having only very general ideas about the values of diversity (with metaphors of salad bowls rather than melting pots, etc.), this movement tended to extend *laissez faire* individualism without consideration as to the quality and justice of the arena into which heretofore marginalized people were to be given entrance. The problem was not that inclusion is a bad thing, but that it is a partial thing. And, in the absence of a positive vision of a pluralistic society, multiculturalism wound up contributing to the relativizing and leveling down of all cultures to the low common denominators of unrestrained capitalism, social science, and management—in short, to a new form of colonizing. This critique, which was leveled at Second Wave Feminism as well as the early Multicultural Movement, was painful and confusing, because it served to diminish efforts to insure equal access, to insure the first generation political rights which the United Nations Universal Declaration of Human Rights referred to as a prerequisite or co-requisite for the achievement of second generation socioeconomic and cultural rights.

I can clarify this ambiguity by reference to a striking experience I had during this time. Sitting in a university-sponsored multicultural seminar of faculty who were charged to think about how to make our university community more diverse, an impressive array of cultures and life ways was represented. And as we talked in this laboratory atmosphere, there was indeed a development of sensitivity, appreciation and understanding, a hearing and valuing of many voices, a delicate though unfocused pluralism—at least at the individual level in relation to the group of approximately fifteen people who were at the table. But after several weeks of talking I began to observe that the social scientists, quite independent of any identification by race or gender or social class, were the ones most ready to universalize their perspective, to present their way as *the* way for all people. At some moments they quite openly displayed their assumption of superiority and willingness to dismiss perspectives other than their own, both disciplinary and cultural. I began to see how multiculturalism had become a context of opportunity for the extension of social science, and even how its unconscious presumption of superiority represented an extension of Western imperialism. All cultures and life ways were to be united on the field of modern social science, and under its assumptions about the nature of personhood and community, cooperation and adjustment, and the relativity of all deeply held values and visions of the good life. The values of social science, and its organizational extension as management, were being asserted as though they simply corresponded to reality itself, and from the perspective of which virtually all traditional values were regarded as either "dysfunctional" or quaint. And we liberal humanists were, once again, unable to propose any alternative or more complete vision. I recall painfully my own critique at the time being awkward, overly "philosophical," and completely ineffective.

Realizing that it might take a book in itself to fully explain what I take to be the implications of this basic experience, I will only say here that the multicultural wave of the early 1990s was one of those times in history when a beautiful but vague ideal gave rise to its opposite. In the absence of coherence about a vision of the common good, the multicultural stage became the time of a certain *coup d'etat* in our public life—certainly in the life of the university, as managers took over from both faculty and administrators of the past. It was from this point that the public came to be dominated by that combination of social science and that business science which is "management," and hence by calculation and control, the urge to assessment and procedure for everything, the quantification of all interactions, and cost-benefit analysis (or commodification). Under the doctrine of mere inclusion (i.e., inclusion for its own sake, without any clear valuing of diversity, and, in fact, as a form of homogenizing), management emerged to resolve ambiguities and serve as the architectonic discipline.[9] The fact that there were now some women and people of color in the management positions did not really hide the underlying reality—it only made it harder to address its insufficiency, this new catholicity not of doctrine but of procedure, this further reach of the rationalization process which Max Weber had warned of nearly a century earlier.

The third wave is the broad cultural and philosophical movement of Postmodernism. It was so severely critical of Western history, so concerned to avoid the overriding problem of false and imperialistic universalizing, and so suspicious of any meta-narrative,[10] that there was little positive advocacy. This most basic point is well stated by Lindsay Waters, when he speaks of the limitations and dangers of postmodernism in terms of its taking us to a place of "advocating a value-pluralism that denies the existence of a common human nature for the sake of affirming irreducibly distinct forms of life that are incommensurable," a place which "legitimates our giving up on the effort to seek out what makes us similar with others."[11]

Despite limitations and dangers, however, postmodernism had two primary positive consequences in relation to the learning and development of surviving American liberals.

First, it carried the modern urge to liberate beyond the social and political dimension to the cultural, to the issue of second generation rights. In the process it brought light to the problematic nature of the dominant Western worldview. Through the general (and loosely understood) method of "deconstruction," it identified the following as tightly interdependent features of the Western worldview: over-emphasis on a progressively more narrow, dichotomizing, and calculating understanding of reason (logocentrism); male dominance and assumption of the inevitability of dominance-submission relationships (androcentrism, patriarchy, misogyny); a non-relational world in which persons are either completely isolated or mere instances of one body; dualistic displacement of goodness into the temporal and religious "out there" (identifying the Earth and "right here" as a lesser place, a view which is also theologically incoherent with respect to the meaning of both human action and any sense of "God's presence in the world"); and chauvinistic, assuming superiority, chosenness, and license to universalize/colonize. These elements of criticism were severe and deep, and contained very little in the way of positive valuing of the position from which critique was generated, and hence little attention to an alternative and/or corrective to these qualities. But, on the positive side, postmodernism became the vehicle for a kind of awareness and critical self-transcendence which is unprecedented in the history of the human race. [12]

Second, postmodernism recalled something of the grandeur of human life, the human capacity for participating directly in the ongoing creation of reality itself, resulting in a fresh apprehension of how it is that we are created "in the image of God"—as creators, beings through whom reality passes directly, as co-creators. This occurred through postmodernism's association with hermeneutical awareness: awareness that life interpretations or worldviews are unavoidable, expressions of our local and contingent circumstances, and matters of choice and responsibility. This awareness certainly has its dangers, insofar as it can be taken—in an immature understanding—to imply relativism, and hence the erosion of any sense of a commonly shared world, the slide into nihilism, and the "culture wars" of competitive social construction as a next and ever deeper extension of the problematic Western individualism. But, on the other hand, it also served liberationist movements and the rooting out of ancient oppressions. And it counseled modesty about the claims of any tradition and a sense of responsibility for one's chosen life-interpretation, as well as openness to further growth and the possibility of a pluralistic world in which we can learn through encounters with others who are different.

Beyond its deep ambiguities, postmodernism contains the possibility that the Enlightenment project, as evidenced by the critique and self-transcendence which pours forth from it (as well as against it), is still alive, and, like America, expanding the scope of its vision beyond the limitations of its earlier articulation. Postmodernism can be seen as modernism and the Western heritage overcoming itself and moving on, through a phase of critique it may or may not survive, struggling now to include such previously excluded dimensions as those of sentiment, the feminine, the ecological, the Eastern.

I want to identify one final wave of change as particularly significant to the liberal spirit and its process of coming to terms with the consciousness agenda and the need for radical change/development that became unavoidable in the late sixties. This wave is dialogue. It is the wave that is washing up on the beach of the present.

In my own experience, the dialogue movement dates back to a 1982 Danforth Fellows conference presentation by John B. Cobb, Jr., and to reading his book which was published in that same year: *Beyond Dialogue: Toward a Mutual Transformation of Christianity and Buddhism*. Cobb spoke very persuasively of the need to "review the past with eyes that are open to the greatness and goodness of other Ways," and about dialogue as transformative practice, one that cultivates an ever-expanding global memory.[13] There followed in the mid-1980s a series of North American Buddhist-Christian Encounters, led by Cobb and his Buddhist partner, Masao Abe.[14] In 1985 Abe published his own book, *Zen and Western Thought*, a work which is strikingly parallel to Cobb's, striking in both similarity and difference.[15]

The movement of inter-religious and intercultural dialogue began to be prominent in both American and world culture in the later 1990s, achieving a high level of recognition in 2001 when the United Nations General Assembly designated that year as the Year of Dialogue Among Civilizations.[16] By this time, dialogue was beginning to be understood to entail a new paradigm of relationship between persons, religions, and societies, and as a practice which itself has religious significance—in terms of its implications for self-transcendence, growth, and intimacy. This movement has become persuasive because many people have come to experience dialogue—parallel with what I have earlier called the relationship of mutuality (and democracy)—as convening of the space in which we can: (1) learn from each other about the range and depth of *human* experience, and learn at the level of *trans*-formation rather than just *in*-formation, actually drawing from and incorporating the wisdom of the other; (2) come to awareness in a non-defensive way of the limitations and blind spots in our own traditions; (3) make contact with the dignity and effectiveness of our traditions as living options in the present; and (4) engage in a continuous practice of conversational encounter, as a kind of hygiene through which we can let go of that which is false or egotistical in our lives and traditions and move toward enlightenment or maturity. The underlying assumption is that neither modern life nor the traditions in isolation provide sufficient ways to preserve and cultivate the human spirit. "Dialogue," in this sense, indicates the creative intersection between traditional wisdom and contemporary vitality.

Through involvement with the dialogue movement, liberalism found a way beyond the negativity of postmodernism, into participation in a positive meaning of multiculturalism, and a way of responding to James Luther Adams' challenge to articulate "the will to mutuality."

RETURN OF RELATIONAL LIBERALISM?

From the perspective of world dialogue, we discover liberalism to be a local and particular expression of a worldwide spirit of human hope and aspiration, an expression, like others, with both dignity and limitation.[17] This means that we in America do not need to impose, absolutize, or universalize—or be inhibited by the fear of doing these things. Rather, the world dialogue gives us a context in which liberalism can be revitalized, as well as some friends in other traditions who are doing something analogous. Freed from the problematic Western-style universalizing of the Traditional Period, we can now move to a deeper apprehension of liberalism as one among many expressions of the human spirit on the planet, trusting not in any one formulation of that spirit, but rather in the spirit itself as it is manifest in and through the world dialogue and its plurality of voices.

This appears to be one of those subtle and decisive movements on which history turns. With it we are released from the liberal guilt of having imposed our ways in the past (and fearing we will do the same in the future), and granted the possibility of vigorous presentation (and living) of our own ideals. This profound shift in perspective leads to neither loose universalism nor rigid fundamentalism, and it actually gives us greater access to the vitality and the transformative energy of our own particular traditions (an essential point to which we must return later). With the inter-religious and intercultural dialogue movement we have had fresh and direct experience of the relationship of mutuality, and the "mutual transformation" which is its core. We have had direct experience of democracy and the democratic spirit in a way which radically and critically transcends America, at the same time it illuminates what had been and still could be great about America.

Maybe the easiest way to see this movement, this shift, is through analogy to the person who finally matures to the point where she/he is able to step beyond the pretense of infallibility, and the consequent necessity of defending their identity—even to the point of "preemptive strikes"—against all possible assault. Part of the problem with that orientation, which we call "egotism" in the person and "absolutism" in culture, is that it blocks the one who engages it from their own integrity and energy. The great traditions point this out again and again, and guide us beyond egotism/absolutism to a kind of vulnerability that is actually strength, a letting go of rigidity through which we receive the capacity to move and grow, the kind of openness to spirit that makes it possible for us to be faithful to our own integrity.

I think it is not overstating to suggest that the future depends on the difference between the way of world citizenship that is indicated by the word "dialogue" and the imperialist way associated with egotism, absolutism, and the ideological orientation—which now come to vivid awareness, as we become conscious of their dangers and begin to envision a more mature way beyond them. We need awareness that those values which the modern West assumed to be self-evidently universal are actually parochial; that other values—for example, "'Asian values' such as sympathy, distributive justice, duty consciousness, ritual, public-spiritedness, and group orientation" are also universalizable values; and that due to the plurality of partial insight in the world, the dialogue of civilizations is "both necessary and desirable."[18] The same is being said for feminist values, including those of nurture and care, and for "right brain" values of immediacy, spontaneity, holistic awareness, and intuitive knowing.

However, the fact that our ancestors universalized from their local position does not mean that this local is without worth, or that appropriate response to inappropriate universalizing in the past is to withdraw altogether in the present (or, worse yet, to assume that our guilt is helpful to anyone). It is time to join Tu Weiming and others who are about the project of reappropriating what is great in the world's traditions. For when we renounce the effort to universalize that which is actually particular, we find that the energy that had been expended previously in abstracting and enforcing superiority is restored to us. We are freed to penetrate to the depth, where the particular opens onto that space which is both the source of our energy and also the arena of our common humanity. In that deep and radiant space of endless alternations of similarity and difference, we are able to both receive wisdom from others and gain access to our own. Through dialogue as transformative practice, we are able to grow together in both similarity and difference, creating a planet of maximum diversity within a harmonious whole. It is impossible to overemphasize the importance of this distinction— which may be understandable only from the standpoint of maturity, from the *experience* of it—between *abstracted/thin/universalized particularity* and *deep/thick particularity which opens onto the universal/common.* We begin to recover (or perhaps truly discover for the first time) our common humanity, beyond the reduced uniformity of the modern, and the incommensurabilities of the postmodern.

There are just a couple of other things I want to say about dialogue and the subtradition of relational liberalism, as we come to the conclusion of discussion of the four waves of discovery and challenge—with the possibility that American liberalism has completed its own journey of leaving the world in order to address the consciousness agenda identified in the late sixties, and is now returning in the form of dialogical engagement. First, perhaps liberalism has learned to accept the limitations and imperfections of its own way of articulating and enacting the larger democratic spirit, at the same time as it has also learned how to share with some vigor the wisdom of the West. Perhaps a revived liberalism, a fully relational liberalism, is now ready to share in the worldwide adventure of democratic transformation that is both similar and different across the globe—and quite distinct from the reduced and imperialist form in which "democracy" is identified with Western individualism and market economy.

Second, it seems clear that liberalism failed because it became disconnected from its spiritual grounding in relationality, the public space, and the common good. It drifted toward not only the "secular" (which, we should recall, historically *has* exhibited what I refer to as the religious commitment to encounter with the other in the open space of democracy/dialogue), but also toward the materialist worldview, and hence toward devaluation of the public space as anything more than arena of exchange and instrumental value. As a result of this reduction, the value dimension was excluded from common life, including considerations as to the common good and civic virtue. And in our post-modern times, awareness of these developments has led to views of human nature that swing unsteadily, as Reinhold Niebuhr points out, between the naïve optimism or "sentimentality" on one side, and cynical pessimism on the other. Gone was the ability to sustain the conscious decision to believe in the goodness of the people without becoming a naïve dreamer. Gone was the energetic realism of Niebuhr, James Luther Adams, and earlier liberals who were able to be effective even in the midst of tragedy, able to value the world and the effort to improve it—without insisting that it become their world, their theocracy.

We need "reappropriation;" we need to revive through reappropriation of a great subtradition in the West and in America, as our own local form of the larger democratic spirit and vision of human thriving. We need to make contact with and actually *experience* the goodness of that life-way which I refer to as "relational liberalism"—and, in the broader world context, "dialogue." Perhaps the subtradition of relational liberalism had to leave America in order to be rediscovered; America had to be experienced from a point of remove, to be re-visioned and reclaimed—"reappropriated"—from within the global dialogue which becomes both possible and necessary in our time. We had to become world citizens, engaging the same educational/developmental movement we later advocated for our students. Isn't this how we grow, by rediscovering what is closest to home within ever larger fields of reference?—like the dunce going out, looking for fire, only to find it in the lighted lantern at the end of his/her arm.

NOTES

1. Reinhold Niebuhr, *The Children of Light and the Children of Darkness: A Vindication of Democracy and a Critique of its Traditional Defenders* (London: Nisbet & Co., Ltd, 1945), p. 15.

2. See "Leaving in the Sixties: From Social Action to Cultural Crisis," in Rowe, *Leaving and Returning*, pp. 38–52.

3. Robin Morgan, *Going Too Far* (New York: Vintage, 1978).

4. See my "Toward a Postliberal Liberalism," pp. 51–70.

5. See my anthology, *Claiming a Liberal Education.*

6. See my anthology, *Living Beyond Crisis: Essays on Discovery and Being in the World* (New York: Pilgrim Press, 1980), as an attempt to pull together the most significant statements of that era.

7. For example, in 1979 William James College was designated by the U.S. Office of Education as a demonstration project for the integration of liberal and career education.

8. See "The Traditionalist Eighties: Reconsidering the Modern Project," in *Leaving and Returning*, pp. 72–93.

9. See my "A Humanities Response to Managerialism."

10. Here I note the profound irony of postmodernism's failure to notice the massive and yet largely unaddressed universalizing going on with the managerialism just discussed.

11. Lindsay Waters, "The Age of Incommensurability," in *boundary* 2 28:2, 2001, pp. 151, 163.

12. See David Ray Griffin's several volume SUNY Press "Series in Constructive Postmodernism Thought" as a significant exception to the negativity of postmodernism. Another major effort to address and go beyond the postmodernist critique is Judith M. Green, *Deep Democracy: Community, Diversity, and Transformation* (Lanham, MD: Rowman & Littlefield, 1999).

13. John B. Cobb, Jr., *Beyond Dialogue: Toward a Mutual Transformation of Christianity and Buddhism* (Philadelphia: Fortress Press, 1982), pp. 1, 52.

14. In my *Rediscovering the West* I discuss the dynamics of these Encounters at some length because I have seen them as pioneering of the broader movement that followed.

15. Masao Abe, *Zen and Western Thought.* See also Donald W. Mitchell, ed., *Masao Abe: A Zen Life of Dialogue* (Boston: Charles E. Tuttle, 1998), and *Buddhist-Christian Studies,* vol. 28, 2008, both of which contain essays of mine on Abe and "the dialogue breakthrough" which he pioneered with John Cobb.

16. The major document associated with this proclamation is Giadomenico Picco, ed., *Crossing the Divide.*

17. A good example of limitation is pointed out in the work of Reinhold Niebuhr cited at the beginning of this chapter, *The Children of Light and the Children of Darkness.* He says that "American history encourages the illusion that the nation was created purely by constitutional fiat and compact. This is an illusion because the constitution was the end and not the beginning of a historical process," p. 113. In other words, we Americans tend to place too much emphasis on formal agreement and constitution, and to overlook the importance of organic conditions in the formation and maintenance of a democracy.

18. Tu Weiming, "Beyond the Enlightenment Mentality: A New Perspective on Confucian Humanism," lecture delivered at Grand Valley State University, Dec. 5, 2003.

Chapter Ten

American Clash and Revival

In the sixties, middle-class children began to rebel against the emptiness and hypocrisy of American society. But this was only the beginning. As the dream of the modern was unmasked and made subject to critique, the America which had been dominant in its infectious spreading to all other societies on the planet came under severe criticism—both from within and from without. Much of it was resentful, as other societies began to realize (often initially through American self-criticism) that "the American dream" was neither really available to them, nor (in retrospect) desirable, and in any case not sustainable for all people on the planet. Internal criticism was variously expressed as loyal opposition, shrill protest, "gorilla" (or cultural) protest, as well as debilitating guilt, defensive/aggressive assertion, and corrosive cynicism.

Ironically, it was America, which had been the carrier of the modern to the rest of the world, which generated some of its deepest protest and at the same time became most vulnerable to its limitations. These factors account for the fragility of America at this point in the human drama, despite its deceptive monopoly on "hard" military and economic power. They also underline the importance of recovering and reviving the American democratic spirit as a vision that predates America's captivity to modern values, beginning in the late 19th century. From a world perspective, America is the bearer of a vision which could easily be lost in the turbulence of our time. We need to recover and revive the democratic spirit, both as a world spirit and as inspiration of the best of American experience.

AMERICAN CLASHING

A necessary element of the vocation of reappropriating the democratic spirit is clear awareness of what has happened. One way to understand the cumulative effect of the discoveries and criticism signaling the breakdown of the modern worldview is in terms of a separating of the constituent strands out of which American culture had been woven, and their coming into a state of conflict with one another, such that the "clash of civilizations," which some take to be the world condition, actually characterizes the American condition as well. The three strands are: Individualism, Collectivism, and Relationalism. In this chapter we will look at discovery of the limitations of the Individualist/Consumerist strand insofar as it had come to dominate American life in modern times, the Collectivist/Fundamentalist reaction that occurred with initial discovery of these limitations, and the ways in which conflict between these two strands of American politics and culture can be understood in terms of the absence of the third strand which is needed to integrate and stabilize the influences of the other two. Finally, we will need to think about that third strand, the Relational/Democratic—as pluralistic, and involving a developed capacity centered on how we choose to live rather than only on what we think, and as distinctively but not uniquely American.

Individualist

The distinguished 20th-century philosopher, Alfred North Whitehead, said that the energizing idea of Western history is that of "the essential greatness of the human soul."[1] This general idea has found specification in different ways at different times and places in the history of the West. In America today, the idea is specified as the remains of the Enlightenment ideal. I say "remains" because essential features of the original Modern vision of a democratic society were lost in the Western rush of modernization, with the dominance of the Natural Rights view of individual and society, and its further shaping under the influence of the scientific paradigm. Those features from an earlier understanding which were lost are: the intrinsic value of relationship and community (rather than the merely extrinsic, instrumental, or exchange value), the trust that each will go beyond their immediate self-interest and contribute to "the common good," and the understanding that a healthy society is only possible if each acts out of their "*enlightened* self-interest" within a community of persons who are "in the maturity of their faculties" (John Stuart Mill). These essential democratic understandings were present in the early Enlightenment, but were leached out of the soil of modern life by the quantifying and mechanizing forces of science, the seductions of consumerism and entertainment, the reducing and relativizing forces of secularism, the horrors of war and unremitting competition. Under the influence of these conditions, America came to elevate the natural rights liberalism of Hobbes and Locke, a strand of American culture which locates reality in the autonomous, rights-bearing individual and their capacity for independent initiative, and to understand democracy—and all other relationships—as a social contract among such individuals, a freely chosen agreement and a construct based on overlapping but *individual* interests.

Social contract and the negative freedom of individual rights (i.e., freedom *from*—so the individual could do whatever they wanted, in the absence of much encouragement to consider what freedom is *for*) continued to drift away from community, mutuality, and awareness of social and cultural discriminations which make it impossible for many to be "an individual." Contradictions began to appear: freedom that is empty, persons who are reduced to the least common denominator sameness of consumers and worshipers of celebrity, terrible isolation that exits right alongside "mass society," Alexis de Tocqueville's "tyranny of the majority," and the generalized homogenization of culture that somehow coexists with social fragmentation. In our time this ideal of natural rights individualism has been deconstructed as one which is radically insufficient and generative of moral disease.

Collectivist

Alongside the idea of social contract, of autonomous individuals entering into civil society out of conscious awareness of their interests, modern and American social thought have also contained a collectivist strand which locates reality in an organic view of society as a whole, within which appeal can be made to what the Modern theorist Rousseau called "the general will," and to what later was called the common will, or the will of the people. In the distinctiveness of American history, the collectivist counterpart to the individualist social contract has frequently been understood as "civil religion," that set of symbols and rituals by which the nation maintains contact with its deepest shared values, whether these be understood as "In God We Trust" in the abstract Deist sense, or in terms of the consumer life which is celebrated in TV commercials. In the collectivist view, democracy is conceived in terms of continuous adjustment so that social and political structures more fully reflect the general will—the reading of which, of course, is crucial.

By the late 20th century, the Collectivist strand had been so overgrown by individualism and polluted by modern, consumerist values that there arose movements of reaction in which right wing groups could claim the collective dimension of American society with amazingly little protest. It was the manner of this claiming that identified these American movements as manifestations of a worldwide wave of reaction against perceived limitations of the modern, a shaking off of the modern which was similar in this respect to the youth protests of the 1960s.

As a potential within many human religions and cultures, fundamentalism is the reactive attempt to reject the modern altogether and reassert some version of tradition, the attempt to escape and *go back.*[2] It begins in realization of the moral relativism and obvious decadence of modern life, its shallowness and ignorance of the deeper dimensions of human beings and reality itself. Out of this realization and the frustration which often accompanies it, fundamentalism involves renunciation of individual capacity and uncritical recoil into *authority* and a "tradition" that is rigid, literalist, and judgmental as it is applied to a modern present which is judged to be totally lost. Priority of the authority aspect and surrender of the individual in fundamentalism, the desire and the need for answers to basic life-questions on which it preys, and susceptibility to peculiar and often dangerous interpretation of traditions, as well as frequently unconscious assertions of the purposes of the particular authority rather than the tradition they claim to represent. Fundamentalism becomes attractive because it speaks to the suddenly vivid perception of modern limitations, and especially to the loneliness and unhealthiness of modern individualism and its moral disease. Providing an alternative to the endless competition and "incessant striving" of individualism, as well as to the complexity, overwhelming choices, and endless indefiniteness of modern life, makes fundamentalism a very persuasive option for many, and a very powerful force in the world.

American Fundamentalism is not the only reaction to excessive or misplaced individualism, and neither is it the only expression of American collectivism. There are many sincere and energetic groups and programs working on the restoration of community life, whole schools of thought and action oriented to "communitarianism"[3] and revival of civic republicanism and "civic virtue."[4] But certainly the predominant and most influential form of communal response to the limits of secularism and what liberalism has become is fundamentalism. And I suggest that we cannot understand fundamentalism until we can understand how good people can find it attractive. It should also be said that fundamentalism shares much with another cultural and political phenomenon with which we became familiar in the 20th century and vowed not to forget: Fascism.[5]

There is one other thing that needs to be said about American collectivism, and that has to do with the influence of the corporation and the increasingly multinational corporation in American life. Within what I have earlier referred to as the ideology of corporate capitalism and its influence on all sectors of American life, including government itself, we have a form of collectivism—and even what some have referred to as a "capitalist fundamentalism," or "free market fundamentalism"—which is difficult for many Americans to see precisely because of ideological investment (see chapter 2). For corporate capitalism maintains close association with the individualist ideal from which it arose, in the image it projects through advertising as well as in the legitimating understanding of the corporation as super-person. This is especially the case in its essential ties with the advertising and public relations industries, as well, of course, with market economy itself. Together these serve to hide the impact of the corporation in political decisions and shaping America—and the world—according to its values. This impact includes the fact that the multinational corporation has come to overshadow the nation state as the dominant political entity. Perhaps the most poignant expression of this new political entity and its tendency to remain invisible to many Americans is its use of "globalization" and "democracy" as Trojan horses in service of the neo-liberal ideology of free market economy. Hence collectivization in the form of homogenization and leveling down proceed largely unquestioned, as capitalism in its later stages leads not only to isolated individualism but also to a tribal kind of collectivism.

Relationalist

It has been observed that the genius of America lies in an illusive and essential quality that some have even called "thirdness."[6] This quality is dynamic, relational, and the locus of an energy that is not available to either individuals in isolation or groups with one mind. Another term for the essential quality is democracy, understood as a way of life which cannot be established as a mere mixture or a balance between individual and communal dimensions, but which is truly a third thing.

From the Relationalist perspective, democracy is not primarily a form of government, but a way of living which is centered on creative relationality. It can be manifest across the whole spectrum of our experience in life, with self, nature, intimate others, family, and immediate community, with workplace and nation state, the larger world of other peoples and cultures, even experience with God and the broadest horizons of life. From this perspective, democracy as a form of government is a set of arrangements which is discovered in specific social/historical circumstances to be most effective in protecting and cultivating the democratic way of life. Democratic government fades and inevitably becomes something else when it is not sustained by direct and continuous *experience and practice* of democratic life.[7]

John Dewey said that "A democracy is more than a form of government; it is primarily a mode of associated living, of conjoint, communicated experience."[8] The democratic way of living is grounded in a certain kind of relationship, the relationship of *mutuality* in which individualist and collectivist dimensions are affirmed simultaneously. We experience the relationship of mutuality as good in itself, as *intrinsically* good. This is to say that we *experience* democratic relationship as space in which we can appear in our full distinctiveness, as the location of genuine or soul-affirming self as distinct from ego, self as subject rather than object, as well as the location of emergent discovery, possibility, and freedom from the constraints and determinisms that otherwise obscure and prohibit our real life. The open space of mutuality is where we encounter the other as well, in their integrity and uniqueness—also as person rather than thing. So significant is the open space for democracy that it can be thought of on the analogy of a temple or holy place in the traditional religions, as a space in which the divine becomes manifest. Perhaps a less dramatic way of making this point is to say that mutuality becomes the locus not only of the liberal negative freedom—that which must be protected, but of *positive* freedom as well, mutuality as human thriving.

America itself was founded on this understanding, which is most evident in the American tradition of "religious freedom." For part of the genius of American history and "religious freedom" or pluralism has been a certain synergy between the particular religions and a public, common, or civic religion. With the help of Deism and Transcendentalism, Americans have been able to maintain and thrive in their different and particular religions, while at the same time valuing—each from their own standpoint—the religious significance of the open, democratic space that is shared by all. This worked as long as there existed two key affirmations which floated between at least some of the particular religions and overlapped the civil religion, providing the basis of the American separation between church and state and a shared religious valuing of the public. The first is that while God is absolute, particular interpretations of God are not; all interpretations are imperfect because of the imperfection of the human beings who are doing the interpreting. This acknowledgment of the limitations of tradition leaves room for growth and development in the religious sphere, redeems religions from the idolatry of their own formulations, and counsels a certain openness to other views. The second affirmation is that God works through others outside of one's immediate community of belief, and that insight sometimes comes from surprising places—the stranger, the other, or the fellow citizen. Democracy is possible among those who recognize the religious significance of the open space, with the other as well as with those of one's own more particular affiliation. This recognition, of course, is absent in both the fundamentalists who cover over the open space with their claims to infallible knowing, and those individualists who deny the existence of such a space altogether.

The genius of American culture is that it provided a way for public life to have religious significance without requiring theocracy. It affirmed mutuality. The critical relationship of mutuality, and its intimate, religious connection to the democratic way of life, is made vivid in contrast with two other modes of relationship, those of *exchange* and those of *authority*—

corresponding with Individualist and Collectivist strands. Neither relationships of exchange nor those of authority value mutuality. In relationships of exchange, we remain isolated and an object: we are valued for what we can do or provide, even as we regard the other in this light also, in terms of their use. In relationships of authority, on the other side, the rule is that of dominance and submission: we submit in light of the superior wisdom or skill of the other from whom we can learn, or by whom we are controlled when their interests and power is so much greater than our own that neither mutuality nor exchange are possible. Certainly all lives contain all three kinds of relationship—or at least those of exchange and authority. For without exchange we are limited in terms of making promises, agreements, and "social contracts," and without authority there can be no discipline. But the democratic vision insists that we are incomplete (and actually in danger) unless these relationships lead to, are stabilized by, and serve the relationship of mutuality. Neither exchange nor authority are responsive to *who* we are as a human being, though both correspond to aspects of *what* we are, in the same way that the Individualist and Collectivist strands are necessary but not sufficient aspects of a democratic society.

But the relational vision of democracy has been so profoundly buried by the structures of modern life that it is rarely available to people today. We see fullness of the democratic vision occasionally in some feminist and environmental perspectives, in some voluntary associations and civic groups, in some programs and instances of intercultural and inter-religious dialogue, and in experiences of great friendship or collegiality that appear like flowers growing improbably out of cracks in the hard rock of contemporary life. There is also some strong evidence of democracy's return among public intellectuals who are beginning to be heard in our day. Here I mention six of these—and their highly recommendable work—who have been strong conversation partners for me in the shared vocation of making real democracy available in contemporary life: Cornell West and his *Democracy Matters*, Elizabeth Minnich and her *Transforming Knowledge*, Jacob Needleman and his *American Soul*, Martin Marty and his *The One and the Many*, Sor-hoon Tan and her *Confucian Democracy*, and Jeffrey Stout and his *Democracy and Tradition*. But these works are not read by many.

In the absence of widely available resources for cultivating the democratic way, resources that are woven into education, community, and family life, it is no surprise that Individualistic and Collectivist strands of the American fabric would separate and each make claims to the whole, rather than being held in dynamic tension by the Relational strand. In our forgetfulness of democracy as an *experience,* a way of living, and a vocabulary of organizing and prioritizing in daily life, non-democratic social and political forms can even claim to *be* democracy—the term having positive connotations, while few remember its real meaning. In the world since World War II, this phenomenon is represented by the widespread preference for "democracy," understood as the procedural or thin form of government—sometimes also called "liberal democracy" or "Western-style democracy"—that guarantees constitutional protections, free elections, public debate, and the right of individuals to be free from authority in order to enter the exchange relationship of free market capitalism. Certainly this political form is preferable to many others, including the tyrannies and authoritarianism that many societies struggle to escape. But the exchange or social contract orientation should not be confused with democracy in the full sense of that term, and the limitations and instability of procedural democracy need to be understood. Procedural democracy is a "system" that embraces competition and exchange within a market economy and society, on the assumption that individuals are equally "free" and that the "invisible hand" of the system itself will take care of the common good. It does not value mutuality or intrinsic relationship, including such qualities as "citizenship" or "the common good," as anything other than an expression of market activity, and it denies the existence of structural inequalities within the system. It is amazingly trusting of the system, and hence is liable to devolution without people noticing, either into plutocracy—rule by the rich, or into what Erich Fromm, Vaclav Havel, and others have referred to as a "megamachine" or "post-totalitarian system" in which everyone adapts and "functions" in a new kind of authoritarian collectivism that Hannah Arendt calls "the rule of nobody."[9] Without explicit valuing of mutuality as the locus of our humanity, we can slip back into authoritarianism—even with "democratic" banners flying.[10] This is why some visionaries such as Oswald Spengler and Friedrich Nietzsche have said that democracy inevitably leads to tyranny; that when the discipline which is necessary to an open society is leached away by the strictly negative understanding of freedom as protection of private life, an invisible vulnerability sets in. They point to the irony and the tragedy of the Modern, Western revolt against historic authoritarianism: it led to an even more severe form of collectivism than the one from which escape was sought, such that some claim the whole of the modern project of freeing the individual was mistaken.[11]

REAPPROPRIATING THE AMERICAN VISION

The hope of America lies in reappropriating the democratic tradition through revitalizing the Relational strand, which can move the Individualist and Collectivist strands from clash to harmony. And it is this sub-tradition which can convene and maintain the open space through which the democratic spirit might be present and active in both persons and society. In a world of multiple simultaneous crises, this solution at first appears to require a leisure which is not ours.

We have come repeatedly in the conversation of this book to *development,* and the theme of an enlarged and deepened maturity as necessary to the changes in society which need to occur if we are to avoid succumbing to moral disease and be able to actualize the potential America represents. I have previously suggested that this is the same issue which John Stuart Mill was addressing when he said that democracy is only possible among persons who are "in the maturity of their faculties." It is what Elizabeth Minnich was pointing to when she said it is "necessary for all groups to achieve self-knowledge, developed from within rather than imposed from without." And, to identify someone who speaks of this theme as an imperative not only for Americans but for the world at large, the great 20th-century Zen *sensei* and dialogue pioneer, Masao Abe says

> We must enter the third historical age of mankind, namely, the age of Self awakened cosmology. We each must awaken to the root of world evil and historical evil deeply within the self and—in the identical foundation of self, the world, and history—we must awaken to the original Self which has broken through the ego. We must take the cosmological 'expanse of Self-awakening' which opens up therein as the new foundation of mankind and, transcending peoples and national boundaries, we must proceed to build a *solidarity of Self-awakening* which includes mankind in the broadest sense. We must build a cooperative society of mankind within the universe. Herein lies the practical task of all mankind today. [12]

The democratic tradition is a tradition which can acknowledge the modern loss and facilitate reconnection to the more particular traditions, saving us from the relativistic quality of individualism on one side, and the fascist tendencies of post-traditional collectivities on the other. Again, the democratic tradition is pluralistic in nature. It is a tradition of many traditions, each acknowledging its limitations and a willingness to grow through a dynamic life with others who are both the same and different. [13] David Bromwich describes the essential quality of a pluralistic tradition in an insightful way as the "non-restrictive" liberal understanding of tradition, and he notes its weakness in our time:

> A tradition on this view, far from being fixed forever, may be shaped by the voluntary choices of readers and thinkers. Indeed, it exists not only as something to know but as something to interpret and reform. But a difficult paradox holds together the idea of a non-restrictive tradition. Before it can be reformed intelligently, it must be known adequately; and yet, unless one realizes first that it *can* be reformed, one will come to know it only as a matter of rote—with the result that the knowledge of tradition will seem as

unimaginative a business as the knowledge of an alphabet or a catechism. Difficult as it is, the liberal understanding was for a long time promoted by American politicians, shared by public servants, exemplified by artists, critics, and freelance citizens. The process of sifting the tradition still continues, however, it is weaker now than it has been for several generations. [14]

It is especially important to understand that pluralism is quite different from relativism and the "liquid" quality of the modern, and it is difficult to conceive intellectually (requiring that we take care not to miss it by imposing the intellectualist bias of needing to generalize from either the individual or the communal dimension, missing the relational on both sides); it requires honoring the paradox to which Bromwich refers—and to which I keep pointing throughout. Hannah Arendt speaks of pluralism as a matter of faith: "The unity of mankind and its solidarity cannot consist in a universal agreement upon one religion, or one philosophy, or one form of government, but in the faith that the manifold points to a Oneness which diversity conceals and reveals at the same time." [15]

This very simultaneity between the particular and the universal (and difference and sameness) can be seen as the aspiration of American culture when it has been at its best. Maybe we see this most dramatically in the vitality of immigrant groups before assimilation has occurred, or in groups such as African American and Chinese American in which assimilation does not occur so easily, whether because of racism or conscious choice. For America was founded, however ambiguously, on the cultural energy which is released when universal and particular dimensions come together and are affirmed simultaneously. The universal elements insist that the particular traditions should confess their own limitations and the possibility of growth beyond their formulations and rituals, along with the possibility of insight coming from the stranger or the other; while the particular traditions insist that those universal aspects respect practice and the necessarily individualized dimensions of transformation.

But, again, without direct and continuous *experience* of the paradoxical character of mutuality/relationality, this simultaneity is not possible—or even identifiable. [16] Without this *experience,* antinomy, Catch 22, dilemma, gridlock, etc. are inevitable, as they are for any culture (or relationship) whose mysterious yet crucial middle ground of relationality has been eroded, eclipsed or otherwise lost, whose vision has been obscured or displaced by the modern distraction. For the dialogical kind of pluralism is more than just intellectual position. It is as well—and more fundamentally—a quality of character, a disposition, a form of association, and, as I have proposed, a stage of growth.

To be as clear as possible about the dialogical character as the type of pluralism which represents the Relational Strand and a new stage in the developmental movement we are attempting to track, I return to Martin Marty, who concludes his discussion of the unity and diversity of American culture and its essential "cohesive sentiment," by recommending that we "start associating, telling, hearing, and keep talking."[17] This indicates a character quite different from that of the two other types of pluralism (toleration and universalism), both of which are more abstracted from the living, pulsing complexity of full relationship, whether in intellectual positions or mystical pursuits. William Connolly, to point to another example of full or deep pluralism, speaks of it in terms of a "bicameral orientation to citizenship," and the cardinal American civic virtues of "agonistic respect" and "critical responsiveness." The first one adopts out of "respect for the relative opacity of their faith to others and in acknowledgment of their own inability, to date, to demonstrate its truth," and the second "takes the form of *careful listening and presumptive generosity.*"[18] Again, the pluralism of democracy is fully relational, and not predicated on shared beliefs or a universalized metaphysic—as visions of unity tended to be in the traditional West, and as universalist pluralism still is in the post-traditional period. Rather, it is predicated on both the shared need for reappropriation of traditional practice as remedy for the modern condition, and dialogue as a shared practice.[19]

This is also to say that, in the fullness of the democratic tradition, the diversity of limited human persons and cultures is understood to be *real*: each symbolizing and responding to the Jamesian "unseen order" or the soul-affirming possibility as best they can, according to the particularities of their local circumstance, including their methods of practice. Again, this is quite distinct from traditional/historical Western senses of a shared life which were predicated on a universalized metaphysic or orthodoxy as the pre-requisite and certification of right relationship.[20] The democratic tradition, by distinction, is founded on commitment to and trust in continuing growth and ever-opening horizons, and the understanding that humans learn and receive insight most effectively through our relationships with "one another"—with those who come to be paradoxically *one* with us at the same time they remain *other,* continuing to develop in their difference as well as in ever deeper commonality. Again, *E Pluribus Unum.*

However, it is hard to see cultivation of this plural union as a remedy for what is actually going on at this point in American culture and politics. As Sheldon Wolin says, "recovering democracy presents a task that runs counter to the political dynamics of our times."[21] Cultivating the essential relationship is something more like an act of faith, of keeping the faith as we have discussed it before, faith in human possibility and the openness of history, an active faith which is manifest as the humble willingness to join together with others to deliberate and act on issues of shared concern, issues of a commonly shared life.

How, then, is it possible to sustain this faith which, as Wolin points out, runs so counter to the dominant dynamics of our times? Reaching back to earlier themes, one answer is that living in the mode of civic virtue is the healthiest way to live with and for ourselves and our neighbors. Another and related answer can be found in William James's arguments with the "scientific absolutists" of his time who claimed to know all based on immediate evidence. James countered their "realism" by insisting that "there are, then, cases where a fact cannot come at all unless a preliminary faith exists in its coming. *And where faith in a fact can help create the fact.*"[22] He counseled a healthy balance between idle dreaming and rigid insistence that things ever shall be as they are now.

So it is that perhaps the best conclusion to this chapter on reappropriation of the democratic spirit in America is with the awakening on which it finally depends. There is no stronger voice on this crucial matter than that of the prophetic pragmatist, Cornell West. He says we must work and hope:

> But we must remember that the basis of democratic leadership is ordinary citizens' desire to take their country back from the hands of corrupted plutocratic and imperial elites. This desire is predicated on an awakening among the populace from the seductive lies and comforting illusions that sedate them and a moral channeling of new political energy that constitutes a formidable threat to the status quo. This is what happened in the 1860s, 1890s, 1930s, and 1960s in American history. Just as it looked as if we were about to lose the American democratic experiment—in the face of civil war, imperial greed, economic depression, and racial upheaval—in each of these periods a democratic awakening and activist energy emerged to keep our democratic project afloat. We must work and hope for such an awakening once again.[23]

Yet we do not know when awakening might come, despite powerful examples from the past when it did come—a list to which we might add the astonishing collapse of the Marxist-Leninist Soviet Empire in the early 1990s. So we work and hope against a backdrop of awareness that the forces which are so powerfully against democracy in the present may not be so powerful as they seem.

The remaining chapters of this book, then, need to push the question as to the meaning and direction of faithfulness to the democratic spirit and "helping the fact" as deeply as possible, into the tissues of how we actually live. In doing this it might help to keep in mind Dewey's earlier inspirational statement about "the common faith of humankind," and ours being the responsibility of "conserving, transmitting, rectifying and expanding the heritage of value we have received that those who come after us may receive it more solid and secure, more widely accessible and more generously shared than we have received it."

NOTES

1. Whitehead, *Adventures of Ideas*, p. 19.
2. See Martin E. Marty and R. Scott Appleby, eds., *Fundamentalisms Observed* (Chicago: University of Chicago Press, 1990).
3. For an inclusive collection of representatives of this tradition, see Markate Daly, ed., *Communitarianism: A New Public Ethics* (Belmont, CA: Wadsworth, 1993).
4. See projects associated with American higher education discussed in chapter 13.
5. On the connection between fundamentalism and fascism in America, see Chris Hedges, *American Fascism: The Christian Right and the War on America* (New York: Free Press, 2006).
6. Josiah Royce, *The Problem of Christianity*, ed. John E. Smith (Chicago: University of Chicago Press, 1968), pp. 273–295.
7. See A. D. Lindsay, *The Essentials of Democracy* (Oxford: Claredon Press, 1977), where he is lucid on the differences between articulations of democracy arising from actual experience of it, as distinct from those which arise from theorizing.
8. John Dewey, *Experience and Education* (New York: Macmillan, 1938), p. 87.
9. Erich Fromm, *Escape From Freedom* (New York: Holt, Rinehart & Winston, 1941), Vaclav Havel, "The Power of the Powerless," p. 54, and Hannah Arendt, *Eichmann In Jerusalem: A Report on the Banality of Evil* (New York: Viking, 1963), p. 295.
10. See Sheldon Wolin, *Democracy Incorporated* as a major caution against this possibility.
11. See, for example, Alasdair MacIntyre, *After Virtue* (Notre Dame, IN: University of Notre Dame Press, 1981), p. 111.
12. Abe, *Zen and Western Thought*, p. 260.
13. I have an unpublished anthology, entitled *Democracy and Post-Traditional Wisdom: A Tradition Beyond Traditions*, in which I have collected works from Western authors who have come to an understanding which is parallel to the one I offer in this chapter.
14. David Bromwich, "The Future of Tradition: Notes on the Crisis of the Humanities," in *Dissent*, Fall 1989, pp. 541–542. For full presentation of Bromwich's understanding of tradition, see *A Choice of Inheritance* (Cambridge, MA: Harvard University Press, 1989).
15. Arendt, "Karl Jaspers: Citizen of the World?," p. 257.
16. Again, see A. D. Lindsay, *The Essentials of Democracy*, on the necessity of ongoing and direct experience of democracy in order to keep it alive.
17. Marty, *The One and the Many*, 225. See also Marty's *Creating Cultures of Trust* (Grand Rapids, MI: Eerdmans, 2010).
18. William E. Connolly, *Pluralism* (Durham, NC: Duke University press, 2005), pp. 3, 123, 126.
19. I attempt to articulate this understanding in "Masao Abe and the Dialogue Breakthrough," in *Buddhist-Christian Studies*, 28 (2008).
20. On the key question as to whether commonality or engagement of transformative practice requires shared belief, we might consider Socrates in the *Phaedo* when he says, after discussing several metaphysical possibilities: "No sensible man would insist that these things are as I have described them, but I think it is fitting for a man to risk the belief—for the risk is a noble one—that this, or something like this. Is true about our souls and their dwelling places, since the soul is evidently immortal, and a man should repeat this to himself as if it were an incantation" (114d). A soul-affirming metaphysic can be an essential support in the movement from ego to soul affirmation/actualization—or it can be a distraction. See the contemporary dialogue on this question between Henry Rosemont and Huston Smith in Henry Rosemont, Jr., *Rationality and Religious Experience: The Continuing Relevance of the World's Spiritual*

Traditions (Chicago: Open Court, 2001), and Rosemont and Smith, *Is There a Universal Grammar of Religion?*, p. 181. I also cite the recent and not-yet-published work of my colleague, Peimin Ni, "An Alternative to Universalism—Confucian Vision of Holism."

21. Sheldon Wolin, *Democracy Incorporated*, p. 276.
22. William James, "The Will to Believe," in McDermott, p. 731.
23. Cornell West, *Democracy Matters*, p. 23.

Chapter Eleven

Pragmatism Revisited

I read the last chapter, and see it is short and non-programmatic. After a moment of longing for some kind of Master Plan, I return to awareness that this is not possible—because of the breadth and depth of the issues before us, their dynamic and interdependent character. And there is another reason: what is most essential to our being able to address the issues of our era is not a One Best Plan, but rather for each of us to pick up the developmental challenge and do our part within the dynamic tensions and paradoxical simultaneities which hold together healthy community and personhood—on the understanding we have discussed before, that naming—or theorizing—these tensions (individual and community, etc) is necessary but not sufficient, since what it takes to bring them into harmonious stability varies greatly from one context to another, one person to another, one community to another. Therefore, what I do to pick up the developmental challenge will be quite different from what you do, at the same time there is some degree of objectivity as to whether either of us is really doing our part or not.

The claim of this chapter is that there are great riches in the matter of how to address the developmental challenge contained within the American heritage—and that pragmatism, as extension of the Socratic tradition and relational liberalism, is a direct expression of that heritage.

Pragmatism is at the very center of America's best possibilities, despite being misunderstood as whatever works (for me, as a further extension or legitimation of competitive individualism), simple instrumentalism, or modern relativism dressed up and legitimated with fancy talk. Perhaps this is due to the fact that pragmatism is extremely difficult to articulate, especially in a world of shrill ideologues who still need to absolutize, cynical nihilists, and a fearful public with a short attention span. It is very difficult to tell these people to focus on development and practice. This developmental dimension of pragmatism underlines, again, both the importance and the challenge of articulating the meaning and value of pragmatism.

Articulating pragmatism often goes awry when more academic interpreters dismiss the above "whatever works" understanding as a completely mistaken form, a kind of embarrassing cousin who must be hidden, thereby consigning the "higher" or "true" pragmatism to the universities and discussions so subtle that they become disconnected from the reality of American culture, its actual joys and sorrows. This dichotomizing dismissal cuts off the possibility of appealing to the lower forms of pragmatism on the basis of the higher, as that "higher" form falls into the irony of exemplifying the very split between thought and action pragmatism had originally set out to overcome.

The point is that pragmatism, long before it becomes a "philosophy," indicates a quality of American culture, one which—like all qualities of culture and character—has more elevated and more debased forms. The challenge in articulating pragmatism, by its own most basic principles, is to speak in a way that not only describes but also elevates, even inspires. Pragmatism is not really pragmatism if it retires from the actual drama of life, into either the cave of scholasticism or the strip mall of opportunistic individualism.

Here is the challenge of American culture itself at this point in history: to articulate America's vision in a way which is something more than only effective problem-solving and the flexibility to think fresh in new situations. These, to be sure, are major and most welcome virtues, but we still need articulation of a broader vision which resonates with our most noble inclinations, helping us by persuasion rather than command to move beyond both blind ideology and crude individualism, into a world of meaning and value which is real, sustainable, and compassionate. This articulation is necessary to America and the restructuring which is signaled by the Obama administration. For this nation is uniquely founded on the conscious holding of an idea of freedom, and is thereby a most ambitious proposition containing both possibilities and dangers which are not to be found in nations built on the conquest of traditional aristocracies. As with any ambitious ideal, if pragmatism fails to articulate its best meaning of freedom, it becomes susceptible to degradations which are not possible among those who hold to lesser ideals. Perhaps what I imply here is that pragmatism can never hold itself exempt from the inward and outward work of overcoming on which it is predicated.

So what is it, this pragmatism?

Pragmatism, in the full sense of that term indicates encounter with the post-traditional experience of Nothingness I have described earlier, and the decision to move beyond despair with the conscious choice to affirm life as a gift. It involves, again quite consciously, the decision to adopt beliefs in support of life affirmation, without any metaphysical certification as to their correctness, and with acknowledgment of these beliefs being limited in that they inevitably reflect, at least in part, our local situation and limited capacities for symbolizing and articulation. Further, pragmatism also entails a willingness to alter these beliefs in the ongoing adventure of living, according to their effectiveness in maintaining, supporting, and deepening life-affirmation, as we learn and grow along with others who share in the post-traditional, post-doctrinal condition—and affirmation.

It really comes down to the decision as to whether life is worth living, a decision on which terrorists and other nihilists, including even some who would fight against them, have come down negatively. This is why understanding of pragmatism requires going back to the root, existential moment. James, to take America's leading example, contemplated suicide, somehow finally decided to "go a step further" to "posit life," and to built pragmatism on this decision and the discoveries which followed from it,[1] chief among which is that our "will[ing] to believe" is sometimes a prerequisite for that in which we believe (like love and justice and God) to be present and active on this planet. It is in this sense that he remarked that our philosophies might be the most momentous reaction of the planet upon itself.

It is impossible to get ideology or doctrine out of this orientation, one which is so entirely dependent on a developmental movement and an intensely existential decision and its individualized consequences. Pragmatism is indeed difficult to communicate: it is not ideological, but neither is it relativistic; it is not metaphysical, but neither is it ungrounded; it cannot be formulated, but it can be identified. This sounds a little like Daoism or Zen, and indeed it is, insofar as pragmatism points to a locus of vitality which is and must remain ineffable, requiring us to resist the human temptation of control and closure. Pragmatism is acutely aware that succumbing to this temptation results in obstruction of the very reality to which it responds; it is acutely sensitive to the dangers of idolatry, to worshipping the symbol rather than that to which it points. Pragmatism is faithfulness to the source of life, and is ever vigilant to the human tendency to fixate on that which flows from the source in a way that causes us to lose touch with the source itself.

Hence pragmatism is, above all, responsive to the dynamics of life in its immediacy. It is indeed a "problem solving" approach, but, much more than that, it is life affirming. James put it this way:

> . . . she 'unstiffens' our theories. She has in fact no prejudices whatsoever, no obstructive dogmas, no rigid canons of what shall count as proof. She is completely genial. She will entertain any hypothesis, she will consider any evidence. . . . Her manners are as various and flexible, her resources as rich and various, and her conclusions as friendly as those of mother nature.[2]

Pragmatism, like America itself, is post-traditional. It is informed by a critique of Western culture as it developed over the centuries, and it contains a strong injunction for humans to grow up and live with an aliveness and a maturity which are rare in the human past. Further, the maturity envisioned by pragmatism is profoundly pluralistic and relational, which is to say it is quite different from both traditional authoritarianism and tepid modern toleration with its negative and private freedom of live and let live. The pluralism inherent to pragmatism is a more vigorous pluralism of mutual growth, dialogue, and democracy—in John Dewey's sense of a way of living together and communicating. It is a pluralism in which our principles and commitments very much matter, yet do not need to be absolutized. Contradictory though it may sound at first, all one must do to enter the creative space of this pluralism is to acknowledge one's limitations, including limitation in the capacity to formulate principles and commitments, and hence also the possibility of growth in this capacity.

Pragmatism is post-traditional in that it arises—as a sentiment and a way of living before it becomes a "philosophy"—out of a sense of the failure, misdirection, or insufficiency of traditional lifeways. This sense is strongly associated with the problem of intellectualism and the ideological life-orientation, as the deep tendency of Western people to withdraw from the immediacy of lived life, into static and closed conceptual systems which then wind up constraining rather than supporting life, doing violence to life in the name of conceptual order. Pragmatism arises out of despair of this deadly tendency, and acute awareness of its inevitable consequences if left unchecked, consequences like fascism, technological determinism, and the sociopathic personality. After two millennia of traditional abstraction from life, and obsession with imposing order and control from the outside, pragmatism is centered on return—to value and meaning located in the deep textures of life itself. It answers a question which has lain dormant in Plato for many centuries, namely the question as to why—apart from compulsion—the enlightened being would return to live in the cavelike darkness of the world. For pragmatism, withdrawing attention from the immediate urgency on the surface of life, and development of capacities of reason, reflection, self-transcendence, and purpose are necessary but not sufficient. The necessary functions of abstraction come to healthy fulfillment not on the detachment of Mount Olympus, but rather in the midst of the ever-changing, ever-ambiguous, ever-struggling world. Here they interact with others in the pluralistic space of democratic problem-solving, discovery, and growth, with others who may have come to different conclusions and who just may have seen more clearly than we have on some issues.

Further, pragmatism affirms that the spirit we need in life, as source of guidance, motivation, and healthy growth, comes not from obedience to command from on high and correspondence to a displaced and static metaphysical order, but from the depth of connection with a continuous flow of gift-full and even redemptive energy which is already present in our lives and the world—if only we would be alert to its presence. Pragmatism, then, as a philosophy of return, does not reject the human need of abstraction, principle, and moral/political direction. Rather, it evaluates abstraction by its fruits, in relation to consequences *in life*, ever mindful that the old Western dream of achieving a single, final set of absolutized abstractions has past. Clearly it takes a significant degree of development to even acknowledge passage of this most basic dream.

Pragmatism begins, beyond despair of the post-traditional and modern world insofar as they are still driven by the abstracting and life denying momentum of the traditional, with the conscious decision to *choose life* against the odds of what the world has become, to affirm the gift quality of life, and the resulting attempt to live in and through direct contact with the deepest and utterly ineffable wellspring of life itself—what pragmatism's most profound articulator, William James, called "pure experience." The assumption here, one which is commonly shared by the world's great traditions, is that human beings are capable of this: that each person, each in their unique way, is capable of bearing the goodness of life directly into the world, within "the paradoxical plurality of unique beings." Here also, coming full circle, is the perception of possibility which inspires the decision and choice with which pragmatism begins.

Though the utterly crucial decision to live in a life-affirming way may occur first in some dramatic moment of one's life, it also occurs repeatedly and with ever greater refinement as we grow and mature in our capacity to be faithful to life—in never-ending cycles of self-transcendence or (as Nietzsche put it) self-overcoming. In the process, pragmatism acknowledges that we will necessarily and inevitably have a "philosophy" in the sense of an articulation of principles and commitments, and our understanding of the value, meaning, and purpose which provide the guidance and discipline we need—at least until we reach the point where we are able to body forth gift in pure form, unpolluted by ego, as in the Chinese ideal of *wu wei* (the action on non-action), or the Christian ideal of "it is no longer I who live, but Christ who lives in me" (Galatians 2:20).

But between now and full embodiment of that ideal, we will have a philosophy, a life-interpretation, which is to say some articulated principles and commitments by which we stand, and a practice through which our transformation is occurring—again, both necessarily and inevitably. But no philosophy is perfect, nor is the one which is appropriate to you necessarily the one which is most effective for me at this point in my own journey. Actually, from the standpoint of the ideal just stated, the very fact of our having a philosophy at all is testimony to our incompleteness. So we need to be especially careful not to freeze our philosophies into static and absolutized positions. It is essential to remember that the lure of certainty—what James called "the queerest idol ever invented in the philosophic cave"[3] —is profoundly self and life defeating. Our philosophies must be understood not as perfect reflections of a reality which is outside of and prior to life, but rather as aids to our growth. We need to be mindful of Socrates' modesty about human knowing, his "human wisdom" of "knowing nothing," and his understanding of philosophy as a practice oriented to purification.

Philosophies need to be evaluated and refined from the perspective of their consequences for growth and creativity, justice and sustainability, their responsiveness to the ever-emerging possibilities and dangers of lived life, their capacity to contribute to a world which is more like gift and less like constraint. Here is an answer to the question which is often put to pragmatism: "Consequences for what?" Is our philosophy life affirming in the broadest and deepest way possible, or does it still contain taints of rigidity and the ultimately destructive ego wish for certainty and complete control?

Alfred North Whitehead expresses the spirit of pragmatism and its energetic recommendation that we adopt a philosophy that is more dynamic and immanent, more feminist and/or process oriented: "We live in a world of turmoil. Philosophy and religion, as influenced by orthodox philosophic thought, dismiss turmoil. Such dismissal is the outcome of tired decadence."[4] With the passage of the traditional period in human history, the habit of dismissing turmoil on the playing field of life becomes dangerous, as some frustrated players become susceptible to fanatical visions and/or extremist schemes which dismiss through absolutizing and denial. However, passing of the traditional also offers the opportunity of participation in that pluralism in which the one great principle of life-affirmation is ever more completely approximated through continuous democratic evaluation of its necessarily local manifestations.

All of the above is very demanding—developmentally. Lao Tzu said, at the very opening of the *Dao Te Qing,* that "the Dao that can be named is not the eternal Dao." Again, the gift quality of life is radically ineffable, and as humans we constantly face the threat of idolatry, worshipping the symbol rather than the source of life to which the symbol points. So pragmatism, like the Eastern philosophies which can help in the articulation of it, both requires and cultivates an order of maturity which is rare in human history. It is developmental and practical to its core. However, pragmatism itself does not claim any special access to this maturity. Rather, it affirms, in the best sense of American "religious freedom," the capacity of many traditions to facilitate and guide this transformative process, according to the needs of particular people in particular social-cultural-personal circumstances. It is in this way that pragmatism can be spoken of as a tradition beyond traditions, and as pluralistic in essence—even as it simultaneously affirms our deep commonality in what James calls "the common mother," our Earthbound condition and our commonly shared wish to live in "intimacy" rather than "foreignness."⁵

CONVERSATIONAL ASIDE: A NEW UNIVERSALISM

*Far from being relativistic, pragmatism, with its ever deeper and broader life-affirmation, leans in the direction of a new universalism, one which is distinctly pluralistic—toward what some ecofeminists refer to as a "situated universalism."*⁶

The universalism of pragmatism is consistent with the earlier proposal of dialogue as a commonly shared element of practice, one which is paradoxically necessary in order to gain healthy access to the greatness of (or through) one's particular tradition. It is consistent as well with what we have heard from Tu Weiming, about the values of the modern Enlightenment having become universal, such that the common agenda is one of broadening and deepening them through "the globalization of local knowledge" in dialogue

Note that we are talking about a kind of universalism which is beyond any particular doctrine, any one best, complete, or final formulation. We are speaking of a universalism in which any articulator of it needs to have developed to the point where they are able to acknowledge the inherent limitations and partial nature of their articulation, and be willing to develop further in both theory and practice through hearing the articulations of others, as well as through hearing one's own (and responses to it) in the presence of the other who is different—as a locus of increasing clarity and effectiveness of articulation.

It is especially important for Americans, in the process of the post-traditional (and post-postmodernist) reappropriation, to understand the difference between this kind of universalizing and the hegemonic universalizing of the past, which was doctrinal and presumed the superiority of its articulator. Because of this past, many Westerners are shy about any kind of universalizing in the present, fearing it will turn out to be, perhaps in some new and subtle way, repetitive of deep habits which have not yet been overcome. They find it safer to remain in critique or incommensurability. But shyness can be dangerous too, blinding us to the inevitability of universalizing, and to new forms which are perhaps even more problematic than those of the traditional era (for example, the contemporary universalizations of management, entertainment, and consumerism).

Awareness of these factors can perhaps lead Americans to a new appreciation of pragmatism, as a magnificent source of the post-traditional, pluralistic universalizing. I hope this has been demonstrated in the previous chapter through the philosophy of William James.

*We can also see pragmatism as a source through John Dewey. The contemporary philosopher and educational leader from Singapore, Sor-hoon Tan, helps us in this. She recommends Dewey as a cure for "antidemocratic culturalism." By this term she means the defense of the identity of a minority, nation state, or civilization against democratizing pressures through a conception of "culture" as a fixed body of norms and practices which "almost invariably becomes reductionist, essentialist, static, and hegemonic."⁷ What is needed, according to Tan, is a more dynamic and nuanced understanding of culture, and it is at this point that she turns to Dewey. He defines culture as a humanizing process involving the ongoing attempt to affirm individual and communal dimensions simultaneously, and as inherently democratic both in this aspiration and in the generalized belief in the human possibilities by which culture is energized. This democratic understanding then, involves moral universalism, since all cultures are involved in a process of learning what it means to be human. But for the same reason it is a non-ethnocentric universalism; it is not anchored in any particular image or ideal state of "human nature," but rather in the universality of aspiration to something like thriving or flourishing (or "intimacy"). Neither is it relativistic. It is sufficiently definite that it can serve in the evaluation of cultures, as "living together in ways in which the life of each of us is at once profitable in the deepest sense of the word, profitable to himself [sic] and helpful in building the individuality of others."⁸ In Dewey's universalism, no one is ever exempt, either due to ethnocentric superiority or to relativistic impotence, from the ongoing evaluation and inquiry which leads to continuous improvement. And here is the possibility of a democratic future: "It is a culture that must be achieved on a worldwide scale if it is to be achieved at all, but not by coercion, economic domination of country over others, or by the hegemony of one culture over others."⁹ Is it not refreshing to embrace this vision? One (and one's culture) does not need to be perfect, but neither does it need to be nothing. Pragmatism offers a way beyond dichotomy, and the dualisms which have infected modern Western thought and culture.*¹⁰

NOTES

1. This is from the journal entry of April 30, 1870, in *The Writings of William James*, p. 8.
2. William James, "What Pragmatism Means," in *The Writings of William James,"* pp. 389–390.

3. James, "The Will to Believe," in *The Writings of William James,* p. 734.

4. Alfred North Whitehead, *Modes of Thought* (New York: Macmillan, 1938), p. 80.

5. William James, *A Pluralistic Universe, ed., Richard J. Bernstein,* pp. 133–134.

6. Karen J. Warren, *Ecofeminist Philosophy: A Western Perspective on What It Is and Why It Matters* (New York: Rowman & Littlefield, 2000), pp. 113–115.

7. Sor-hoon Tan, "Reconstructing 'Culture:' A Deweyan Response to Antidemocratic Culturalism," pp. 34–35.

8. *Ibid.,* p. 47.

9. *Ibid,* p. 48.

10. *Ibid.,* p. 35.

Chapter Twelve

Democratic Life, American Hope

A Meditation on/from the Practical Turn

PRACTICE IN THE POST-TRADITIONAL ERA

The paradox of universality and particularity, of each requiring the other in order to be fully activated and vital in the present, is not resolvable apart from the movement to *practice*. Apart from practice—"the return to life" as *an act*—universality and particularity freeze in opposition, as yet another form of either-or in our transitional era. Anything anyone claims as "universal" will be reduced immediately to the particularity of its articulation, and any particularity will be seen as radically "incommensurable" with all other particularities—each claiming its own universality. Freezing in opposition is a function of issues being addressed from the perspective of modern values and the intellect alone, the intellect disconnected from heart and soul and body. The intellect alone leaves us in a thicket of antinomy, until we can finally accept that paradox is gateway to what is vital in life, and discover through practice a way to activate universal and particular dimensions simultaneously—and to understand that the proper function of the intellect is to *point to* rather than contain "the life in living."

To state the issue from the side of universality, the commonly shared crisis of modern life leads us to see that what the great traditions and visions of full humanity have in common is the understanding that an intervention, the cultivation of a "second nature," is a necessary condition of human maturation and well-being. With humans, something very particular must be done, a transformative practice which is specific to both tradition (and/or subtradition) and person must be engaged. To state the same point from the side of particularity, we must move beyond abstracted universalizing and empty entertainment—and get to work.

In the post-traditional 20th century, we have had a hermeneutical revolution, a revolution in understanding the function of interpretation, its limitations as well as the fact that interpretation is inescapable, intimately connected with human capacity for action and growth, and religious in that it reflects (and even transmits) what we take to be ultimate in life. In our time we have met the imperative of a new way of living and of continuous growth. We have discovered the requirement of a fundamental change in consciousness with regard to how we treat the natural world, and that this in turn depends on a fundamental change in how we treat ourselves, how we constitute and cultivate our selves and each other. In support of this change, in our century we need a *praxiological revolution*, a revolution in how we conceive of, evaluate, and support practice. We need to mature beyond the Western sense that practice is simply application or implementation of that which has been settled elsewhere, either in an antiseptic intellectual environment or as the dictate of unquestionable authority. We need an understanding of practice which embraces interpretation, and evaluates it in relation to its ability to inspire and direct the transformation of both individual and society in the direction of well-being and the common good. From the perspective of my own particular tradition, this means we need to pick up on and continue the pragmatic revolution, and reclaim philosophy and liberal education as practice.

Practice is inevitable in human life: the question is not whether or not there shall be practice, but rather which one, and whether it is conscious, subject to critical refinement, and conducive to well-being. Meanwhile, interpretation is necessary for practice, and inevitable also, unavoidable—for better or for worse. If we don't interpret, if only to ourselves, how could we even remember those experiences which we take to be important? Interpretation without consciousness of practice is an unexamined practice of questionable value (as the lives of some Western philosophers demonstrate with their unexamined practice of intellectualizing); while practice without ownership of its interpretive dimension is practice which belongs to someone else—is oppression or mere training.

Before going further, we need to notice something utterly basic which has been presupposed in all that has been said so far. It has to do with our condition as post-traditional people, and one of the most basic ways in which our life-circumstance is radically different from those of our ancestors. The vast majority of our ancestors were born, lived, and died within the enclosure of a tradition, and what they knew as a more or less stable frame of reference with respect to metaphysics, trustworthy authority, and role assignment/ expectation. But they were not conscious of being enclosed; what for us is "a tradition" or "an interpretation" was for them the way things are. This is a simple point, and yet one with such wide-ranging implications that it can be hard to see. Perhaps this is because there is a correlative point with respect to "self:" consciousness of "tradition" arises right alongside of consciousness of and responsibility for self, in an expanded order of choice and responsibility which would have been quite literally unthinkable for the vast majority of our ancestors. I think Robert Bellah, in his classic essay, "Religious Evolution," makes this point most clearly: "modern religion is beginning to understand the laws of the self's own existence and so to help man take responsibility for his own fate," including "growing awareness that it [i.e., traditional religious language] is symbolism and that man in the last analysis is responsible for the choice of his symbolism."[1] The implication here is that, while those of our ancestors who were privileged to engage transformative practice were able to turn themselves over to recognized authorities who would direct them, we have no such given authorities (or so many that they cancel each other out). Rather, we find ourselves in an enormously ambiguous post-traditional place of both awareness and alienation, a place where we are left to direct our own transformation, where practice must be conscious, and where we must take responsibility for its outcomes. As Bellah goes on to say, this situation has high potential for "pathological distortion" as well as "creative innovation in every sphere." My concern is that we appreciate both the astonishing array of choices we have before us *and* the ambiguities of choice, commitment, and guidance which are also integral to our thriving in post-traditional circumstances.

With all of the above in mind, then, in this chapter I share my own practice and some reflections on practice in general from this perspective. My practice arises from the tradition of liberal education as it has been reappropriated in the post-traditional present, a practice which I take to be intimately associated with the American democratic tradition (in ways I will discuss in the next chapter). More specifically, in this chapter I share through *engaging* my own practice in relation to the issue of practice itself, the issue of our each being able to develop our own practice, one which can grow and develop as we do, and one which includes reappropriation of the wisdom of a particular tradition, identification of the positive values of modernity, and dialogue as a shared practice.

CONVERSATIONAL ASIDE

Here is a brief report on the joy of learning and transformation from the perspective of liberal education as it is reappropriated as a transformative practice in the post-traditional present, a report on its essential dynamic:

In each part of the course, we begin inquiry with a real-life question (like that of viable practice in the post-traditional present). In the humanities it is always a question about which any adult already has some kind of answer, whether conscious or not—questions, in the broadest frame, like What is Love, Justice, Truth, Beauty, Goodness, etc.? Recalling what it said over the entrance to the Temple of Apollo at Delphi: "Know Thyself," the first step in any inquiry is to get ahold of your own thinking on the question before us, something that can be accessed simply by asking oneself and listening for sincere response. This step includes toleration of the aporia *experience of realizing that I "know nothing"—or at least of the humble nature of my initial response. Once we have some sense of where we stand, it then becomes possible to turn to sources, to others who present their answers to the same questions, like Socrates, or Lao Tzu, or Aristotle, as well as one's classmates, professor(s), and contemporary sources. These answers make it possible for us to refine and develop our own previous answers, by comparison and contrast, agreement and disagreement, and that mysterious opening of horizons, that* aporia *experience, which real thinking and the presence of others often brings.*

This relational—or dialogical—approach has also been demonstrated to be the most effective environment in which to listen to others and "learn the sources," more effective on several counts than the old method of rote learning through memorization and repetition. Through the back and forth approach to learning, I become more clear and articulate about my own position on matters of importance, at the same time I learn to tolerate the condition of not-knowing (aporia)*, and even to value this condition as an opening through which wisdom enters my life. I learn simultaneously to appreciate and respect the positions of others who are different. Here is the practice through which learning moves beyond in-formation to trans-formation. As I learn from/about others and self, I am also transformed through the spirit in which encounter occurs.*

Through repeated engagement of this process of questioning and answering with both self and others, gradually there emerges a different kind of person. They are in touch with themselves but not self-centered, engaged with others and the world but not coopted; active and yet cooperative, respectful of the space or kind and relationship in which transformation becomes possible, and hence alert to issues and policies with respect to the common good. They emerge as persons who are in "the maturity of their faculties," and, insofar as they become independent learners and continue as lifelong learners beyond college, some become truly magnificent or even enlightened human beings.

Many of my students don't get it at first; in fact, they don't get it at all until they experience *it. Something like "patterned learning" is required, where the student learns by the instructor "taking them through the movement," literally moving body parts in the learning of such things as, for example, the side stroke. We do something quite analogous in the learning of inquiry. The first few times through the process students are often skeptical or resistant, and do not begin to trust the process until they write papers and see for themselves what they have learned—and become.*

The resistance is itself instructive. The predisposition of most contemporary American students is toward either the objective or the subjective pole. These days, the first concerns are usually on the objective side: What are the facts and information we must cover, and What will be "on the test"? When it becomes apparent that something other or more than this is called for, students tend to go to the opposite pole: Oh, so it is all subjective, what we think/feel, our self-expression, or, alternatively, the equally subjective likes and dislikes of the professor. The joy of teaching occurs when students finally break through the objective-subjective dichotomy, and come to what can quite legitimately be spoken of as a new paradigm. They literally move to a new way of conceiving of self, world, and the possibilities between them, moving from opposition to synergy, and from the ideological to the relational, discovering a qualitatively new order of possibility in a relational world—one which lies beyond the objective-subjective opposition. And if the practice is well-rooted, it will—like any genuinely transformative practice—expand from the more narrow and protected environment of the classroom to a way of being and relating in all of life, developing a truly democratic way of living. The more narrow disciplines of reading/listening, writing/speaking, and inquiry/conversation/ dialogue break open into a way of being in the world.

DECISION, OPENNESS, RETURN

Now back to the broader dynamics of post-traditional people adopting and refining transformative practice. For this purpose, let us return once more to statements from Socrates, Confucius, and William James which have become central to our conversation:

Socrates said: we must "risk the belief" in the immortality of the soul in order to live well, and repeat this belief as an "incantation" (*Phaedo*, 114d), or sing it over "the frightened child within" until we have "charmed away his fears" (77e).

Confucius said: "It is not the Way that makes the human great; it is the human that makes the Way great."

William James said: we need to exercise "the will to believe," aware that some realities—including those of an "unseen order" of energy on which humans can draw—depend, at least in part, on the human willingness to sustain the belief in them as a precondition for their being present and effective on this planet and in our lives. In this same vein, he also remarked that our philosophies may well be the universe's most profound reactions upon itself.[2]

The testimony of these three figures is clear: we must decide to believe, take responsibility for our choice, and recognize that choice is unavoidable—that scientism, nihilism, and consumerism, for example, are just as much choices as are traditional orthodoxies. Going way back to chapter one, the adoption of an effective practice must begin with acknowledgment of our need of forgiveness and help, which in turn is predicated on distinction between the two ways of life which exist within us: the ego-driven and the soul-affirming. Yet this distinction cannot be real without choosing to believe that there *is* such a thing as soul—or "non-self," or "relational self"—one way or another to believe in the existence of a larger reality beyond that of the ego, one which embraces, transfuses, and transforms. Practice in our time must be conscious, and it requires "belief" in a dimension of possibility which lies beyond stimulus-response conditioning and power to manipulate. This is perhaps the most fundamental choice upon which human life rests, whether it is given in the unconscious inheritance of traditional culture, or chosen out of post-traditional awareness.

Another way to read these three figures is to say that culture and community ultimately depend on some who consciously *choose* their values and relationships, some who choose to live in good faith and with sincerity. Choice of this order is not dependent on particular forms of culture and community which are thought to correspond with some external—and externally certified—metaphysical principle or commandment. Rather, this way of choosing only happens out of the experience of Nothingness which occurs, as Karl Jaspers points out, when we fully confront the impossible nature of our post-traditional situation and "recall our origin." It is an act of love, analogous to God's act of creation and ongoing presence in the world. This, of course, is saying a lot: that we must (1) come to full awareness of what I have called the moral disease implicit in modern life; (2) withstand the terrible experience of despair and nihilism that accompanies this awareness; and then (3) go beyond the nihilism (go *all* the way and "negate the negation," in the vocabulary of Japanese Kyoto Zen) into the life affirmation that arises only out of Nothingness as love or compassion. And finally (4) we come to understand that this movement has very little to do with whether I am a Buddhist or a Christian, a Muslim or a Confucian—though each of these traditions can support the essential movement to affirmation, as well as provide illumination along the way.

Considered from yet another angle, the statements from Socrates, Confucius, and James imply that the human future depends on a maturity that has been rare in the past, though, as several 20th-century visionaries have discovered, this maturity and its cultivation can be seen as the wisdom at the root of the world's traditions. And it is the only way we can move beyond the moral disease we can now understand as a function of people getting stuck in the developmental process we have been discussing: the movement from absolutism to relativism to universalism to reappropriation, and into the pluralistic/relational/democratic stage and possibly a new axial age. The future depends on maturity, on a public that has crossed a certain developmental threshold such that the significance of care for the common good and civic virtue are acknowledged and activated, and relatedness can be valued as intrinsically good. In order for democracy to take root—in the person, relationship, community, or society—this maturity must be recognized, celebrated, nurtured, and sustained. It requires that form of human cultivation which is recognized in the great traditions, again, as *practice.*

Democracy itself can be seen as one such practice, reflecting Rinehold Niebuhr's famous saying: "Man's capacity for justice makes democracy possible; but man's inclination to injustice makes democracy necessary."[3] But I am really going a step further than this point, to say—along with John Dewey and others in the tradition from which I speak—that democracy itself is a form of practice that is generative of humanity's capacity for justice, as well as the capacity to recognize and let go of the inclination to which Niebuhr refers. Democracy—like dialogue—both requires *and cultivates* the maturity we need.

The maturity of which I speak—and democracy, in the full sense of that term—are grounded in and arise from a very definite and fundamental experience. It is experience of that specific kind of relationship in which mutuality occurs, a synergy of simultaneous openness and definiteness in the presence of the other. For in the fullness of democratic relationship, I discover myself to be more fully and deeply present than I am in those moments of isolated introspection when I try to find and/or create (or "grasp") myself within my self. Mutuality opens me up to the central paradox that is shared in common by the world's religions in the traditional period of humankind—stated here in its Hindu form: *atman* (self) *is Brahman* (God); or, in Christian terms, "It is no longer I who live, but Christ who lives in me" (*Galatians 2:20*). I learn to live this paradox with others first, and only later—as Levinas points out—with myself.[4]

The key is openness, a certain transparency of the ego self. In the democratic relationship (including the relational aspect of democratic personality) we are able to honor, maintain, and expand the open space within and between us as the source of all good things: solution to problems, creativity, personal integrity, and psychological health. Some even identify this crucial open space—or "the beyond" as it has been described above—as locus of the ongoing creation of the universe, again, paradoxically with/ through other human beings. Pointing to the openness in another way, the traditional Chinese quality of *wu wei*, usually translated as "action of non-action," describes the kind of action in which neither genuineness of self (*cheng*) nor the deepest source of life (*Dao*) are eclipsed by ego, and in which both Self (or true Self, as in usage of the Kyoto School as we have seen it earlier via Masao Abe) and the Dao (in Confucianism, the Way) appear simultaneously and as indistinguishable. Right or good action, in these moments, flows freely through us. Here also, I think, is what the Christian Saint Augustine was indicating when he said, "Love God and do what you please," and the more contemporary Robert Pirsig, in his *Zen and the Art of Motorcycle Maintenance,* when he talked about his finally discovering "the silence that allows you to do each thing just right."[5]

It is the greatest challenge of all for human beings to honor, maintain, and expand this kind of openness, as distinct from domination by ego, through rationalization and control on one hand, and indeterminateness and proteanness on the other, both of which are so prevalent as symptoms of loss in modern societies. Proper honoring of openness, without sacrifice of focus, is the issue of growth and maturity. Confucius said:

> From fifteen, my heart-and-mind was set upon learning; from thirty I took my stance; from forty I was no longer doubtful; from fifty I realized the propensities of *tian (tianming)* [heaven;mandate of heaven]; from sixty my ear was attuned; from seventy I could give my heart-and-mind free reign without overstepping the boundaries.[6]

The last stage is that of *wu wei.* To be open—"as a little child" in the Christian tradition—while at the same time maintaining the adult virtues of commitment and constancy, is one way of identifying the magnificence of the fully formed human being; to have "free reign without overstepping." This is challenging in that it requires us to let go not of effort, but of our temptation to think we can contain and control life through our actions. This point is made beautifully in a Hindu saying that the ideal is "not renunciation of action, but renunciation in action." The challenge is for us to *live* the Dao even though it cannot be spoken, which is celebrated as the highest human capacity in the world's great traditions: it is *phronesis* in Greek culture, *ijtihad* in Islamic culture, *sui shi yin yuan* in Chinese culture, and "skillful means" in Buddhism. And it is the root of civic virtue.

Development to this point, again, does not happen "naturally" in humans; intervention is necessary, a discipline of transformation, a yoking (yoga), a practice. It is easy for Westerners especially to overlook this crucial point. Experiences of *wu wei* are easy to *see* and admire, since they speak to the deepest longing of the human soul. In fact, this seeing and vicarious admiration has become a major topic of popular culture. But there is a profound deception in this, the same as that of the preliminary universalism which we discussed in a previous chapter. For the actual *living* of these experiences requires a practice that allows them to be integrated into the deep tissues of our whole being (not just in our heads or emotions or electronic devices). Westerners tend toward admiration while being blind to practice: because of preference for intellectual/theoretical resolution and correctness, because of worldviews and philosophies that are deterministic or otherwise denying of human action as being able to accomplish anything, because of either-or theories of salvation which arise from special revelation, and now because the narcosis of modern culture—with attention deficit and insistence on instant gratification in addition to its orientation to the vicarious, which have made us lazy in the pursuit of human cultivation.

I think it helps, in making this central point about integration and actually living the wisdom we recognize and admire, to observe the theme of *return* in the great traditions: the truly enlightened or mature human being is not the one who is "mystical" (who, for example, flies elegantly through treetops, as in the very beautiful *Crouching Tiger, Hidden Dragon*). The mystical is a preliminary form. Full enlightenment/maturity entails return in humble service to others, and is distinguished by full integration into the *ordinary* structures of existence. The Japanese Zen tradition is helpful on this: "Enlightenment that smells like enlightenment is not enlightenment," or "Easy to meditate in the monastery, more difficult in the home, most difficult in the world." Zen and other traditions affirm the ultimate identity between *prajna* (wisdom) and *karuna* (compassion). Here is the full significance of Karen Armstrong's observation that all of the Axial Age traditions teach compassion.[7] It is the "highest" stage of development; it *is* enlightenment. As Dietrich Bonhoeffer puts it in his articulation of a "religionless Christianity," "being there for others is the experience of transcendence."[8]

To say it another way, with development refinement of the practice occurs, such that there comes to be a *convergence* of the extraordinary and the ordinary, and of the means and the ends of practice. Again in Zen: "First there was a mountain [as perceived through immature, ego/objectification consciousness], then there was no mountain [in mystical realization], and then there was a mountain [in return, the world as perceived against the backdrop of mystical realization]." In Christian terms, "love thy neighbor as thyself" ceases to be a commandment, and instead becomes the best advice as to where we find the vitality and "redemption" in life. With Socrates, we find ourselves "examining both myself and others," as "really the very best thing that a man [*sic*] can do."[9] In Confucianism, *Shu* (holding the heart of the other as analogous to one's own) is the method of becoming a *Ren* person, a fully actualized and truly good person, an authoritative (not authoritarian) person (*Junzi*), a person of sincerity (*Cheng*). In the democratic tradition, practice of civic virtue, as care for and enjoyment of the public space, is both the mark of the mature human being and the pathway to becoming one. In feminist language, this is to speak of "mutuality as core practice."[10]

INTERPRETATION AND ENGAGEMENT

The point is practice, and yet we/I keep generating more interpretation. Articulation and interpretation are *very* important in human life. As with philosophy in its best (though not complete) sense, interpretation such as the above provides reminders of what is really important, pointers toward that which is vital in life, ways of thinking that help us prioritize experiences and grow to greater focus in our genuineness—ways of guiding and developing our practice. If philosophy does not support our being more fully and continuously present in life, it becomes another distraction, one which is more subtle and hence even more dangerous than that of entertainment. Like religion, philosophy can be profoundly distracting when it generates theories of presence that do not actually *cultivate* presence. Here we come back to the Western seduction of knowing that supersedes and substitutes for being, to the temptation of ideology and ultimately of fundamentalism and fascism. Socrates addressed this danger with his insistence that philosophy be understood not simply as intellectual formulation, but as a "charm" and an "incantation," as purification of the soul, and ultimately as "preparation for death and dying" (*Phaedo* again*).* Here we also come to the essential point of pragmatism, and the reason why William James thought that the emergence of pragmatism was just as important in Western history as the Protestant Reformation: our interpretations are to be judged by their efficacy in the transformative process, their consequences in terms of how they locate us in life—whether toward greater intimacy, being at home, being faithful to Earth as our common mother, or toward cynicism and foreignness.[11] And here is the point of contact with Eastern philosophies, where, as in genuine pragmatism, interpretations are embraced and evaluated by the commitment to the larger practice (*Gongfu*) which they serve. Whether interpretations can make us "most right" in some grand competition about the most absolutely correct formulation of the nature of God or the Real—is childishness.

But now it is time to renounce interpretation, insofar as this is possible—or to renounce the simple notion that all issues of practice must be settled at the level of interpretation and then *applied.* We need to commence the praxiological revolution, and begin thinking seriously and directly about practice, and we should pause to take note, once again, of this as a basic imperative of our time. For ours is a time different from previous times, times of settled and apparently reliable authority, when it was possible to simply deliver oneself to an obvious master, group, or institution. But this is no longer possible. There is something basic about the dynamic of our time which requires that our practice be *conscious*. This is extraordinarily difficult because it requires choice about precisely that which we do not yet know, and some significant measure of trust and surrender to those whom we acknowledge as more developed than we. It is difficult because of our individualist bias (we must know everything), and because we know the dangers of religious and cultural leaders who are revealed to be manipulators and predators. No wonder so many people shy away from commitment to a practice, remaining in the warm but shallow waters of universalism, or giving up on cultivation of their humanity altogether.

So when *do* we—or *can* we—step beyond interpretation (which can become the nervous chatter of avoidance) and actually get to practice? Each of the several attempts to get to practice in recent pages has turned back to more interpretation.

Or have they? Perhaps we are engaging practice now, as I have suggested before, a practice of liberal education—which happens to be a practice of much talking, dialogue or conversation, discourse about our choice of the most effective interpretation/belief in relation to maintaining the crucial affirmation to which Socrates, James, and Confucius point. The same can (or should) be said of philosophy itself.[12]

One other thing in the interpretive mode: whatever else it might mean to "get to practice," there is an element of practice which we have discussed at length before which needs to re-enter the picture now, and that is the need to venture beyond the insufficiency of the modern worldview to reappropriate from one or more of the wisdom traditions arising out of the Axial Age. To review quickly what was suggested previously: that (re)connection with and/ or reappropriation from tradition provides (1) a vision of the deep dimensions of human experience, (2) an understanding of the problem of human life and its remedy, and (3) a discipline through which enlightenment, redemption, or access to remedy might occur. So "reappropriation of tradition" is one element of practice.

Descriptions of the great traditions are readily and amazingly available in our time, as are lectures and presentations by their representatives—in what I have referred to elsewhere as "the irony of availability" in our time.[13] But how is one to choose at the level of commitment which is adequate to "connect the tether" firmly enough to support engagement of practice? How to do this without being indiscriminate or seduced into a cult or some other form of false authority? And beyond all this, how can one find ongoing guidance, support, and reliable companionship?

These are big and difficult questions, and ones for which there is no set of easy answers, and certainly no technique. There is risk, and not one but a series of "leaps of faith" are involved in the establishment of healthy connection. I want to propose some specific guidelines as to the dynamics of this connection and how to keep it healthy, but before offering these I have two suggestions. The first is that the traditions themselves are trustworthy in their original, Axial Age presentations, especially those of the texts from a tradition's founding period which have been identified as sacred or "scripture." It is in the later interpretations and appropriations that deviation and strangeness occur. So, with full awareness that this is precisely what many cults and deviant sects *think* they are doing, I suggest connecting the tether to the root of tradition, in their scriptures and early commentary. In doing this, one way to avoid the dangers of slipping into some dangerous, merely idiosyncratic, or ineffective form of connection—or fundamentalism—is to maintain awareness of what was going on with the formation of the traditions in the Axial Age. And here I especially recommend the works by Karen Armstrong, Karl Jaspers, Jacob Needleman, and Huston Smith which have already been cited. In the language of the chapter before last, this is to suggest that we need to maintain the universal dimension, and honor the necessarily paradoxical relationship between universality and particularity. It also points to dialogue as the locus of healthy reappropriation. In this sense, dialogue *is* the paradox, the space and the relationship through which we are able to live or "solve" the paradox.

A second suggestion is that we find mentors who have done what we are attempting to do, pioneers in overcoming the modern limitation through reappropriation of traditional resources. The four I have just mentioned would each qualify in this category.

COMPONENTS OF PRACTICE

Still, many questions remain about how you and I, in the concrete particularity of the lives we live, might establish and maintain healthy practice. In this section, moving closer to the living presence of embodied life, I offer some specific guidelines as to how we might think, choose, and remain conscious in our practice. For the sake of brevity and directness, I will present what I take to be the essential components of practice in the form of a list, with awareness that these items are really overlapping, in no way sequential, and that some come close to contradicting others. These might be thought of as a tightly interdependent set, arrayed in a circular configuration around a center through which the kind of openness I have been describing occurs.

1. Cultivate awareness of/in the gift quality of life, including the sense in which gift is contained within self in such a way that "awareness" entails stewardship.

2. Remember Aristotle's "common sense" advice for the cultivation of virtue: In order for acts in accordance with the virtues to have good effect, they must be (1) undertaken consciously, (2) engaged for their own sake, not for some collateral consequence (like impressing someone), and (3) applied with persistence, or "proceed[ing] from a firm and unchangeable character."[14]

3. Maintain wakefulness—aware of the narcotic quality of modern society; maintain spiritual practice as a basic hygiene, a daily cleansing which removes accumulated obstructions. Meditate, engage mystical prayer, cultivate mindfulness, or contemplation, as it is enacted by one of the great traditions, and move toward integrating this practice into your ordinary life with no taint of "the mystical."

4. Maintain and develop contact with what Medieval Christian mystics called the *magister internus,* the master within, which is to say an internal sense of rightness, in terms of both recommendations received from others and refinements of practice which one discovers out of the practice itself. Learn to listen to and trust that deep voice within, sometimes called "conscience" or *daimon* in the Greek tradition, which knows and discovers and is active in the natural movement of transformation.

5. Beware of temptations of "knowing," especially in the forms of formulating and intellectualizing. Remember, in the great traditions it is understood that ego is not capable of reliable knowing, and that intellect initially is owned by ego (as in "rationalization"), so that, in the words of the classical Zen Master Dogen, "the inconceivable may not be distinctly apparent. Its appearance is beyond your knowledge."[15]

6. Beware also of temptations to false senses of "not knowing," to pretenses to *wu wei* which are actually ego performances.

7. "Reappropriate" and trust one or some combination of particular traditions, including their sources of advice, support, direction, criticism. At the same time, become aware of the limitations or "blind spots" of this/these tradition(s), and that in its past for which it must apologize in the present. Find and connect with an inevitably limited and humbling particularity of tradition and community of transformative practice.

8. Engage dialogue with an "other" tradition, one which brings fresh insight and understanding from the other at the same time it illuminates the dignity of your own tradition(s)—one with which the fullness of dialogue as a religious practice, a metapractice, becomes possible.

9. Remain open to continuous refinement of the practice through the metapractice of dialogue, and also—again—of the movement from practice as a separate and special activity to one which is fully integrated with the whole of your life, your embodied, ordinary life.

10. Find someone with whom you can discuss your practice as a whole, its several components and their relationships to the overall practice.

11. Look to consequences, to "by their fruits ye shall know them" as the best principle of evaluation. While evaluation of our practice is complex, and in many ways beyond the ken of the practioner (see Dogen in number 5 above), there are some broad principles on which we can rely. Following the Christian tradition of identifying "marks of salvation" to distinguish true from false practice within the sanctification process, Paul Tillich provides four: "first, increasing awareness; second, increasing freedom; third, increasing relatedness; fourth, increasing self-transcendence."[16] Henry Nelson Wieman, a great empirical theologian of the Chicago School, also has four: "emerging awareness of qualitative meaning derived from other persons through communication; integrating these new meanings with others previously acquired; expanding the richness of quality in the appreciable world by enlarging its meaning; deepening the community among those who participate in this total creative event of intercommunication."[17]

I look back at the list I have just written. It is so simple and humbling. Of course it only makes sense that I fill in many details from the particularity of my own life, which would be confusing or trite to share here. Practice must be individualized. It is also important to note that our practice keeps developing, so that some subset of these components will be more figural in one phase, and another subset in the next—that the order of priority of this list is highly variable (or, again, best seen in a circular configuration).

In another way, I see my list as too complex. I recall a conversation with Huston Smith in which he identified three elements of his practice: hatha yoga for the body, reading of religious classics for the mind, and meditation for the soul. These seem beautifully sufficient. Actually, after articulating these, he paused, and then added, in all sincerity, a fourth: composting. He collects organic waste from the kitchen, carries it to a compost pile in the yard, and then his wife uses the compost to grow vegetables and flowers.[18] For him this is not mere housekeeping. Maybe his list of four is more helpful than mine; maybe together his and mine point to the importance of our each developing a sensitivity to and an ongoing alertness about our own components of practice.

Perhaps at some time there will be no need of identifying components; we will get to the point where all we need to say to ourselves about our practice is what Augustine said: "love God and do what you please," or Confucius: "give my heart-and-mind free reign." Until that time, we need structure and discipline and continuous refinement.

RESISTANCE, FAITH, AND SURRENDER

Above all, though, we need to begin.

Why is it so difficult to maintain the faith—is this not what it is?—which makes it possible to begin and persist? This brings us to a necessary topic in the discussion of practice, and that is resistance, inhibition, refusal. There is something deep within us which causes us to hold back and avoid our own growth and thriving. Of course this is part of ego, which can be very subtle in the invention of reasons why practice is unnecessary, even dangerous, or may be put off until another time.

At the deepest level, there seems to be something about the human being itself which *refuses*, refuses thriving and the gift quality of life altogether, including its cultivation through practice. The gift is given, yet humans hide from it, obstruct and deflect, try to channel it into schemes of comfort, control, and self-aggrandizement. Ego again. It is as though ego prefers the perverse security of neurosis and failure to the indeterminateness of freedom, the unwell-being of "eternal return" in repetition of self and other-defeating patterns, the false humility of unworthiness—which so often alternates with its secret twin, which is arrogance. In fact, it is not all that unusual for we humans to maintain habits of refusal and self-censorship which require far more energy than do the disciplines of transformation.

This, of course, is the case with societies as well as individuals, most obviously in traditional societies where some few people were privileged with resources of actualization, and many others were defined as less than fully human and thereby excluded from the cultivation of their humanity. At a more subtle level, some post-traditional criticisms of Western culture take note of factors which have served to alienate even those who are privileged from the question and the resources of transformative practice. These factors include root ideas about religion which define salvation as an all or nothing, either-or thing: either you are among the elect or not, either you are predestined for heaven or not, either you believe or you do not. In Western history, this orientation was usually associated with two other ideas which reinforce the tendency to overlook practice: a "final" rather than ongoing or "process" view of creation, and an image of God as radically transcendent and known primarily through his giving of commandments and judgments. Within the frame of these ideas, there is little attention to practice, either before or after the singular act of submission, a state which can be given very definite and often exploitative direction when guided by ecclesiastical and/or political figures claiming to know and mediate the will of God/Allah.

The positive side of this package of ideas is that it emphasizes *grace,* salvation as God's miraculous act of—in the words of Paul Tillich— accepting those who are unacceptable (perhaps analogous to Buddhist insistence that you *are* the Buddha). But, again, in the mainline understanding in which this act is interpreted through the ideas just discussed, it is extremely difficult to answer the question as to how or why we should (or *can*) *do anything,* leading Alfred North Whitehead and others to identify doctrines of the atonement (or lack thereof) as the chief weakness in Christianity.[19]

As Charles Hartshorne, David Ray Griffin, and others have observed, these limitations in the mainline understandings of faith and surrender have driven many Western people to atheism.[20] They have also driven to rejections of "religion" in favor of simple or romanticized views of "spirituality," as well as interest in Asian approaches to practice. And they have provoked the emergence of an effective alternative in the more empirical and naturalistic ways of speaking which are found in process philosophy, feminist theology,[21] and pragmatism within the American tradition.

Which brings us back to our old friend William James. He presents an understanding of faith and practice which is based on ordinary and natural experiences which are quite familiar to most of us—despite the fact that mainline culture has done little to identify these experiences as significant, and to cultivate them through forms of practice. His is a vision of spirituality which can be cultivated in the normal and natural immediacy of life, rather than exclusively from above and outside. The experience he lifts up in his mature work as *the most* significant in religious life is "the experience of new ranges of life succeeding upon our most despairing moments." There are moments in our actual, ordinary lives when we experience *being faithful,* where faith is understood as a state of having access to a deeper or finer energy, the unseen order, or the presence of God or the *Dao*—as in living in good faith, or living in truth, or in sincerity. From this perspective, practice becomes doing what we can in the present to be open to these self-evidently good and desirable experiences as they may occur in the future, letting our lives be transformed by them, moving from their being extraordinary experiences to their being the ordinary environment in which we live our lives.

But we should expand the definition of religious experience beyond what happens after or through the despairing moments to which James refers—lest we wind up cultivating these in an unnecessarily ascetic or even morbid form of practice. The moments we value can also be naturally occurring experiences of "the silence that allows you to do each thing just right," of profound insight, or of deep appreciation of the goodness which abides in the midst of ordinary life, moments of "flow" or "peak experience." These moments in which we experience being faithful are moments when we experience the identity of our will with that of another which is paradoxically both "wholly other" and "more near to ourselves" than our ordinary ego identity. They are moments when the "unseen order" breaks through, guiding and energizing our lives, often without any overt drama at all, transforming, enabling us to live through an energy vastly larger than our own. In our practice we engage faith not only in the goodness of the unseen order through which these experiences arise, but also in the capacity of those traditions and disciplines which we appropriate so that we might develop toward more continuous sustaining of those experiences—and faith in ourselves as beings who are capable of being more than we presently are, as bearers of that which is ultimate in life.

However, especially given the radical and potentially dangerous nature of this last point from the standpoint of the traditions, it is necessary to conclude this discussion of practice with the root theme of compassion and return. Martin Luther King says it well in terms of our remaining faithful to "the first law of life":

> From time immemorial men [*sic*] have lived by the principle that "self-preservation is the first law of life." But this is a false assumption. I would say that other-preservation is the first law of life. It is the first law of life precisely because we cannot preserve self without being concerned about preserving other selves. The universe is so structured that things go awry if men are not diligent in their cultivation of the other-regarding dimension. [22]

He goes on to say that "we are in the fortunate position of having our deepest sense of morality coalesce with our self-interests." Again, there is no distinction between the means and ends of practice. The maturity of practice entails this awareness: that the ordinary is the locus of maturity and enlightenment, and that love/compassion is the vital center of the ordinary.

NOTES

1. Bellah, "Religious Evolution," p. 42.
2. James, *A Pluralistic Universe*, p. 272.
3. Rinehold Niebuhr, *The Children of Light and the Children of Darkness*, vi.

4. Emmanuel Levinas, *Totality and Infinity: An Essay on Exterioriy,* Alphonso Lingis, trans. (Pittsburgh, PA: Duquesne University Press, 1969).

5. Robert M.Pirsig, *Zen and the Art of Motorcycle Maintenance* (New York: William Morow, 1974), p. 242.

6. Confucius, *Analects* 2:4, in *The Analects of Confucius*, pp. 76–77.

7. Armstrong, *The Great Transformation.*

8. Dietrich Bonhoeffer, *Letters and Papers from Prison* (New York: Macmillan, 1976), p. 381.

9. Speaking broadly of Western history, it is important to note that as early as Plato the dimension of return (and hence the possibility of democracy as well) was eclipsed by intellectual system and authority, knowing and command. As Plato's career progressed, from relatively simple reporting on the doings and sayings of Socrates in the early dialogues to his own interpretation in *The Republic,* the relational dimension was lost. The only way to get the enlightened one to return as the Philosopher King to that Cave of Ignorance which is the world was *compulsion.* By contrast, with Socrates the relational principle—or the principle of return—is integral to enlightenment itself, essential to both its pursuit and its completion. It is as though the democratic principle of Socrates has been remembered dimly in Western history, and even rediscovered from time to time, but not supported in thought due to the dominance of Platonic doctrine. But on the other hand: for the possibility that there is an internal principle of return in Plato, and for a more subtle reading of *The Republic,* see Mitchell Miller, "Platonic Provocations: Reflections on the Good in the *Republic,* in *Platonic Investigations,"* ed. Dominic J. O'Meara (Washington, DC: Catholic University of America Press, 1986), pp. 190–193.

10. Caroline Whitbeck, "A Different Reality: Feminist Ontology," in Carol C. Gould, ed., *Beyond Domination: New Perspectives on Women and Philosophy* (Totowa, NJ: Rowman & Allanheld, 1983), p. 65.

11. James, *A Pluralistic Universe,* p. 128.

12. Pierre Hadot, *Philosophy as a Way of Life* (Malden, MA: Blackwell Publishing, 1995).

13. Ironic because relatively few actually take advantage of the availability, because, in addition to the machine-like speed with which we live today, the abundance of options tends to result in paralytic response to choice. This is related to earlier comments about the possibility that the traditions are not only available in our time, but more purely or intensely available than they have been at any time since the Axial Age—heightening the irony.

14. Aristotle, *Nicomachean Ethics,* Book II, 4:30, 1105b. In *The Basic Works of Aristotle,* ed., Richard McKeon (New York: Random House, 1941), p. 956.

15. Dogen, *Moon in a Dewdrop: Writings of Zen Master Dogen, ed.,* Kazuaki Tanahashi (San Francisco: North Point Press, 1985), p. 15.

16. Paul Tillich, *Systematic Theology* (Chicago: University of Chicago Press, 1967), vol. 3, p. 231.

17. Henry Nelson Wieman, *The Source of Human Good* (Carbondale: Southern Illinois University Press, 1946), p. 58.

18. From a series of interviews at Smith's home in the Winter and Spring of 1999. Recordings and videos are housed with the Smith papers in Berkeley.

19. Whitehead, *Adventures of Ideas,* p. 170.

20. David Ray Griffin, "God in Process," in David Stewart, ed., *Exploring the Philosophy of Religion,* Sixth Edition (Upper Saddle River, NY: Pearson Education, 2007), p. 177. This piece of Griffin's is also an excellent, short presentation of the process view of Whitehead, Hartshorne, and Wieman, arising from the Chicago school of empirical theology.

21. For a prominent example, see Rosemary Radford Ruether, *Sexism and God Talk: Toward a Feminist Theology* (Boston: Beacon Press, 1983).

22. King, *Where Do We Go from Here?,* p. 180.

Chapter Thirteen

Liberal Education as Democratic Practice

CLAIMING A LIBERAL EDUCATION

Liberal education is the most prominent, effective, and well-supported form of democratic practice in American life. Liberal education is not only *preparation* for democracy, it *is* democracy insofar as it entails direct exercise and development of those interdependent arts which are at the heart of both democracy and human maturity: engagement of ourselves and each other in relation to the issues of our public or common life, the developed ability to both state one's own position and at the same time be open to the positions of others—*and* open as well to the new or expanded truth that emerges from the dialogical encounter of a community or relationship in which diversity and unity are mutually enhancing, and supportive of continuous learning, growth, and good policy decisions.

Many things, of course, are labeled "liberal education," since the term itself, like "democracy" or "dialogue," carries favorable connotation. But I want to say that this label is inappropriate unless the educational form to which it is affixed shows substantial commitment to the core practice just described. Without this core, education becomes mere transmission of what Alfred North Whitehead calls "inert knowledge," all "impression" without the necessary "expression" in William James' articulation, the "the beauty parlor" conception of art and ideas according to John Dewey, or "the banking concept" of education in Paulo Freire.[1] It becomes intellectualism severed from cultivation of the whole person and the virtues of compassion and civic virtue, an intellectualism which is expressed not only as the ivory tower academics which Americans love to hate, but more pervasively today as people who live in the cold environment of technique, procedure, money, and management—in mechanism alone, severed from the beating heart of real life. Failed liberal education devolves into either equipping elites with the trappings of "culture," or training of workers—training in either case, not education as transformation, as *e-ducare,* the leading out or drawing forth of the genuine self from the morass of ego. Without that crucial core which is shared with democracy, education becomes mere content without engagement with any part of us other than mind; without the depth dimension which leads us beyond mere knowledge to practical wisdom (*phronesis*).[2]

Awareness of the intimate connection between democracy and liberal education enables us to appreciate a great strength of America which is often overlooked. For America is blessed with an amazingly rich and pluralistic system of higher education, and one which is centered on the commitment to liberal education. Excluding vocational, technical, and paraprofessional programs, this commitment is evident to varying degrees across the broad spectrum of institutions which award the baccalaureate degree. Certainly liberal education is tepid in many programs, at best a kind of lip service paid to the requirement that students take "distribution" or "general education" courses on their way to specialization in the major. In many public and private colleges and universities liberal education is spoken of as becoming "well-rounded," or developed as a "whole person" and someone who has become a "lifelong learner." Other places more ambitiously engage students in active learning, experiential learning, service learning—all this variously mixed in the name of liberal education. The American system of higher education is highly diverse, but within and under and through the diversity, it is held together by the commitment to liberal education—which, again, can be seen as a profound expression of the democratic spirit in America.

Considering the great diversity of approaches to liberal education in American higher education, two factors immediately stand out. First, what works in one place does not necessarily work in another. After surveying liberal education as it is practiced more or less successfully in different settings—demographically, institutionally, pedagogically, one is drawn to a conclusion that may be uncomfortable for some: liberal education is both real, as in something that is either present or not, and yet at the same time something for which there is no one formula, no universal technique, no single scale by which to measure its intensity (which is why, as Whitehead pointed out long ago, the current enthusiasm for "assessment" through quantitative measures and standardized teaching is dangerous: it is yet another universalization which violates the local circumstances in which alone life can be lived with richness and grace. It is scientism in the process of eclipsing the humanities side of Western culture). In this respect liberal education is like love, justice, beauty, goodness, truth and those other essential qualities of life—including democracy—that insist on remaining ineffable; very real but not susceptible to any final or universal statement, always working together with the "local knowledge" of particular situations. It is an art and not a science.

The second thing is that a student (and/or a professor) could *miss* a liberal education even in those colleges and universities that are most vigorous in its practice. Liberal education can never be done *to* one. Just because a college or university has a great curriculum or an excellent faculty, this does not guarantee that liberal education is occurring. It requires choice and conscious engagement by both students and professors; it must be identified as something valuable, and a commitment must be made. A liberal education must be *claimed.*[3]

IDEAS AND RELATIONSHIPS

My statements above are predicated on a reappropriation which has not yet been made explicit, a deeper understanding of the meaning and value of liberal education—and, given the radical claim of equivalency between liberal education and democracy with which this chapter began, of democracy as well. What follows, then, is a reconsideration of liberal education from the standpointof our post-traditional moment.

Liberal education is grounded in a simple point which has been basic to human culture in the Traditional Period of human history (from the Axial Period of the first millennium B.C.E., to sometime in the 20th century), and yet which was put into eclipse by the bright lights and glitter of modern society: that human beings are different from other life forms (so far as we know) in that the mature form does not unfold out of the natural process without cultivation, without a discipline of transformation which is consciously employed for the purpose of bringing human beings to the fullness of their development.

Throughout history and across cultures there has been a great variety of methods for intervening in the natural process to introduce a discipline of cultivation—through many activities and functions, some physical, some intellectual, some more oriented to arts, some to ideas, others to ritual performance, all spiritual in the sense that they envision a transformation of ordinary human capacities. Beneath the variety there has always been attention to *practice,* as the kind of activity that gives rise to nothing less than the fullness of ourselves. And along with this attention there has been distinction between this fundamentally human kind of activity and the other activities in which we engage for *productive* reasons, in order to make or cause or control. As distinct from the productive activities, the cultivation of humans has been articulated in the West as "an end in itself," or as something that is "good for its own sake." These potentially confusing phrases point to a central truth in human life as it was envisioned in traditional cultures: that cultivation of the mature form of human being requires renunciation of all extrinsic or instrumental purpose. Coming to the fullness of who we really are is good in a way that is quite independent of whatever pleasure or pain might follow as a consequence, whatever advantage or disadvantage, whatever gain or loss as measured by the society in which one lives.

Zooming in to the Western tradition of liberal education in particular, there have been two primary and inter-dependent media for the predominant Western discipline of transformation which has been called liberal education: ideas and relationships. Holding these two together has been the challenge, and it is possible to distinguish many of the typical problems of Western education and culture by what happens when they become separated. The history of education, especially in the post-traditional 20th century, exemplifies this in the tension between "traditional" and "progressive" (sometimes "experiential" or "alternative"—often defined negatively, in opposition to the "traditional" approaches to liberal education). The traditional is criticized as being only delivery of ideas to be memorized and banked away for future use—as all idea and no relationship. But meanwhile the progressive approach is discovered to have a tendency toward becoming incoherent and/or relativistic, to degenerate into either reflecting the whims of popular culture and politics or an unexamined ideology of opposition—as all relationship of the immediate moment and no guiding ideas. And, of course, this tension in education can be seen as manifestation of a fundamental dichotomy which runs throughout Western culture itself, in the tension between theory and practice, mind and body, conservatives and liberals, Plato and Aristotle, even Athens and Jerusalem.

The vision of complementarity or synergy between ideas and relationships presupposes a mature understanding of each. And likewise, the oppositions and either/ors that make up so much of Western history can be seen as a function of falling back into immature understanding.

Ideas in the mature sense are not just intellectual constructs, concepts, or knowledge in the usual sense of those terms. In fact, it is precisely the usual sense of those terms which has led to intellectualism, mentalism, Cartesianism, or the logocentrism which we discover in the postmodern condition to be the root of so many problems in the history of the West. Ideas in the full sense indicate those questions or issues or insights into reality on which our existence depends, and the articulation of them in such a way that they bring us to the critical state out of which transformation occurs, a state which can be described as *aporia* and *wonder,* a state in which we can actually tune ourselves to greater harmony with reality. *Aporia* is a state of not-knowing, a state of being beyond knowing as it has been experienced in the past, of "knowing that I know nothing" in the Socratic sense. This is not, however, a state of ignorance or skepticism, but rather a state in which one experiences something like the *source* of knowing as distinct from merely things which are known. It is a state of wonder—as in Socrates' "philosophy begins in wonder" (*Theaetus, 155d*), again, as a state of being energized through direct contact with source, with a quality of life that is more like a verb than a noun, with an indescribable but essential *energy* which is paradoxically both the energy of the universe and the energy of one's own genuine self. Ideas in the full and nonderivative sense can be thought of on the analogy of valves, as openings through which the basic life-energy flows, so that the joy of real thinking can be understood by its proximity to creativity itself (way beyond the simple moving around of inert concepts).[4]

Relationship, in its own full sense, points to that space in the world where one is able to appear and be active as one's own real self, which is at the same time the space in which ideas can come alive and be radiant. What is envisioned is a particular kind of relationship, one which is beyond transaction or exchange, manipulation, command, power and interest, negotiation and contract—the usual senses of relationship which in the West drive toward either sad isolation or dangerous fusion, either individualism or collectivism (see previous chapters). As with ideas, the doorway to understanding the kind of relationship that is essential to liberal education (and democracy) is paradox: within the relationship in which commonality and distinctiveness are maximized together simultaneously we experience being present in our genuineness; in mutuality we experience thriving, and the locus of our fulfillment as human beings. And yet without the discipline and definiteness of ideas, as well as their inspirational quality, relationality loses discipline and direction, becomes susceptible to the "whatever" relativism and insincere pleasantness of our era.

In the vision of liberal education and democratic society, ideas apart from relationships become hard and closed objects, basically weapons and/or containers, while relationships without ideas drift toward either sentimentality or manipulative opportunism—either way, unanchored by well-examined commitment and purpose.

The classical statement of proper unification of ideas and relationship, and the practice through which they each come to fullness, is Socrates in "The Apology." The center of it is his famous statement about the unexamined life being not worth living. Actually, his statement is much more full than this, and can be seen as the core practice of both liberal education and democratic culture:

> I tell you that to let no day pass without discussing goodness and the other
> subjects about which you hear me talking and examining both myself and
> others is really the very best thing that a man [*sic*] can do and that life without
> this sort of examination is not worth living.[5]

What is he saying? First of all, there is the huge claim that "this sort of examination" is "the very best thing" that a person can do. For Socrates, this examination is the central discipline of human transformation; all other goods in human life follow from this root practice. Second, the currency of examination is "goodness and the other subjects," which means ideas, and those ideas in particular that really matter to us, ideas, as I suggested before, on which our lives depend. Note, again, that the idea of "goodness" for Socrates was not an abstract or merely academic subject, but rather a matter of immediate and practical concern. In the same dialogue he distinguishes goodness from both wealth and fame as goals around which people tend to organize their lives. Ideas, in the Socratic understanding, are much closer to *values* than they are to the merely conceptual. Also note—especially in contemporary America—that ideas are quite different from inner psychological states: ideas converge and bring us to that which is common, while psychological states claim uniqueness and lead to isolation—to "the infinite regress of motive," as Hannah Arendt put it.[6] Indeed, the contrast between Socrates' method and those prevalent contemporary forms of therapy which are oriented to exploration of psychological states becomes most clear when we compare results, and specifically results in terms of what kinds and intensities of energy become available through the process. We see that many forms of therapy are only further extensions of the control-oriented Western individualism, and that their libratory energy is often low.

But, again, in order for the power of ideas to be released they need the specific kind of relationship which is invoked by Socrates. In the quotation from the *Apology,* the necessarily relational context of our intercourse with ideas is indicated by his reference to "examining both myself and others." It is not examining self only, not introspection or isolated reflection. But neither is the kind of relationship Socrates points to one in which we simply receive what is handed down from authority. Rather, it is mutual. In this relation I am able to say what I really think about the idea we pursue together; goodness, justice, love, and subsets of these—as long as they are of real concern in our lives, and not merely academic subjects or intellectual puzzles. And in the warmth of mutuality I am able to withstand the crucial moment of *aporia* or wonder, when you help me discover that I do not in fact know what I thought I knew. And it is precisely at this moment when the synergy between idea and relationship begins to release an energy within the self which is the source of real growth. It is the energy Socrates speaks of as access to the "divine sign," *daimon,* or "inner voice," which we can interpret as the fundamental genuineness, integrity, or authenticity of the person.[7] Practice of the examined life is "the very best thing a person can do" because it gives birth the fully developed person. This is why Socrates was known as a midwife.

To fully appreciate the vision of Socrates in the present, I think it helpful to consider those more recent advocates of liberal education who have spoken of it as initiation into the conversation out of which democratic culture is woven. One powerful example is Michael Oakeshott:

> Perhaps we may think [of the components of a culture] as voices, each the expression of a distinct and conditional understanding of the world and a distinct idiom of human self-understanding, and of the culture itself as these voices joined, as such voices could only be joined, in a conversation—an endless unrehearsed intellectual adventure in which, in imagination, we enter into a variety of modes of understanding the world and ourselves and are not disconcerted by the differences or dismayed by the inconclusiveness of it all. And perhaps we may recognize liberal learning as, above all else, an education in imagination, an initiation into the art of this conversation in which we learn to recognize the voices. [8]

Note that in recent years this same art is sometimes referred to as "dialogue." But the most basic point is that liberal education is a stream of possibility for both self and world that runs from Socrates into the present. As such, it needs to be understood as one of the world's great traditions of human cultivation and transformation. Indeed, it is the close association between liberal education and a certain understanding of philosophy in the West that has led Huston Smith, one of our greatest interpreters of the Traditional Period of human history, to refer to "Western Philosophy as a World Religion." [9] It is religious in that liberal education and Socratic philosophy are in their essence oriented to transformation and enlightenment. Envisioning what is possible through the co-presence of ideas and relationships, or through engagement of the conversational/dialogical practice which is common to liberal education and democracy, consider Socrates' statement: "Acquaintance with it must come rather through a long period of attendance on instruction in the subject itself and of close companionship, when suddenly, like a blaze kindled by a leaping spark, it is generated in the soul and at once becomes self-sustaining." [10] Is this not very close to what other traditions describe as enlightenment?

CONTEMPORARY AGENDA

But presentation of historical and transhistorical ideals is of limited value unless we also think in more proximate terms about how they could come to life in the present. "Reappropriation" requires identification of vitality in both past *and* present. Again, liberal education must be "claimed," reappropriated fresh in each generation, as what David Bromwich has called a "non-restrictive tradition."

Turning to the present, then, I want to focus on the conversation about liberal education as it is occurring within three of the primary national associations devoted to its support, associations from which a great number of local colleges and universities draw language, direction, and often whole programs of institutional and curricular development: The American Association of Colleges and Universities (AAC&U), the Society for Values in Higher Education (SVHE), and the Council on Public Liberal Arts Colleges (COPLAC).[11] There is amazing consistency between them in terms of how they see a necessary linkage between liberal education and democracy, in ways which are entirely consistent with the Ideas-Relationships view I have just presented. It is with this close association in mind, then, that I share my reading of the underlying and tightly interdependent themes of liberal education in America today. I want to state each of them as compactly as possible, hoping for a useful panorama. There are five:

1. *Diversity/Inclusion:* Reflecting what I have called America's third great crisis, the crisis of second generation economic, social, and cultural rights, the movement beyond toleration, as a neutral acceptance, to the positive affirmation of difference, alterity, otherness, is a major theme. The AAC&U, for example, speaks of "diversity and inclusion as a multi-layered process through which we achieve excellence in learning; research and teaching; student development; institutional functioning; local and global community engagement; workforce development; and more." In curriculum development discussions especially, there is much concern with the dynamics of moving beyond toleration, as well as beyond a later stage (generally corresponding with the universalism stage discussed in chapter 8) of diversity as friendliness or appreciation—the "Pizza, Sushi, Falafel" approach referred to before (in chapter 9). This approach is sometimes recognized as containing a new and hidden imperialism of modernization or homogenization, a dissolving of otherness or reduction of it to the level of modern "lifestyles," or to the laws of social science. The concern is to move into a stage of full affirmation in which otherness is preserved and enhanced at the same time self and the encounter (or the public space) is enhanced also. Breaking through the antinomy of unity and diversity, or the "Catch 22" of forms of unity which suppress diversity versus diversity which is chaotic, is sometimes acknowledged as the challenge, and meeting it is often taken to be essentially a developmental challenge.

2. *Democracy:* This theme, in the tight interdependence of all five themes, is linked closely to the diversity theme, as in this AAC&U statement: "[it] is our conviction that democracy cannot fulfill its

aspirations without acknowledging diversity and that diversity finds its moral compass in democratic values and principles." Democracy is usually understood to be deliberative democracy, "[which] engages citizens, encourages participation and collective action, and leads to meaningful, sustainable change." According to SVHE, the challenge is "to create intentionally designed and ongoing opportunities for identifying, studying, deliberating, and acting on problems with social and ethical implications and to draw from the work of experienced community builders and practioners in deliberative democracy."

3. *Sustainability/Global Perspective:* This theme, already evident in the SVHE program mentioned above, represents direct response to environmental crisis, the necessity of cultivating an interdependent, global perspective, and "sustainability" as something more than maintenance of the status quo. These elements are stated clearly at the beginning of a COPLAC program entitled "Sustaining Democracy, Sustaining the Environment: The Liberal Arts Mission:" "A vital question facing our democracy is how we as individuals, as a nation, and as global citizens, can preserve the environmental richness we have and alleviate environmental deprivation where that exists." Here "sustainability" is similar to "diversity" in that the term indicates a positive ideal that is not yet fully articulated, one which is associated with both democracy and developmental challenge. Sustainability is, in a way, an aesthetic ideal—of maximum diversity within a stable system, and envisions simultaneity with democracy such that it is possible to have both sustainability without authoritarianism and democracy without environmental degradation. Again, the implicit ideal is not yet fully stated, and is probably not stateable in traditional Western intellectual formulation because it entails the vital paradox of a certain kind of community and relationship, and a developmental and experiential threshold on the near side of which it cannot make sense.

4. *Service/Civic Engagement:* This theme, in its broadest sense, is well-stated in a AAC&U program: "This type of learning engenders connections between scholarship and public questions, considers alternative frameworks for judgment and action, draws meaning from experience, critiques theory in light of practice, and evaluates practice in light of new knowledge." At a deeper level, though, this theme indicates something like what I have been referring to as "civic virtue," indicating that care for the commonly shared life and the open space of encounter which at the same time is understood to be the best thing a person can do to cultivate their own humanity. Here is the theme of "return" we have discussed earlier in relation to religious practice. Usage of the terms "civic engagement" and "service" in this

sense indicate something larger than simply volunteering, something very much like the kind of experience and relationship which are understood to be implicit in "diversity," "sustainability," and "democracy." And it seems very distinctive of our era that in this fourth theme the emphasis is not on the *definition* of these terms, but rather on their *enactment.* Here traditional forms of understanding are no longer seen as necessary and prior to the doing of it, the practice. This is evident in the AAC&U document just cited, in which the relationship between theory and practice is much more complex and dynamic than it was in the "epistemology prior" orientation of liberal education and Western culture generally which came to prevail in the traditional period, where intellectual resolution in theory was taken to be a necessary pre-requisite for its subsequent application in practice. Now, it seems, necessary principles of guidance and purpose can come from shared commitments and dense relationship, rather than from an external and static intellectual formulation (without, at the same time, denying the value of "new knowledge").

5. *Development:* This theme is inclusive of the others, and like the others it contains several layers. At one level it reflects the tendency to define liberal education not in the more traditional terms of subject matter and knowledge to be acquired, as in terms of skills and qualities to be developed. This is associated with certain key terms which are often present in the discussion: "critical thinking," "reflexivity," "learning how to learn," and "dialogue." At a level deeper than individual qualities to be developed, these terms center on the same critical threshold mentioned above, on the far side of which it becomes possible to live a kind of life which is responsive to diversity, sustainability, and democracy as envisioned in the previous themes. And this, in turn, involves growing into the more complex and dynamic orientation to the intellect just mentioned in discussion of the previous theme, and greater attentiveness to the wisdom which arises out of practice and relationship.

Probably the work most influential among educators on the crossing of this threshold is William Perry's *Forms of Moral and Intellectual Development in the College Years.* Perry describes a developmental movement which occurs in the passage through college, as a sort of curriculum underneath the more formal curriculum of catalogues and courses and majors. It progresses through three stages: (1) Absolutism, which presupposes that for every question there is a right answer and a known authority; (2) Relativism, which presupposes many answers to all questions, each as good as the other, and all a matter of nothing more than personal preference and power—driving to the nihilism we have been discussing throughout; and (3) Commitment, which centers on "an affirmation made in a world perceived as relativistic, that is, *after* detachment, doubt, and awareness of alternatives have made the experience of personal choice a possibility."[12] Commitments, then, are acts of choice which "require the courage of responsibility, and presuppose an acceptance of human limits, including the limits of reason."[13] In terms of the earlier discussion, commitments can be seen as arising from the experience of Nothingness as source.

It is my suggestion that it is precisely the crossing of this developmental threshold which makes it possible for us to grow beyond intellectualism and the world of ideology, to enter a relational/democratic world. In this world it becomes possible to decide for commitment—including those to other persons, vocational, cultural, and political purposes, and forms of practice—while at the same time maintaining awareness of their limitations, the possibility of further refinement and growth, and being able to thrive in relationships of simultaneous similarity and difference—beyond the antinomy of reductive sameness or complete incommensurability. Here we have what some call a "paradigm shift," and the very transition to a relational world I have been pointing to throughout this text.

Concluding discussion of the five themes, I want to mention a significant omission, namely the dialogical/comparative approach to reappropriation which is advocated throughout this book. For example, Western reappropriations of Socrates can appreciate the depth of his vision of transformation through the conversations of "the examined life" when they see him alongside Confucius, with his claim that "when strolling in the company of just two other persons, I am bound to find a teacher." And likewise, the full implication of Confucius' vision of the power of sincerity (*Cheng*) to well order both self and world might be appreciated more broadly when seen alongside the Socratic claim to "know nothing" and being guided by an "inner voice." In other words, the only way to nurture mature human beings in our era is to let the meaning of this nurturance remain an open question—a real question rather than just a "whatever," a question which both reflects and honors the pluralistic nature of our shared humanity itself, as the kind of question about which there are more than one right answer, the kind of room into which there is more than just one door.[14]

A DEMOCRATIC CURRICULUM

How to understand this report and interpretation in relation to reappropriation of the democratic spirit in America?

I think it is important to see liberal education functioning not only for individuals, but also for American culture as a whole. Certainly liberal education serves an important representative function, especially insofar as it is widely available and practiced—to greater or lesser degrees of intensity. There is a remarkable sense in which it is a medium for engagement, deliberation, and working through of the most basic imperatives and challenges of American life, including those mentioned earlier in the larger conversation of this book: the most general imperative of adopting a new way of living, and the three subsidiary imperatives of growth, otherness, and the adoption of an effective practice.

Liberal education, in this way, can be seen as a sort of metacurriculum of American culture; with classrooms among the most effective and healthy public spaces we have in America at this point. This is the case in both the idea and the relationship aspects of liberal education which were discussed earlier in this chapter. The primary ideas are those of democracy, diversity, development, and sustainability; and relationships center on the aim of including the widest possible diversity of fellow-learners, not only within educational institutions but also in the broader local and global communities.

We have seen liberal education addressing two issues in particular, two of which are arguably the deepest and most basic issues of America culture in our time.

The first issue is that of inclusion and diversity. We have seen the sense in which liberal education is a context of experimentation and discovery within the third great crisis of American history, the crisis of expansion into affirmation of second generation rights. There is an ideal of unity in diversity which is present in the larger discussion of liberal education, though it is one which is not yet fully articulated and embraced in practice. But the effort and the intention is clearly present—as is the ideal itself though in ways which are often hazy or misplaced. It is a work in process. And certainly there are failures. I recall, for example, Erin O'Connor's account of the controversy surrounding reading Barbara Ehrenreich's *Nickel and Dimed: On (Not) Getting By in America*in freshman orientation programs at a number of colleges and universities. She says that "on both sides of the debate [about the appropriateness of this reading], a book's politics are assumed to matter more than its scholarly merit or literary quality," and she concludes by sharing the fear that "in the name of eliminating 'bias,' American education has been reduced to a banal exercise in multicultural appeasement."[15]

The second issue is that of moving past the ideological conflict which so typifies our time, to discover the proper role of the intellect. Should the intellect be the primary organ in human life, expressed as both technological control and the generation of fixed and rigid ideological positions which define the person? Or rather, should it serve something larger and somewhat illusive from the strictly intellectual perspective?—whether that larger quality be conceived in terms of the common good or the well-being of the individual? I have gone so far as to suggest that discussions about the practice of liberal education entail the developmental movement from traditional/absolutistic/intellectualist culture, which becomes dangerously ideological in our time, to a relational worldview. In educational terms, we are talking about movement past the 20th-century antinomy of "traditional education" which simply delivers intellectual products, versus "alternative education" which is overly-loaded toward feelings and mere self-expression.[16]

In the relational paradigm the proper role of the intellect can be seen as one of *pointing and supporting.* It can point to those adjustments of action and practice which contribute to the maximizing of democracy, diversity, development, and sustainability. In this frame, the intellect can never *contain* the essential relationship of mutuality and communication in a theory or technique, but it can support the kind of action which makes this relationship more widely accessible; it can bring critical resources of historical precedent, relevant knowledge, and evaluative insight. No longer an idol of purity, control, and transcendence of life, the intellect now *enters life* and takes up a profoundly significant supporting role. Far from diminishing the importance of ideas, this decisive shift allows ideas to be redeemed from the merely conceptual, so that they can be restored in their transformative power—as openings through which democratic life can be nourished and inspired, allowing relationships to grow beyond their constraint in the *laissez faire* exchange of Western individualism.

In the midst of the crises of our time, it is easy to overlook or take for granted the enormous contribution of liberal education to the nourishment and maintenance of a democratic society. I conclude this chapter by sharing the words of Martha Nussbaum, a fellow citizen and colleague who reminds us in a most helpful way of the grandeur of what we are doing in America, of the close relationship between education and democracy, and of how America might be valued in the world community:

> Our country has embarked on an unparalleled experiment, inspired by these ideals of self-command and cultivated humanity. Unlike all other nations, we seek a higher education to contribute a general preparation for citizenship, not just a specialized preparation for a career. To a greater degree than all other nations, we have tried to extend the benefits of this education to all citizens, whatever their class, race, sex, ethnicity, or religion. We hope to draw citizens toward one another by complex mutual understanding and individual self-scrutiny, building a democratic culture that is truly deliberative and reflective, rather than simply the collision of unexamined preferences. And we hope in this way to justify and perpetuate our nation's claim to be a valuable member

of a world community of nations that must increasingly learn how to
understand, respect, and communicate, if our common human problems are to
be constructively addressed.[17]

Indeed, the genius of America itself can be taken to exist in the interplay
between "complex mutual understanding" and "individual self-scrutiny," one
that must be taught and modeled in both political life and education. For the
complex mutuality of democracy is impossible without the mature or
transformed person. And at the same time, self-scrutiny goes astray without
democratic values of social transformation, the dignity of all people, and
conversation among the people as the best place to find wisdom—without
the "complex mutual understanding." Democracy and liberal education need
each other, for both completion and continuous correction. Indeed, as we
have seen from the contemporary discussion of liberal education, they tend
toward convergence, in something very much like the Confucian ideal of
society as a learning community.

CONVERSATIONAL ASIDE

*But all of the above will be dismissed by that form of nihilism which restricts
value to money and the personal pleasures it can support. For the relatively
large proportion of people of this orientation in America today, talk of ideas
and relationships, and transformation are just ways obsolete institutions
(and professors!) devise to extract money from consumers who should know
better.*

*The "practical" sentiment has crossed America in waves throughout its
history, sometimes as healthy corrective against abstraction and
intellectualism, and as the pragmatic wish to evaluate education by its actual
outcomes. But particularly in our time, it seems, it is concern about money
which is driving the critique. This is especially the case in the wake of the
Great Recession of 2008, and is encouraged by books like Andrew Hacker
and Claudia Dreifus's Higher Education?: How Colleges Are Wasting Our
Money and Failing Our Kids—and What We Can Do About It.[18]*

*While the book is actually a call for reform, the public debate which has
followed turns mostly on the financial utility of a college education, and the
question as to whether it is even necessary. Some, like William Gross,
Managing Director of Pacific Investment Management Company, argue that
American students are wasting their minds by going to college, and that "All
of us who have been there [Duke in his case] know an undergraduate
education is primarily a four year vacation interrupted by periodic bouts of*

cramming or Google plagiarizing."[19] *Others, like David Leonhardt, draw on different statistics, to demonstrate that people with a college degree make substantially more money, even in jobs that do not require the degree.*[20]

With few exceptions, the debate misses altogether the claim that a liberal education is necessary to anything like a democracy, and to the development of the kind of person who is able to live beyond the abyss of modern values. In fact, here precisely is where the nihilists, as those who have committed to the nihilistic conclusion about interest and power—and money—being the bottom line realities on this planet (see chapter 3), will become annoyed. They do not want to hear people like Carol Schneider, President of AAC&U, criticize a recent National Governors Association report which spoke about higher education almost completely in terms of job-creation by saying that "the report might at least acknowledge that governors are elected by citizens and that higher education plays a vital role in building civic capacity."[21] *Neither do they wish to hear people speak about crucial areas of study, such as ethics, where student learning is not easily assessed through quantitative measures.*[22] *And they certainly do not want to hear people like William Deresiewicz speak about a college education building those qualities of character which we see in the leader, as distinct from the mere bureaucrat, qualities of independent judgment, moral courage, and concentrated thinking.*[23]

I think it is important to be aware of the tendency of nihilists to become annoyed. Again, going back to the initial discussion of nihilism, there is a resentment and an impatience to it, and an insistence that others join them in their conclusion. It is as though they dimly recall something they once believed in and then gave up on in disappointment, a sense that they had been betrayed or duped. And the point is that this kind of experience leads to intolerance of those who still believe, and possibly even a wish to dismiss them in some aggressive way.

Awareness of these dangerous tendencies is likely to become all the more pertinent as we realize that the way out of the modern morass (if any) is through reclaiming the deeper appreciation and aspiration in life, a sense of affirmation and commitment to a better life which is shared and much more than material, and compassion as the one reliable guiding value—and the joy of ongoing conversation, both "philosophical" and in the halls of policy, as to how these ineffable values might be more fully embodied on this very fragile planet.

Perhaps awareness of danger goes hand-in-hand with awareness of an irony which is well-articulated by Schneider: "just as myopic policy advisors are urging a narrowing of American higher education, Asian countries are hastening to adapt our signature designs for liberal and general education."[24] *Actually, the same might be said for democracy.*

NOTES

1. Alfred North Whitehead, "The Aims of Education," in *The Aims of Education and Other Essays* (New York: Free Press, 1957), p. 5, William James, *Talks to Teachers on Psychology: and to Students on some of Life's Ideals* (New York: Norton, 1958), p. 39, John Dewey, *Art as Experience* (New York: Capricorn Books, 1958), p. 344, and Paulo Freire, *Pedagogy of the Oppressed* (New York: Continuum, 1998).

2. Note that protests against this orientation in Western culture often merely fly to the opposite pole, as in the objectivity-subjectivity dichotomy discussed in the previous chapter. Much of "alternative education," permissive child rearing, and modern attempts at art "freedom" generally have this quality of an entirely negative, "not this" approach, without any positive conception or ideal.

3. See my *Claiming a Liberal Education*.

4. Once again (as in chapter 1 above), I want to point to the significance of Jacob Needleman's *The Heart of Philosophy*. This work, along with Robert Cushman's *Therapeia: Plato's Conception of Philosophy* (Westport, CT: Greenwood Press, 1958) and Pierre Hadot's *Philosophy as a Way of Life: Spiritual Exercises from Socrates to Foucault*, have made available an understanding of Socrates and Western philosophy which was largely eclipsed by doctrinal readings of Plato in the Traditional Period. A foremost example of the power of Post-Traditional intercultural dialogue and comparative studies to open up the wisdom of one's own tradition, Needleman's work presents Socrates before the anti-relational and intellectualist tendencies of Plato took root.

5. Apology, 38a, in Plato, *Collected Dialogues*, p. 23.

6. Arendt, *The Human Condition*, p. 5.

7. *Apology,* 31d, 40a, in Plato, *The Collected Dialogues,* pp. 17, 24.

8. Michael Oakeshott, *The Voice of Liberal Learning* (New Haven: Yale University Press, 1089, p. 541.

9. Huston Smith, "Western Philosophy as a World Religion," i.e., the Western [Greek] transformative practice alongside that of other world religions.

10. Plato, *Letters* VII241c-d, in *The Collected Dialogues of Plato,* p. 1589.

11. All quotes from these associations in the remainder of this section are from their respective websites as of February of 2008. An updating review of these same websites in July of 2011 revealed little change. The possible exception is greater emphasis on the theme of development, possibly due to the influence of Martha Nussbaum's *Not for Profit: Liberal Education and Democratic Citizenship* (Princeton: Princeton University Press, 2010) which is structured around the distinction between economic development and "human development. "

12. William Perry, *Forms of Intellectual and Moral Development in the College Years* (New York: Holt, Rinehart and Winston, 1968), p. 136.

13. *Ibid.,* p. 135.

14. I delivered a lecture entitled "Confucius, Marx, and Socrates: The Need for Comparative General Education," at Jiao Tong University, Shanghai, PRC, on August 11, 2010. Publications forthcoming.

15. Erin O'Connor, "Misreading What Reading is For," in *The Chronicle of Higher Education,* 9/5/2003, http://chronicle.com/weekly/v50i0202b02001.htm, p. 4.

16. Here I join John Dewey and others in offering progressive education as a middle ground. See especially Dewey's *Experience and Education*.

17. Martha Nussbaum, *Cultivating Humanity*, 294.

18. Andrew Hacker and Claudia Dreifus, *Higher Education?: How Colleges are Wasting Our Money and Failing Our Kids—and What We Can Do About It* (NY: Times Books, 2010).

19. William Gross, "School Daze, School Daze / Good Old Golden Rules Days," www.pimco.com/EN/Insights/Pages/School-Daze-School-Daze, p. 1.

20. David Leonhardt, "Even for Cashiers, College Pays Off, in *New York Times,* "Sunday Review Section," June 26, 2011, p. 3.

21. Carol Geary Schneider, "'Degrees for What Jobs?' Wrong Question, Wrong Answers," in *The Chronicle of Higher Education*, 5/10/211, http://chronicle.com/article/Degrees-for-What-Jobs-Wrong/127328/

22. Peter Schmidt, "The Challenge of Putting a Grade on Ethical Learning," in *The Chronicle of Higher Education*, 7/5/2011, http://chronicle.com/article/The-Challenge-of-Putting-a/128086/?ke

23. William Deresiewicz, "Solitude and Leadership," in *The American Scholar*, 6/29/2011, http://theamericanscholar.org/solitude-and-leadership/print/

24. Schneider, p. 2.

Conclusion

Democracy Somewhere

In 18th-century North America, the vision of a life of liberty and justice for all within the vibrancy and continuous growth of an ever more inclusive community burst into flame. It resulted in the founding of the highly imperfect but very promising American republic, and (a little later) identification of the vision with the term "democracy."

While the promise of this vision persisted in the modern era which ensued, it was largely overshadowed by a more limited dream which also came to be associated with the word "democracy:" the natural rights dream of minimum government in a society in which everyone pursues their own interests and leaves everyone else alone, except to propose exchanges and contracts in the furthering of their interests. Under modern conditions in America and all across the world, this "American dream" of a better life in the material dimension had even stronger appeal than the earlier dream of inclusive community. And under its influence "democracy" came to be all but identified with market capitalism and governmental institutions of the ballot, representation, and protection of individual rights—surely not bad things, but very limited things in relation to the earlier ideal. Democracy as a way of life, as a vision of human development—into the fullness of human beings thriving in a community of diversity, deliberation, and mutual discovery—was all but forgotten.

But then a surprising thing happened in the late 20th century. With the emergence of a somewhat surprising "post-secular" era, there developed awareness that "the American dream" of hyper-individualism and consumption as the primary signifier of well-being is neither sustainable nor desirable—nor democratic. And out of the worldwide search for the good society which followed this awareness, two rather remarkable things happened. First, there was widespread recalling of the original democratic vision as "substantive," meaning as a way of life in which individual and communal dimensions are affirmed simultaneously, rather than only as "procedural" protections of the individual. The vision of governance through deliberation, discussion, and what Amartya Sen calls "public reasoning"[1] reappeared. And, second, it was discovered that the deeper democratic vision is by no means unique to Greece or European America, but truly global in its origins.[2]

These factors cause America to be seen in a different light, now more as one possibility rather than *the* possibility. The materialism of America is no longer so easily equated with the ideal, as a sign of close association with the best society or a democratic life. Now material excess is as likely to be understood as a function of greed and decadence as of God's favor. And the democratic life is no longer seen as unique to America. Peoples have been freed from a certain 20th-century illusion of America, free to find the values and dispositions of the good life within their own cultural heritage.[3]

And yet there remains a radiance to America, a strength and beauty. This is not so much, any longer, a function of standard of living or even quality of life, as it is testimony to America as an imperfect model of harmony among peoples from all over the world.

Both the strength and the beauty are revealed in the refrain at the center of the song of America: "We shall overcome." America has overcome monarchy, slavery, the denial of voting rights to women and minorities, several impossible wars, and to some degree racism, sexism, and classism. Perhaps it will now become capable of overcoming consumerism and the associated limitations of the modern life.

America has always been an improbable work in progress. And that which needs to be overcome has never been entirely external. America at its best exemplifies the self-overcoming which Nietzsche, Elizabeth Minnich, Masao Abe and many others have identified as the chief and most necessary attribute of the post-traditional person—the continuous adventure of reflexivity, re-envisioning, and growth. In our time it becomes clear that America itself needs to overcome the modernity which it exported to the whole world, proving there is something deeper and broader to the American vision than the life of consuming. America needs to preserve the best of modernity within an integration which leaves behind the negative values of the modern which have become so dramatically evident in our time. America needs to grow into a more perfect embodiment of "liberty and justice for all."

In this book I have attempted to speak of this possibility from a decidedly practical perspective, from the critical developmental threshold on which America and the world teeter in the present. For it seems clear that either America will be overcome by terrorists—those resentful others for whom access to "the American dream" is denied, and those who have been radicalized by awareness of its moral and spiritual limitations, its hypocrisy—or America will overcome itself with growth beyond the limited dream with which it came to be identified.

In some ways, the self-overcoming of America seems as simple as making the transition from first to second generation rights orientations—as these have been articulated in the 1948 UN Universal Declaration of Human Rights. The era of "first generation" focus on the autonomy of the individual is passing. This occurs as the negative "natural rights" of the individual (as free from this, free from that) are revealed to be a significant and necessary but ultimately limited in value. As part of the breakdown of the modern era we discover that these values, when asserted by themselves and in the absence of affirming community and relational values as well, are generative of loneliness and injustices associated with cultural dynamics which that earlier ideal could not comprehend. The new "second generation" era is focused on a broader ideal of positive social, economic, and cultural rights of both individuals and groups, based on awareness of the dynamics of culture and ecology, and a vision of the good life in which diversity, inclusion, and dialogue are not merely tolerated, but valued.

To say "simple," though, is not to say "easy." To say that a new worldview, a new paradigm, and a new developmental stage become available in our time is not to say that it will be able to take root sufficiently to inform policy decisions and the actions of everyday life on this planet.

Maybe, out of the turmoil of our period, a more perfect embodiment of this planet's magnificent vision of the good life as simultaneous affirmation of diversity and unity will occur somewhere other than in the USA. However this turns out, it seems appropriate to conclude the conversation of this book with one last attempt to articulate that grand aspiration which we know as democracy, as an ideal which is both American and global, arising from the worldwide struggle which America may have inspired and yet which America cannot control, and from a historical moment in which America may become a stepping stone to the fulfillment of that vision somewhere else.

So here it is, my best attempt at this moment to invoke in words that magnificent vision:

Hannah Arendt speaks of plurality as "the law of the earth."[4] What if infinite plurality really is the bottom line reality on this planet? What if, in William James's terms, we live in "a pluralistic universe," a universe in which even "God" has an external environment, as the necessary context within which it becomes possible to *do anything*, a context which either is or contains an *other* who could be met either as adversary or as friend? What if Martin Buber, in his iconic *I and Thou*, is correct?

> In the beginning is the relation—as the category of being, as readiness, as a form that reaches out to be filled, as a model of the soul; the *a priori* of relation; *the innate You*.[5]

What if relationality is as real as mass and energy, and is, in its most pure form, something like the absolute opposite of a black hole, a pure fecundity bordering on nothing but outer space? What if this is the human meaning of Einstein's famous theory of relativity, and the deep insight which caused him to remark in the end that "God does not play dice"?—that a relative universe is not an arbitrary universe but a relational universe of ever broader and deeper and richer relationships, where there is structure, not chaos, though not the structure of command with which we are familiar? What if the underlying structure is more like what Whitehead described earlier in this inquiry as the movement in orientation to the void (or experience of Nothingness), from enemy to companion?[6]

This, as I have indicated throughout, is the most delicate and crucial developmental threshold of our era. For to remain in "void as enemy" is to languish in moral disease, be susceptible to fundamentalist reassertion of monarchy, and/or at risk of the nihilistic "willing [of] the void"—in either softer forms which are often turned against the self, or the hard and externalized form of physical terror. To cross over from "void as enemy" to "void as companion" is to mature beyond these dangers, into a new kind of stability in which relationality or Bonhoeffer's "being there for others" provides both the discipline and the inspiration we need in order to live in what several European thinkers describe as "a new nobility"[7] or the "existential revolution" of "living in truth,"[8] and what some feminists describe as a new construal of personhood involving "the coinherence of autonomy and mutuality."[9] Does not the way of living which is envisioned by these phrases harken back to being guided in life by the Socratic "inner voice" or "divine sign," by Christ who "lives through me," by the Dao which is manifest in the *wu wei* action of non-action.

Having discovered these basic dynamics, the voice of the traditional absolute monarch would become offensive—understandably, given its association with our earlier inability to tolerate and participate in the open-endedness of freedom which lies beyond the enclosure monarchy provides. The offense would extend beyond the modern revolt against authority, anti-relational patriarchy, and hierarchy. Other forms of dictation would become abhorrent also, including the voice of unitary reason unfolding in the irrefutable—though often misguided—argument of the intellectualist and the technocrat (and the fascist, and the managerialist). And we would become hypercritical of *ourselves* for having been mistaken for so long about what suddenly appears to be so obvious (and yet so hard to articulate within the categories we have inherited), so unresponsive as to be unable to grow beyond a childish understanding which envisions only parental control and adolescent rebellion as the available options, failing to see/experience/name mutuality/democracy as the vastly more vital alternative.

In initial stages of breaking through into a more mature way of understanding ourselves and the universe, we will be awkward, groping for new ways to speak. Such, I feel, is the condition of this manuscript. It starts out speaking of conversation—and yet there is obviously only one voice in the room. Then out of nowhere (beginning in chapter 2) there appear a series of "Conversational Asides" which struggle toward deeper connection with the reader, deeper than that of either authority or entertainment—something more like the friendship kind of relationship. Perhaps the asides are ungainly.

I risk it, though, because my democratic sensibilities tell me that the way we speak with one another is important and inseparable from what we have to say. We need a more circular, conversational genre, understanding talking together as the root of relationship, with writing and other forms of communication following from and more or less supportive of the root conversation. (Who was it that said "Love is talk"?). We need to stop separating *what* we have to say from the *way* we speak, from the quality of our communication and the depth of our encounter. We now know that communication which is only concerned with delivery of the "what" aspect leads to ideological standoff and either gridlock or war, to domination/control rather than understanding or improvement.[10] When will we learn this in America?

The new orientation I'm trying to describe is frightening at first because it makes us vulnerable (as though we could be any more vulnerable than we already are in this life form! No, it makes us *aware* of our vulnerability and responsible for/in this awareness). I think it helps, in the movement to a relational or democratic way of life, if we think of the "what," the content of our message, as a kind of platform or launching pad from which we either communicate or fail to do so—as necessary but not sufficient to the distinctively human act. Then, in those really good moments when communication actually occurs, we find ourselves going beyond preparation and the whatness aspect, into a state of being which can be described as one of speaking not just from our minds with their well-prepared arguments, but our hearts and the sincerity of our commitments—abiding in integrity. We can then go beyond what the mind alone can know and transmit, with a humility which bespeaks healthy awareness of the limitations of our ability to both know and communicate, into what we can *be,* including the capacity to really listen to both other and self, to learn and grow together. In this way we can mature into deeper and more effective awareness of our own commitments, as well as discover together the surprising new life which emerges in our midst when we are together in this way—in the shared commitment to a healthy planet.

It is in this crucial "beyond"—or the openness described above—that the magic of democracy and human thriving and cultivation occur: here we meet the other as other, as both similar and different in ways that are refreshing and helpful. Here we also enter into the open space of discovery, emergent truth, creativity, and novelty, in the adventure of growth which keeps us healthy, moving—alive. It is also in this beyond that we encounter ourselves as beings who are worthy, forgivable, and sometimes bearers of truth and compassion. And we find that the more we live in "the beyond" (like the *aporia* of Socrates or the Nothingness we have discussed throughout) the more we are transformed, expanded and deepened in our capacity for truth and compassion.

What, then, if we thought of the universe itself on these terms, as a relational universe, beginning with the relationship between the One and the many?—where the One remains and becomes more fully One at the same time the many are enhanced in their richness, vibrancy, and goodness. It is only from the intellectualist perspective that One and Many come to opposition. In real life they are two aspects of a single, dynamic reality. Here we find the great lesson and developmental challenge of otherness in our era, as well as whisperings of the democratic spirit.

So it is that with these whisperings I would like to offer what seems an appropriately conversational, nearly choral conclusion to this book:

First, Alfred North Whitehead adopts the vocabulary of the Christian tradition to point to "another suggestion:"

> There is, however, in the Galilean origin of Christianity yet another suggestion that does not fit very well with any of the three main strands of thought. It does not emphasize the ruling Caesar, or the ruthless moralist, or the unmoved mover. It dwells upon the tender elements of the world, which slowly and in quietness operate by love; and it finds its purpose in the present immediacy of a kingdom not of this world. Love neither rules, nor is it unmoved; also it is a little oblivious as to morals.[11]

Whitehead engages "reappropriation," and love is what he finds, definitely a relational quality, perhaps a synonym for democracy (and "the beyond"). He might also have cited the New Testament, Luke 17:21: "The Kingdom of God is in your midst."[12]

Martin Luther King comes to much the same conclusion, saying that "Every nation must now develop an overriding loyalty to mankind as a whole in order to preserve the best in their individual societies," a loyalty grounded in love as "that force which all the great religions have seen as the supreme unifying principle of life."[13] And the voice of Huston Smith (which bears repeating): "But in addition to our own traditions, we listen to the faith of others.... For understanding brings respect, and respect prepares the way for a higher capacity which is love."[14]

Finally, speaking from the depth of her study of the world's traditions as they arose in the Axial Period, Karen Armstrong concludes that we need to "go in search of the lost heart, the spirit of compassion that lies at the core of all of our traditions."[15] She is speaking both of the Axial Age and also of possibilities which are present and necessary in our time, as we rediscover that lost heart—in the understanding of religion as practice, and practice as compassion:

> What mattered was not what you believed but how you behaved. Religion was about doing things that changed you at a profound level. Before the Axial Age, ritual and animal sacrifice had been central to the religious quest. You experienced the divine in sacred dramas that, like a great theatrical experience today, introduced you to another level of existence. The Axial sages changed this; they still valued ritual, but gave it a new ethical significance and put morality at the heart of the spiritual life. The only way you could encounter what they called "God," "Nirvana," "Brahman," or the "Way" was to live a compassionate life. Indeed, religion *was* compassion.[16]

Here we have an inclusive vision of reappropriation, the transformative overcoming on which the future depends, and the practice which can energize our lives. Here we have choosing life, making the way great, and that most embracing form of love which is civic virtue.

NOTES

1. Amartya Sen, *The Idea of Justice* (Cambridge, MA: Belknap Press, 2009). Sen identifies the significance of Rawls and Habermas in this recalling, and others, many of whom have been mentioned in this text already should be mentioned as well, including Fred Dallmayr, John Dewey, J. Ronald Engel, Elizabeth Minnich, Sor-hoon Tan, and Tu Weiming.

2. The influence of Sen is strong on this second point as well. See especially his *The Argumentative Indian,* and "Democracy and Its Global Roots." And note that virtually all of the figures I have cited in the previous note contribute to this understanding as well, implying that the second discovery follows from the first—and that the procedural or neoliberal understanding of democracy as tightly linked to capitalism and laissez faire individualism may be on the wane. This also underlines the milestone quality of the Berger and Huntington anthology I have cited before, *Many Gobalizations: Cultural Diversity in the Contemporary World.*

3. It should be noted that insistence on the integrity of many cultures sometimes leads to assertions of a relativistic culturalism and arguments as to the incommensurability between cultures. But the remedy for culturalism need not be either imperialistic imposition of one culture over all others or the reduction of all to a low common denominator. In fact, one of the most powerful arguments I know of as to the universality of democracy as a truly pluralistic alternative comes as a response to culturalism: Sor-hoon Tan, "Reconstructing 'Culture': A Deweyan Response to Antidemocratic Culturalism."

4. Hannah Arendt, *The Life of the Mind: Thinking* (New York: A Harvest Book, 1977), p. 109. Note also her understanding of the "paradoxical plurality" of the human condition, of our being the same in that each of us is unique. See *The Human Condition,* p. 176.

5. Martin Buber, *I and Thou*, trans. Walter Kaufman (New York: Charles Scribner's Sons), 78.

6. The orientation described in this paragraph is consistent with the *kenosis* (emptying) orientation which we see in some forms of Christianity, Buddhism, and other traditions—on their mystical sides. See Donald W. Mitchell, *Spirituality and Emptiness: The Dynamics of Spiritual Life in Buddhism and Christianity* (New York: Paulist Press, 1991) and John B. Cobb, Jr. and Christopher Ives, eds., *The Emptying God: A Buddhist-Jewish-Christian Conversation* (Maryknoll, NY: Orbis Books, 1991). This same orientation is shared and extended in a dramatically relational direction by Dietrich Bonhoeffer. See *Letters and Papers from Prison.*

7. Bonhoeffer, *Ibid.*, p. 13, and Jaspers, *Man in the Modern Age*, pp. 210–217, in his magnificent concluding section, "Maintenance of Selfhood in the Contemporary Situation," pp. 192–228.

8. Havel, "The Power of the Powerless," in *Living in Truth*, p. 115.

9. Elizabeth Johnson, *She Who Is*, p. 68.

10. On the other end of the continuum, all "way" and no "what" is no less problematic, as we see in so much of commercial culture in which image is severed from idea and principle in its appeal to base instincts and urges, leading to another kind of domination/control. Note the parallel between "what" and "way" in this chapter, and "idea" and "relationship" in the previous chapter (as well as Marshall McLuhan's famous 20th-century discovery that "the medium is the message." Also note that something like this distinction has been the source of considerable discussion in the history of Chinese philosophy. See, for example, previous discussion of Tong Suijin on ti and yong in n230.

11. Whitehead, *Process and Reality*, p. 404.

12. Note the very significant ambiguities involved with translation of this crucial reference, as between more individualist and more relational readings. It has often been translated in the more individually-oriented mode as "The Kingdom of God is within you" (King James Version, New King James Version, and American Standard Version). On the other hand, the more relational reading I present above is found in The New American Standard Bible and Revised Standard Version. The New International Version presents the ambiguity directly as "The Kingdom of God is within (or 'among') you.

13. King, *Where Do We Go From Here?*, p. 190.

14. Smith, *The Illustrated World's Religions*, p. 249.

15. Armstrong, *The Great Transformation*, p. 399.

16. *Ibid.*, pp. xiii–xiv.

Bibliography

Abe, Masao. 1985. "Zen and its Elucidation," in *Zen and Western Thought*, ed. William R. LeFleur, Honolulu: University of Hawaii Press.

Ames, Roger and Hall, David. 2001. *Focusing the Familiar: A Translation and Philosophical Interpretation of the Zhongyong*. Honolulu: University of Hawaii Press.

Anderson, Gordon L. 2009. *Life, Liberty, and the Pursuit of Happiness*. St. Paul: Paragon House.

Annon, Kofi. 2001. Untitled address at Seton Hall University's School of Diplomacy and International Relations, 5 February 2001, retrieved from www.un.org/Dialogue/pr/sgsm7705.htm

Anshen, Ruth Nanda. 1971. "World Perspectives: What This Series Means," in *Physics and Beyond: Encounters and Conversations*, Werner Heisenberg. New York: Harper & Row.

Apatow, Robert. 1998. *The Spiritual Art of Dialogue*. Rochester, VT: Inner Traditions.

Arendt, Hannah. 1958a. *The Human Condition*. Chicago: University of Chicago Press.

———. 1958b. *The Origins of Totalitarianism*. Cleveland and New York: Meridian Books.

———. 1963. *Eichmann in Jerusalem: A Report on the Banality of Evil*. New York: Viking.

———. 1968. "Karl Jaspers: Citizen of the World?" in *Men in Dark Times*. New York: Harcourt, Brace and World.

———. 1977. *The Life of the Mind: Thinking*. New York: A Harvest Book.

Aristotle. 1941. "*Nicomachean Ethics*, Book II, 4:30, 1105b," In *The Basic Works of Aristotle*, ed. Richard McKeon. New York: Random House.

Armstrong, Karen. 2006. *The Great Transformation: The Beginning of Our Religious Traditions*. New York: Alfred A. Knopf.

Barrett, William. 1986. *Death of the Soul*. Garden City, NY: Anchor Doubleday.

Bauman, Zygmunt. 2000. *Liquid Modernity*. Cambridge: Policy Press.

Bellah, Robert N. 1967. "Civil Religion in America." *Daedalus: Journal of the American Academy of Arts and Science* 96(1) (Winter 1967): 1–21.

———. 1970. "Religious Evolution," in *Beyond Belief: Essays on Religion in a Post-Traditional World*, New York: Harper & Row.

Berger, Peter L. and Huntington, Samuel P. 2002. *Many Globalizations: Cultural Diversity in the Contemporary World*. New York: Oxford University Press.

Berman, Morris. 2006. *Dark Ages America: The Final Phase of Empire*. New York: Norton.

Bernstein, Richard J. 1999. "Incommensurability and Otherness Revisited," in *Culture and Modernity: East-West Philosophic Perspectives*, ed. Eliot Deutsch. Honolulu: University of Hawaii Press.

Bok, Sissela. 1978. *Lying: Moral Choice in Public and Private Life*. New York: Vintage,

Bonhoeffer, Dietrich. 1976. *Letters and Papers from Prison*. New York: Macmillan.

Boonin, Leonard. 1969. "Man and Society: An Example of Three Models," in *Voluntary Associations*, eds. J. Roland Pennock and John W. Chapman. New York: Atherton Press.

Bowers, Fredson and Skrupskelis, Iqnas K. 1977. *A Pluralistic Universe: Works of William James*. Cambridge, Massachusetts: Harvard University Press.

Bromwich, David. 1989. *A Choice of Inheritance*. Cambridge, MA: Harvard University Press.

Buber, Martin. 1970. *I and Thou*, trans. Walter Kaufman. New York: Charles Scribner's Sons.

Caldwell, Christopher. 2009. *Reflections on the Revolution in Europe: Immigration, Islam and the West*. New York: Anchor Books.

Campbell, Joseph . 1972. *The Power of Myth*. New York: Bantam.

Cobb, Jr., John B. 1982. *Beyond Dialogue: Toward a Mutual Transformation of Christianity and Buddhism*. Philadelphia: Fortress Press.

Cobb, Jr., John B. and Ives, Christopher, eds. 1991. *The Emptying God: A Buddhist-Jewish-Christian Conversation*. Maryknoll, NY: Orbis Books.

Confucius. 1998. The *Analects of Confucius*, 15/29, trans. Roger T. Ames and Henry Rosemont, Jr. New York: Ballantine.

Connolly, William E. 2005. *Pluralism*. Durham, NC: Duke University press.

Cushman, Philip. 1990. "Why the Self is Empty: Toward a Historically Situated Psychology." *American Psychologist* 45(5) (May 1990): 599-611.

Cushman, Robert. 1958. *Therapeia: Plato's Conception of Philosophy*. Westport, CT: Greenwood Press.

Dallmayr, Fred. 2010. *The Promise of Democracy: Political Agency and Transformation*. Albany, NY: SUNY Press.

Daly, Markate, ed. 1993. *Communitarianism: A New Public Ethics*. Belmont, CA: Wadsworth.

Dean, William. 1974. "The Rise of the Professional Intellectual," in *The Religious Critic in American Culture*. Albany, NY: SUNY Press.

Deresiewicz, William. 2011. "Solitude and Leadership." *The American Scholar*, June 29, 2011, retrieved from http://theamericanscholar.org/solitude-and-leadership/print/

Deutsch, Eliot, ed. 1991.*Culture and Modernity: East-West Philosophic Perspectives*. Honolulu: University of Hawaii Press.

Dewey, John. 1927. *The Public and Its Problems*. Chicago: Swallow Press.

———. 1934. *A Common Faith*. New Haven: Yale University Press.

———. 1938. *Experience and Education*. New York: Macmillan.

———. 1958. *Art as Experience*. New York: Capricorn Books.

———. 1966. *Democracy and Education*. New York: Free Press.

Didion, Joan. 1961. *Slouching Toward Bethlehem*. New York: Farrar, Straus and Giroux.

Dogen, Eihei. 1985. *Moon in a Dewdrop: Writings of Zen Master Dogen, ed.*, Kazuaki Tanahashi. San Francisco: North Point Press.

Eck, Diana. 2000. "Dialogue and the Echo Boom of Terror: Religious Women's Voices after 9/11," in *After Terror: Promoting Dialogue among Civilizations*, eds., Akbar Ahmed and Brian Forst. Cambridge, UK: Polity Press.

Elshtain, Jean Bethke. 1995. *Democracy on Trial*. New York: Basic Books.

Engel, J. Ronald. 2002. "The Earth Charter as a New Covenant for Democracy," in *Just Ecological Integrity: The Ethics of Maintaining Planetary Life,* eds. Peter Miller and Laura Westra. New York: Rowman & Littlefield.

Fingarette, Herbert. 1972. *Confucius: The Secular as Sacred*. Long Grove, IL: Waveland Press.

Fowler, James W. 1995. *Stages of Faith: The Psychology of Human Development and the Quest for Meaning*. San Francisco: Harper & Row.

Frank, Thomas. 2004. *What's the Matter with Kansas: How Conservative Won the Heart of America*. New York: Metropolitan Books.

Freire, Paulo. 1998. *Pedagogy of the Oppressed*. New York: Continuum.

Fromm, Erich. 1941. *Escape From Freedom*. New York: Holt, Rinehart & Winston.

———. 1968. *Revolution of Hope: Toward a Humanized Technology*. New York: Harper Colophon.

Fukuyama, Francis. 1992. *The End of History and the Last Man*. New York: Free Press.

Gadamer, Hans-Georg. 1988. *Truth and Method*. New York: Crossroad.

Gilding. Paul. 2011. *The Great Disruption: Why the Climate Crisis Will Bring on the End of Shopping and the Birth of a New World*. New York: Bloomsbury Press.

Green, Judith M. 1999. *Deep Democracy: Community, Diversity, and Transformation*. Lanham, MD: Rowman & Littlefield.

Greenberg, Irving. 1997. "Seeking the Religious Roots of Pluralism: In the Image of God and Covenant." *Journal of Ecumenical Studies* 34(3) (Summer 1997): 385- 394.

Griffin, David Ray, ed. 2005. *Deep Religious Pluralism*. Louisville, KY: John Knox Press.

————. 2007. "God in Process," in *Exploring the Philosophy of Religion*, ed. David Stewart. Upper Saddle River, NY: Pearson Education.

Gross, William. 2011. "School Daze, School Daze / Good Old Golden Rules Days." Retrieved from http://www.pimco.com/EN/Insights/Pages/School-Daze-School-Daze

Habermas, Jurgen. 2001. "Moral Consciousness and Communicative Action," in *Moral Consciousness and Communicative Action*. Cambridge, MA: MIT Press.

Hacker, Andrew and Dreifus, Claudia. 2010. *Higher Education?: How Colleges are Wasting Our Money and Failing Our Kids—and What We Can Do About It*. New York: Times Books.

Hadot, Pierre. 1995. *Philosophy as a Way of Life: Spiritual Exercises from Socrates to Foucault*. Malden, MA: Blackwell Publishing.

Hall, David L. and Ames, Roger T. 1999.*The Democracy of the Dead: Dewey, Confucius, and the Hope for Democracy in China*. Chicago: Open Court.

Hallie, Philip. 1979. *Lest Innocent Blood Be Shed*. New York: Harper & Row.

Havel, Vaclav. 1989. "Power of the Powerless," in *Living in Truth*, ed. Jan Vladislav. London: Faber and Faber.

Hedges, Chris. 2006. *American Fascism: The Christian Right and the War on America*. New York: Free Press.

Heller, Joseph. 1996. *Catch 22*. New York: Simon & Schuster.

Hershock, Peter D. 2001. *Reinventing the Wheel: A Buddhist Response to the Information Age*. Albany, NY: SUNY Press.

Hick, John. 1995. *A Christian Theology of Religions*. Louisville: Westminster John Knox Press.

Hillesum, Etty. 1981. *An Interrupted Life: The Diaries of Etty Hillesum 1941–1043*. Trans. Arno Pomerans. New York: Washington Square Press.

Huntington, Samuel. 1996. *The Clash of Civilizations and the Remaking of World Order*. New York: Simon & Schuster.

Huxley, Aldous. 1944. *The Perennial Philosophy.* New York: Harper Colophon.

Jaggar, Alison. 1989. "Love and Emotion in Feminist Epistemology," in *Inquiry* 32(2): 151-176.

James, William. 1902. *The Varieties of Religious Experience*. London: Longman, Green, and Co.

————. 1958. "The Gospel of Relaxation," in *Talks to Teachers on Psychology; and to Students on some of Life's Ideals.* New York: Norton.

————.1971. "A Pluralistic Universe," in *Essays in Radical Empiricism and a Pluralistic Universe*, ed. Richard J. Bernstein. New York: Dutton.

Jaspers, Karl. 1953. *The Origin and Goal of History.* New Haven: Yale University Press.

————. 1957. *Man in the Modern Age*. Garden City, NY: Anchor Books.

Jonas, Hans. 2001. *The Phenomenon of Life: Towards a Philosophical Biology*. Chicago: University of Chicago Press.

Johnson, Elizabeth. 1993. *She Who Is: The Mystery of God in Feminist Theological Discourse*. New York: Crossroad.

Kariel, Henry. 1970. *Frontiers of Democratic Theory*. New York: Random House.

Kegan. Robert. 1982. *The Evolving Self: Problem and Process in Human Development*. Cambridge, MA: Harvard University Press.

Khan, Si and Minnich, Elizabeth. 2005. *The Fox in the Henhouse: How Privatization Threatens Democracy*. San Francisco: Berrett-Koehler.

King, Jr., Martin Luther. 1967. *Where Do We Go From Here: Chaos or Community?* Boston: Beacon Press.

Kupperman, Joel J. 1999. *Learning from Asian Philosophy*. New York: Oxford University Press.

Laing, Ronald David. 1960. *The Divided Self.* New York: Penguin.

Lasch, Christopher. 1979. *The Culture of Narcissism*. New York: Norton.

L'Engle, Madeleine. 1979. *A Circle of Quiet*. New York: Seabury press.

Leonhardt, David. 2011. "Even for Cashiers, College Pays Off." *New York Times,* June 26, 2011, "Sunday Review."

Levinas, Emmanuel. 1969. *Totality and Infinity: An Essay on Exterioriy,* trans. Alphonso Lingis. Pittsburgh, PA: Duquesne University Press.

Li, Chenyang. 1999. *The Tao Encounters the West: Explorations in Comparative Philosophy.* Albany, NY: SUNY Press.

Li, Chenyang, ed. 2000. *The Sage and the Second Sex.* Chicago: Open Court.

Lifton, Robert Jay. 1980. "The Survivor as Creator," in *Living Beyond Crisis: Essays on Discovery and Being in the World,* ed. Stephen Rowe. New York: Pilgrim Press.

———. 1993. *The Protean Self.* New York: Basic Books.

Lincoln, Abraham. 1894. "Address in Independence Hall. Philadelphia, Pennsylvania February 22, 1861." in *The Complete Works of Abraham Lincoln, v. 6,* eds. John G. Nicolay and John Hay. New York: Francis D. Tandy Company.

Lindsay, A.D. 1935. *The Essentials of Democracy.* Oxford: Claredon press.

MacIntyre, Alasdair. 1981. *After Virtue.* Notre Dame, IN: University of Notre Dame Press.

Marty, Martin E. 1997. *The One and the Many: America's Struggle for the Common Good.* Cambridge: Harvard University Press.

Marty, Martin E. and Appleby, R. Scott, eds. 1990. *Fundamentalisms Observed.* Chicago: University of Chicago Press.

McCumbr, John. 2001. *Time in the Ditch: American Philosophy in the McCarthy Era.* Evanston, IL: Northwestern University press.

McDermott, John J., ed. 1977. *The Writings of William James.* Chicago: University of Chicago Press.

Meadows, Donella H. 1972. *The Limits to Growth.* New York: Signet.

Miller, Mitchell. 1986. "Platonic Provocations: Reflections on the Good in the *Republic,*" in *Platonic Investigations,* ed. Dominic J. O'Meara. Washington, DC: Catholic University of America Press.

Minnich, Elizabeth. 1990. *Transforming Knowledge.* Philadelphia: Temple University Press.

Mitchell, Donald W., ed. 1998. *Masao Abe: A Zen Life of Dialogue.* Boston: Charles E. Tuttle.

Mitchell, Donald W. 1991. *Spirituality and Emptiness: The Dynamics of Spiritual Life in Buddhism and Christianity.* New York: Paulist Press.

Morgan, Robin. 1978. *Going Too Far.* New York: Vintage.

Needleman, Jacob. 1982. *The Heart of Philosophy.* New York: Alfred A. Knopf.

———. 2002. *The American Soul: Rediscovering the Wisdom of the Founders.* New York: Tarcher/Putnam.

Ni, Peimin. 2001. *On Confucius.* Belmont, CA: Wadsworth.

———. 2004. "Reading Zhongyong as a Gongfu Instruction: Comments on Focusing the Familiar." In *Dao: A Journal of Comparative Philosophy* 3(2) (June 2004): 189–203.

———. 2010. "Kung Fu for Philosophers." *New York Times,* December 8, 2010, Opinionator.

Ni, Peimin and Rowe, Stephen. 2002. *Wandering: Brush and Pen in Philosophical Reflection.* Shanghai and Chicago: Dongfang and Art Media Resources.

Niebuhr, Reinhold. 1945. *The Children of Light and the Children of Darkness: A Vindication of Democracy and a Critique of its Traditional Defenders.* London: Nisbet & Co., Ltd.

Nietzsche, Friedrich. 1956. "The Genealogy of Morals," in *The Birth of Tragedy and the Genealogy of Morals,* trans. ed. Francis Golffing. Garden City, NY: Doubleday Anchor.

Nishitani, Keiji. 1982. *Religion and Nothingness.* Berkeley: University of California Press.

Noddings, Nel. 1984. *Caring: A Feminine Approach to Ethics and Moral Education.* Berkeley: University of California Press.

Noyce, Phillip. 2010. *Salt.* Columbia Pictures.

Nussbaum, Martha. 1997. *Cultivating Humanity: A Classical Defense of Reform in Liberal Education.* Cambridge, MA: Harvard University Press.

———. 2010. *Not for Profit: Liberal Education and Democratic Citizenship.* Princeton: Princeton University Press.

Oakeshott, Michael. 1989. *The Voice of Liberal Learning.* New Haven: Yale University Press.

O'Connor, Erin. 2003. "Misreading What Reading is For," in *The Chronicle of Higher Education,* 9/5/2003, http://chronicle.com/weekly/v50i0202b02001.htm

Paris, Peter. 1995. *The Spirituality of African peoples: The Search for a Common Moral Discourse.* Minneapolis: Fortress Press.

Perry, William. 1968. *Forms of Intellectual and Moral Development in the College Years.* New York: Holt, Rinehart and Winston.

Picco, Giandomenico. Ed. 2001. *Crossing the Divide: Dialogue among Civilizations.* South Orange, NJ: Seton Hall University School of Diplomacy and International Relations.

Pirsig, Robert M. 1974. *Zen and the Art of Motorcycle Maintenance.* New York: William Morow.

Plato, 1985. "Apology" in *The Collected Dialogues of Plato,* ed. Edith Hamilton and Huntington Cairns. New York: Pantheon Books.

Poirier, Richard. 1999. "Why Do Pragmatists Want to Be Like Poets?" in *The Revival of Pragmatism: New Essays on Social Thought, Law, and Culture,* ed. Morris Dickstein. Durham: Duke University Press,

Progoff, Ira. 1956. *The Death and Rebirth of Psychology.* New York: Julian Press.

Rich, Adrienne. 1979. "On Lies, Secrets, and Silence," in *Living Beyond Crisis: Essays on Discovery and Being in the World,* ed. Stephen Rowe. New York: Pilgrim Press.

Rieff, Philip. 1968. *The Triumph of the Therapeutic.* New York: Harper Torchbooks.

Riesman, David. 1961. *The Lonely Crowd.* New Haven: Yale.

Rorty, Richard. 1998. "Habermas, Derrida, and Philosophy," in *Truth and Progress: Philosophical Papers.* Cambridge: Cambridge University Press.

———. 1999. "Trotsky and the Wild Orchids," in *Philosophy and Social Hope.* London: Penguin Books.

Rosemont, Jr., Henry. 1991. A *Chinese Mirror: Moral Reflections on Political Economy and Society.* La Salle, IL: Open Court.

———. 2000. "On Freedom and Equality," in *The Aesthetic Turn: Reading Eliot Deutsch on Comparative Philosophy,* ed. Roger T. Ames. Chicago: Open Court.

———. 2001. *Rationality and Religious Experience: The Continuing Relevance of the World's Spiritual Traditions.* Chicago: Open Court.

Rowe, Stephen C., ed. 1980. *Living Beyond Crisis: Essays on Discovery and Being in the World.* New York: Pilgrim Press.

———. 1989. *Leaving and Returning: On America's Contribution to a World Ethic.* Lewisburg, PA: Bucknell University Press.

———. 1992. *Claiming a Liberal Education: Resources for Realizing the College Experience.* Needham Heights, MA: Ginn Press.

———. 1994. *Rediscovering the West: An Inquiry into Nothingness and Relatedness.* Albany, NY: SUNY Press.

———. 1996. "Toward a Postliberal Liberalism: James Luther Adams and the Need for a Theory of Relational Meaning," in *American Journal of Philosophy and Theology* 17(1) (January 1996): 51-70.

———. 2002. *Living Philosophy: Remaining Awake and Moving Toward Maturity in Complicated Times.* St. Paul, MN: Paragon House.

———. 2003. "Cultivating Mutual Growth: A Socratic Approach to the Post 9–11 World," in *Harvard-Yenching Academic Series,* vol. 3. Beijing: SDX Press.

———. 2005. *Globalization and Dialogue between Civilizations.* Jiangshu: Jiangshu Jiaoyu Press (original in Chinese).

———. 2007. "A Humanities Response to Managerialism: Democracy, Diversity, and Liberal Education in the Shade." *The International Journal of the Humanities* 5(2007): 95–102.

———. 2008. "Masao Abe and the Dialogue Breakthrough." in *Buddhist-Christian Studies* 28 (2008): 123–125.

Royce, Josiah. 1968. *The Problem of Christianity,* ed. John E. Smith. Chicago: University of Chicago Press.

Ruether, Rosemary Radford. 1983. *Sexism and God Talk: Toward a Feminist Theology.* Boston: Beacon Press.

Schneider, Carol Geary. 2001. "'Degrees for What Jobs?' Wrong Question, Wrong Answers." *The Chronicle of Higher Education,* May 10, 2011, retrieved from http://chronicle.com/article/Degrees-for-What-Jobs-Wrong/127328/

Schmidt, Peter. 2011. "The Challenge of Putting a Grade on Ethical Learning." *The Chronicle of Higher Education*, July 5, 2011, retrieved from http://chronicle.com/article/The-Challenge-of-Putting-a/128086/?ke

Schrag, Calvin O. 2002. *God as Otherwise Than Being: Toward a Semantics of the Gift*. Evanston, IL: Northwestern University Press.

Sen, Amartya. 2003. "Democracy and Its Global Roots," in *The New Republic*, Oct. 6, 2003, 35.

———. 2005. *The Argumentative Indian: Writings on Indian History, Culture and Identity*. London: Penguin Books.

———. 2009. *The Idea of Justice*. Cambridge, MA: Belknap Press.

Sheehy, Gail. 1974. *Passages: Predictable Crises of Adult Life*. New York: Dutton.

Skinner, B. F. 1971. *Beyond Freedom and Dignity*. Indianapolis: Hackett.

Slater, Philip. 1970. *The Pursuit of Loneliness*. Boston: Beacon Press.

Smith, Huston. 1976. *Forgotten Truth*. New York: Harper Collins.

———. 1991. *The Illustrated World's Religions*. San Francisco: Harper.

———. 2001. *Why Religion Matters: The Fate of the Human Spirit in an Age of Disbelief*. San Francisco: Harper.

Snow, Charles Percy. 1959. *The Two Cultures and the Scientific Revolution*. Cambridge: Cambridge University Press.

Stivers, Richard. 1994. *The Culture of Cynicism: American Morality in Decline*. Oxford: Blackwell.

Stout, Jeffrey. 2004. *Democracy and Tradition*. Princeton: Princeton University Press.

Sturm, Douglas. 1998. "Crossing the Boundaries: Interreligious Dialogue and the Political Question," in *Solidarity and Suffering: Toward a Politics of Relationality*. Albany, NY: SUNY Press.

Swidler, Leonard. 1990a. *After the Absolute: The Dialogical Future of Religious Reflection*. Minneapolis: Fortress.

———. 1990b. "Death or Dialogue: From the Age of Monologue to the Age of Dialogue." Lecture at Grand Valley State University, May 20, 1990.

Tarnas, Richard. 1991. *The Passion of the Western Mind*. New York: Ballantine.

Tan, Sor-hoon. 2004. *Confucian Democracy: A Deweyan Reconstruction*. Albany, NY: SUNY Press.

Tan, Sor-hoon and Whalen-Bridge, John. 2008. *Democracy as Culture: Deweyan Pragmatism in a Globalizing World*. Albany, NY: SUNY Press.

Tillich, Paul. 1952. *The Courage to Be*. New Haven: Yale University Press.

———. 1967. *Systematic Theology*: vol. 3. Chicago: University of Chicago Press.

Tong, Shijun. 2000. *The Dialectics of Modernization: Habermas and the Chinese Discourse of Modernization*. Sydney: Wild Peony.

Tu, Weiming. 1985. *Confucian Thought: Selfhood as Creative Transformation*. Albany, NY: SUNY Press.

———. 1993. "Toward the Possibility of a Global Community," in *Ethics, Religion and Biodiversity*, ed. Lawrence Hamilton. Cambridge: The White Horse Press.

———. 2000. "Implications of the Rise of 'Confucian' East Asia." *Daedalus: Journal of the American Academy of Arts and Sciences* 129(1) (winter 2000): 195–218.

———. 2003. "Beyond the Enlightenment Mentality: A New Perspective on Confucian Humanism," lecture at Grand Valley State University, Dec 5, 2003.

Toulman, Stephen. 1990. *Cosmopolis: The Hidden Agenda of Modernity*. Chicago: University of Chicago Press.

Tracy, David. 1989. *Plurality and Ambiguity: Hermeneutics, Religion, Hope*. San Francisco: Harper & Row.

Waldenfels, Hans. 1980. *Absolute Nothingness: Foundations for Buddhist-Christian Dialogue*, trans. J. W. Heisig. New York: Paulist Press.

Warren, Karen J. 2000. *Ecofeminist Philosophy: A Western Perspective on What It Is and Why It Matters*. New York: Rowman & Littlefield.

Waters, Lindsay. 2001. "The Age of Incommensurability." *Boundary* 2 28(2) (2001): 133–172.

Weber, Max. 1958. *The Protestant Ethic and the Spirit of Capitalism,* trans. Talcott Parsons. New York: Charles Scribner's Sons.

Weintraub, Karl J. 1966. *Visions of Culture.* Chicago: University of Chicago Press.

Weinstein, James. 1968. *The Corporate Ideal and the Liberal State.* Boston: Beacon Press.

Welch, Bryant. 2008. *State of Confusion: Political Manipulation and the Assault on the American Mind.* New York: Thomas Dunne Books.

West, Cornell. 2004. *Democracy Matters: Winning the Fight against Imperialism.* New York: The Penguin Press.

Whitbeck, Caroline. 1983. "A Different Reality: Feminist Ontology," in *Beyond Domination: New Perspectives on Women and Philosophy,* ed. Carol C. Gould. Totowa, NJ: Rowman & Allanheld.

Whitehead, Alfred North. 1925. *Science and the Modern World.* New York: Free Press.

———. 1933. *Adventures of Ideas.* New York: Free Press.

———. 1938. *Modes of Thought.* New York: Macmillan.

———. 1957. "The Aims of Education," in *The Aims of Education and Other Essays.* New York: Free Press.

———. 1960. *Religion in the Making.* Cleveland: Meridian Books.

———. 1969. *Process and Reality.* New York: Free Press.

Whitman, Walt. 2010. *Democratic Vistas: The Original Edition in Facsimile,* ed. Ed Folsom. Iowa City: University of Iowa Press.

Wilberg, Peter. 1998. "Modes of Relatedness in Psychotherapy." Retrieved from www.meaningofdepression.com

Wieman, Henry Nelson. 1946. *The Source of Human Good.* Carbondale: Southern Illinois University Press.

Wilshire, Bruce. 1990. "A Specimen Case of Professionalizing a Field of Learning: Philosophy," in *The Moral Collapse of the University.* Albany, NY: SUNY Press.

———. 2002. *Fashionable Nihilism: A Critique of Analytical Philosophy.* Albany: SUNY Press,

Wolin, Sheldon. 2008. *Democracy Incorporated: Managed Democracy and the Specter of Inverted Totalitarianism.* Princeton, NJ: Princeton University Press.

Yankelovich, Daniel. 1999. *The Magic of Dialogue: Transforming Conflict into Cooperation.* New York: Simon & Schuster.

Zakaria, Fareed. 2008. *The Post-American World.* New York: W.W. Norton.

Index

About the Author

Stephen C. Rowe is one of the founding faculty of William James College (1971–1982) at what is now Grand Valley State University, a public university deeply committed to liberal education. He is also the founding chair of the Liberal Studies Program (GVSU's option for individualized interdisciplinary and problem/issue defined majors), and long-time chair of GVSU's pluralistic Philosophy Department. Rowe is a graduate of the Social Ethics Field at the Divinity School of the University of Chicago, also with work in Philosophy and the Committee on Social Thought, and an activist with roots in the American traditions of pragmatism and democratic social change. He is author of many books, some published in China, England, India, and Japan, as well as the United States, and has been involved with the intercultural dialogue movement, especially in relation to the Japanese Kyoto School and Third Epoch Confucianism—and more recently in relation to Chinese efforts to develop general education. The winner of various teaching and service awards, Rowe's books include *Leaving and Returning: On America's Contribution to a World Ethic* (1988), *Rediscovering the West: An Inquiry into Nothingness and Relatedness* (1994), *The Vision of James* (1996), and *Living Philosophy* (2002). He continues to teach and write in Grand Rapids, Michigan.

CPSIA information can be obtained
at www.ICGtesting.com
Printed in the USA
LVOW12*0733071017
551575LV00009B/92/P